LABOR-ENVIRONMENTAL COALITIONS

Lessons from a Louisiana Petrochemical Region

Thomas Estabrook

Work, Health, and Environment Series
Series Editors: **Charles Levenstein and John Wooding**

CRC Press
Taylor & Francis Group
Boca Raton London New York

CRC Press is an imprint of the
Taylor & Francis Group, an **informa** business

CRC Press
Taylor & Francis Group
6000 Broken Sound Parkway NW, Suite 300
Boca Raton, FL 33487-2742

First issued in paperback 2018

ISBN 13: 978-0-89503-307-9 (hbk)
ISBN 13: 978-0-415-78435-1 (pbk)

Visit the Taylor & Francis Web site at
http://www.taylorandfrancis.com

and the CRC Press Web site at
http://www.crcpress.com

Library of Congress Catalog Number: 2006049894

Library of Congress Cataloging-in-Publication Data

Estabrook, Thomas.
    Labor-environmental coalitions : lessons from a Louisiana petrochemical region / Thomas Estabrook.
        p. cm. -- (Work, health, and environment series)
    Includes bibliographical references and index.
    ISBN-13: 978-089503-307-9 (cloth)
    ISBN-10: 0-89503-307-0 (cloth)
    1. Working class--Louisiana--Political activity--Case studies. 2. Louisiana Labor-Neighbor Project--Case studies. 3. Oil, Chemical, and Atomic Workers International Union--Case studies. 4. Paper, Allied-Industrial, Chemical and Energy Workers International Union--Case studies. 5. Petroleum chemicals industry--Environmental aspects--Louisiana--Case studies. 6. Environmental protection--Louisiana--Citizen participation--Case studies. I. Title.

    HD8079.L8E88 2006
    331.88'12233820976309049--dc 22

                                                            2006049894

Cover photograph by Jenny Bauer

Dedication

For Sibylle, Elias, and Jonah

Table of Contents

Acknowledgments

I am grateful for the engagement, cooperation, and support of many people over many years during the research and writing of this book. The idea of creating a book from a doctoral dissertation originated with Jody Emel, one of my doctoral advisors in geography at Clark University. Yet the book would have remained simply a concept without the faithful support and confidence of John Wooding and Chuck Levenstein of the University of Massachusetts Lowell, as editors of the Baywood *Work, Health and Environment* book series, who helped me transform the dissertation into a product for a wider audience.

I thank the leadership and staff at Baywood Publishing and associated companies, particularly Stuart Cohen, Bobbi Olszewski, Julie Krempa, Claire Meirowitz, and Angelo Giovanniello for their support and hard work on the book manuscript and production.

Eduardo Siqueira of UMass Lowell and Eduardo Machado, visiting scholar from Bahia, Brazil, offered important analysis as we wrote a collaborative article comparing the Louisiana and Bahia, Brazil coalition experiences. Danny Faber and the Boston area working group of the journal *CNS* provided a critical forum for the book's ideas. Danny Faber of Northeastern University, Phil Brown of Brown University and Susan Moir of UMass Boston reviewed the manuscript in its last stages, offering very helpful comments to make the book more widely accessible.

During my tenure in Louisiana in 1991-92, and subsequently on numerous visits and through countless correspondences, I owe my sincere gratitude to many people. I was highly motivated by the words and accomplishments of the late Tony Mazzocchi, labor-environmental coalition-builder extraordinaire, whose work helped to lay the foundation for the Louisiana Labor-Neighbor Project. The late Ernie Rousselle of OCAW set an inspiring example of moral leadership in co-founding the Labor-Neighbor Project and providing seasoned guidance throughout the project's existence. The late John O'Connor, then chairperson and founder of the National Toxics Campaign, provided invaluable commitment and support. Richard Miller, OCAW organizer during the BASF campaign, gave me extensive support and insight into organizing, the BASF lockout, and Louisiana politics. The brothers and sisters of OCAW Local 4-620 (now United Steel Workers) put their trust in me as an organizer on the Louisiana

Labor-Neighbor Project. Duke King, OCAW leader, was particularly instructive about the project over the years. OCAW leaders Bobby Schneider, the late John Daigle, Robbie Robinson, Leslie Vann, Esnard Gremillion, and Jerrome Summers shared their invaluable perspectives. Willie Fontenot—gracious host in Baton Rouge, an exemplary bridge-builder of the Labor-Neighbor Project and the Louisiana grassroots environmental movement—offered continuous crisp analysis of Louisiana environmental politics. Dan Nicolai, director of the Labor-Neighbor Project, was a generous host and lent his expert analysis on numerous visits to Louisiana, and by phone, throughout the 1990s. Jenny Bauer provided the use of excellent photographs for the book as well as hospitality during visits to Baton Rouge. Stan Holt, organizing advisor to the Labor-Neighbor Project for many years, shared his sage advice and understanding of the dynamics of the project and the essentials of organizing. Darryl Malek-Wiley of the Sierra Club and Marylee Orr of the Louisiana Environmental Action Network provided vital analysis and ongoing support. The late Amos Favorite shared his stunning stories of life as a civil rights, community and union leader in Ascension Parish. Numerous other community and union leaders and organizers worked with me, including Pat Bryant, Ben Clark, Ida and Emanuel Sharper, Albertha Hasten, Irma Rixner, Chris and Kay Gaudet, Donna Carrier, Hubert Armond, Rev. Welma Jackson, Izeal Morris, Les Ann Kirkland, Nina Shulman, Zack Nauth, and Fred Brooks. Audrey Evans, Peter Evans, Marcus Carson, and Anna Mattssen were generous hosts.

Richard Peet, David Angel, Jody Emel, and Dianne Rocheleau of Clark University, and Michael Heiman of Dickinson College, and John Wooding of UMass Lowell all gave valuable guidance as my geography dissertation committee. Richard Peet deserves special recognition for helping me develop my theoretical framework, and for his expert comments, editorial input, and overall advice on version one of this book. Fellow grad students Scott Carlin, Kirsten Dow, Melissa Gilbert, Brad Jokisch, Doreen Mattingly, Paul Robbins, Kevin St. Martin, Lydia Savage, Phil Steinberg, and Seth Tuler contributed important ideas to the research. Margaret Pearce created the excellent maps used in this book. Jeff Mitchell, dissertation brother-in-arms, provided indispensable, lively solidarity and advice during the writing of version one. My brother Chuck Estabrook lent broad support that helped rescue version one of the book on numerous occasions.

Craig Slatin, Paul Morse, and Wayne Sanborn, my supervisors at The New England Consortium at UMass Lowell, gave me the flexibility and support to fit book writing into a hectic work schedule. Lending much moral support and advice were my colleagues at The New England Consortium: Bill Benn, Bob Burns, Marcy Goldstein-Gelb, Jim Celenza, David Coffey, Diane Doherty, Judy Elliot, Mike Fitts, Jane Fleishman, Claudie Grout, Judy Martineau, Bernie Mizula, Therese O'Donnell, Jimmy Smith, John Thoma, and Aaron Wilson. Other friends and colleagues at UMass Lowell have also lent assistance, particularly through their work building institutional partnerships: Ken Geiser, Joel Tickner, Rafael

Moure-Eraso, David Kriebel, Margaret Quinn, Bob Forrant, Linda Silka, Chris Tilly, Lenore Azaroff, Cathy Crumbley, Marian Flum, Christina Holcroft, Mike Prokosch, Charley Richardson, Cora Roelofs, Susan Shepherd, Jamie Tessler, Robin Toof, Dan Toomey, Dave Turcotte, and Susan Winning. In New England I have benefitted from the inspired efforts of numerous leaders, activists, and friends to forge labor-community coalitions: Lee Ketelsen, of Massachusetts Clean Water Action; Marcy Goldstein-Gelb, and the leadership of MassCOSH; Russ Davis, Rand Wilson, and the leaders of Massachusetts Jobs with Justice; the leaders of the labor advisory committee of the Alliance for a Healthy Tomorrow, Ed Collins, Susan DeMaria, Steve Gauthier, Tolle Graham, Brian Mayer, Mary Vogel, Aaron Wilson, and Kim Wilson; as well as Anneta Argyres, Karla Armenti, Ted Comick, Nancy Lessin, Sanford Lewis, Susan Moir, Fred Rose, Beth Rosenberg, and Rich Youngstrom.

Beyond Massachusetts I have gained much from the inspired activism and leadership of many coalition-builders, including the many engaged activists and educators in the occupational health section of the American Public Health Association, Beverly Wright of the Deep South Center for Environmental Justice, Robert Bullard of Clark Atlanta University, Jose Bravo of the Just Transition Alliance, Nick DiCarlo, Jim Mahan, and Cathy Walker of the Canadian Auto Workers, Diane Heminway of United Steel Workers, Les Leopold and Paul Renner of the Labor Institute, and Ted Smith of the Silicon Valley Toxics Coalition.

Finally, I thank my family for enduring my many distractions from our collective life. This book has been a constant presence throughout the lives of my sons, Elias and Jonah. My partner Sibylle has been superhuman through it all. My deepest gratitude goes to them.

CHAPTER 1

Labor and Environment:
Out of Crisis, a Progressive Spark*

Since the early 1980s, coalitions of labor, community, and environmental groups have emerged in response to environmental and occupational health problems and rapidly deteriorating conditions for organized labor, working people and the poor. These coalitions are part of a global popular struggle challenging the destructive consequences of the globalization of capital. They are part of the rise of community-based, working class environmentalism. They are closely related to the emergence of a wide variety of labor-community alliances focused on job preservation and creation, a living wage and economic development, a process which has forced the previously separate notions of "community" and "labor" more to overlap, while remaining respectful of differences. The environmentalism redefined by the working class grassroots—including women, people of color, and labor—has little to do with protection of wilderness and the natural environment. It has everything to do with protecting human health and improving economic well-being.

A dominant feature of working class environmentalism is the emphasis on the protection of, and restitution from damage to, community health, as exemplified by the antitoxics activism at Love Canal and Times Beach, and the environmental justice activism in Warren, North Carolina. A less common tendency of working class environmentalism is the focus on increasing democratic power and control over production decisions and the distribution of industrial wealth, a position expressed by coalitions such as the Labor-Community Strategy Center in Los Angeles. Many labor-community coalitions have arisen partly as tactical and strategic responses by both local labor unions and communities to protect and expand union jobs in an era of dwindling rank-and-file membership and political power for unions. Within this context these coalitions have increasingly defined the environment and the local economy, environmental and economic justice, as

---

*All endnotes are at the end of each chapter.

interlocking. The extent to which workers and community members are able to forge common self-interests to wage a united struggle against violations of workers' rights, contamination of workplace and community, and local under-development, is a fundamental question addressed by this book.

This book examines the social and geographical conditions under which one of the most well-established labor-environmental coalitions in the United States, the Louisiana Labor-Neighbor Project, emerged and achieved success. It looks at problems the 16-year-old Project faced as it developed; the degree to which it came to address a broader economic agenda; and the impacts it had on occupational and environmental health, both policy and practice, as well as economic development. Examining closely a single historical case of labor-community collective action helps illustrate general problems and issues experienced by many labor-community coalitions elsewhere in the United States.

The Louisiana Labor-Neighbor Project, which went into hibernation in 2002, represented a multiscaled collaboration of labor and environment to fight forces at once local and global. This study assesses how the community process interacts with the global process to define the dynamics of the local struggle. "Environmentalism," "community," "working class," and "labor" are all concepts that have important geographic significance.

The problem of labor-environmental collaboration at the local level is in essence a problem of capitalist development versus local collective action. This book examines local labor-environmental collaboration in terms of how social relations—economic, ideological, and geographic—shape collective action and capitalist response. The Louisiana Labor-Neighbor Project resulted from a larger economic crisis within global capitalism that led corporations to cut labor costs and avoid or reduce environmental and health and safety costs. The economic crisis is rooted in the destructive and exploitative tendencies of capitalist development, which are potentially destabilizing for capital by undermining the basis of expanding capital accumulation, particularly the health and economic security of workers and communities, as well as environmental quality. At the same time, threats to worker, community and global health present political opportunities for new forms of social movements and collective action. While corporations may have a seemingly large supply of workers, communities, and nature to use in their accumulation practices, capitalist development ultimately faces real limits, in part forced upon it by social resistance and government regulation. The crisis of global capitalism, therefore, is a major factor in the emergence of new forms of collective action.

To understand the role of ideology—a system of language, ideas, culture, and the consciousness that arises from—in shaping the Louisiana Labor-Neighbor Project requires that we look at how labor, community, and social movement groups have defined the concepts of environment, community, and working class. Since the establishment of American urban ethnic communities in the mid-19th century, there has been a conceptual separation of workplace and community, in part connected to actual spatial separation of the two in many places (Katznelson, 1981).* In urban settings, "environment" was generally a community but not a workplace concept, and the linking of the two was more the exception than the rule. In contrast, in many rural and small town settings such as coal mining and mill communities, where worker and community health were intimately related, integrated definitions of environment and health were maintained. In both urban industrial and rural contexts there was a history of attempts to link workplace and community environments, as during the Progressive Era when activists regarded health as socially defined, thereby linking workplace and community environments; working-class interests were central to the public health movement of that era.

The concepts of working class and labor, as well, have changed over time, and today hold different meanings and relevance than thirty or forty years ago. In the past, "Labor" has too often regarded itself in opposition to women and oppressed social groups in the community, resulting from the gender division of labor, in which men, who dominated "labor," were involved in the production sphere, while women were defenders of the reproduction sphere, or community (Cobble, 1993; Nast, 1994). The gender division helped maintain the split between community space and production space. Yet this view of labor in opposition to women and community is gradually changing, given the transformation of the labor movement during the past decade. Labor-community coalitions face the challenge of redefining "labor" to be more inclusive of people of color and women.

The concept of "community" is vague and relative, tied to specific social and historical contexts. For instance, organized workers have typically defined themselves as a community of workers, particularly during periods of increased solidarity. Indeed, for workers, the "community of workers" may serve as the primary community. Such a community can be local, regional, national, or international, depending on the extent of the workplace struggle. Community can also refer to a local urban or rural residential community; a community of social movement activists, geographically local or extensive; and organized, multiclass constituencies such as oppressed groups, liberal churches, and liberal elected public officials. In this study "community" refers to residential community, unless otherwise specified. In certain instances I refer to environmental community, religious community, and labor community. In recent labor-community coalitions, the "community" is often comprised of multiclass groups with middle class or professional leadership, who are generally poorly experienced at social mobilization. In contrast, unions tend to have a unified class base and a clear, narrow set of goals; as such, they generally provide the sustaining impetus in labor-community coalitions (Mantsios, 1998; Moody, 1988; Yates, 2001). Yet at the same time, unions are weakened by racial and gender discrimination and business unionist bureaucracy. The coalition process itself represents potential for

*All references start on p. 211.

both unions and communities to confront their separate weaknesses. On the one hand, community partners in labor-community coalitions, particularly those steeped in civil rights activism and neighborhood direct-action militancy, provide useful models for unions to challenge their own internal weaknesses, particularly their exclusivity. On the other hand, unions may bring a democratic organizational process to coalitions, including the need for specific sets of attainable goals.

The impact of historical changes in defining labor, community and environment needs to be explored in the context of capitalist development. The development of the Louisiana Labor-Neighbor Project involved significant new definitions of environment, health and community. Environment is conceptualized by workers and community to include community and workplace health, as well as economic development, such as public services, while community is defined to include industrial workers. By comparison, capital's definition of environment and community works to its advantage, dividing workers from residential community when necessary.[1]

Further, struggles over community and working class identity and over health, in the context of capitalist development, are geographic. Identity and health are increasingly defined in more places and on various scales, which fundamentally alters the way labor, community, and the environmental movement view themselves and their grievances against capital and the state. As capital becomes more globalized, the crisis it creates and fosters are increasingly challenged by new forms of local and multiscale collective action. The growing inability of state institutions to confront crisis creates openings for labor and community to experiment. As such, worker and community collaboration occurs at a level not seen since the 1930s. The Louisiana Labor-Neighbor Project succeeded because of the multiscale nature of collective action, involving national-level organizations working closely with community-based and local union organizations and taking advantage of primarily local state political opportunities. That is, the project succeeded because it tied together the politics of multiple local places to challenge capital's domination of space. Yet the project eventually failed because it no longer effectively mobilized resources at multiple scales.

LABOR-COMMUNITY COLLABORATION IN THE LITERATURE

There is a growing body of literature on labor-community collaboration, some of which is theoretically informed (Fine, 1998; Jonas, 1998; Wills, 1998). Numerous empirical studies documented aspects of the recent history of these alliances. Brecher and Costello (1990) examine the rapid growth of such alliances in the 1980s in response to the economic and political effects of industrial restructuring, such as job loss and cutbacks in social services.

Several authors have examined labor-environmental coalitions in theoretical depth (Foster, 1993; Keil, 1995; Mann, 1993; Rose, 2000). Rose (2000) considers class tensions in collaborative attempts between workers and environmentalists in the Pacific Northwest, concluding that middle-class/working class alliances are possible but difficult to sustain because of incongruent class cultures. Keil (1995) theorizes the emergence of labor-environmental coalitions in reference to the Toronto-based Green Works Alliance, focusing on the struggles of building a common agenda. Gottlieb (1993) outlines the dynamics and history of labor-environmental coalitions, although others, too, have explored the recent history of such collaboration (Faber and O'Connor, 1993; Grossman, 1985; Kazis and Grossman, 1982; Siegmann, 1985). Foster (1993) provides an important class analysis of logger/environmentalist tensions in the Pacific Northwest. Several other writers (Noble, 1986, 1990, 1993; Wooding, 1990) have made reference to links between community environmental groups and labor over reduced state enforcement of environmental and health and safety standards. None of these studies, however, address the emergence of labor-environmental coalitions in explicitly historical-geographic theoretical terms.[2]

Several theoretical studies, while not speaking directly to coalitions, do speak to the conditions keeping labor and community apart. Katznelson (1981) locates the cleavage between workplace politics and community politics in the cultural traditions of American ethnic communities. Castells (1983) and Saunders (1981) argue that the locus of collective action has shifted from the production sphere to the consumption sphere.

Heiman (1989, 1996) explores the convergence of grassroots working class segments in helping to bring about more effective pollution controls, and pro-vides a clear geographic theoretical analyses of working class environmentalism as a project challenging global capitalism.[3] The environmental justice literature (Bullard, 1993; Faber, 1998; Harvey, 1996; Heiman, 1996; Hofrichter, 1993; Pulido, 1996) is rich with analysis of class- and race-based communities chal-lenging the state and corporations over the destructiveness of polluting facilities. Lerner's (2005) study of environmental justice activism in Louisiana's "cancer alley" examines how one particular community waged a successful international campaign to get Royal Dutch/Shell to finance the relocation of the community out of a heavily contaminated environment. Environmental justice analysis argues that environmental and economic regulation has failed to protect the health and economic well-being of working class communities and communities of color. Environmental justice activists promote a transformation of regulation from the current system of lax environmental enforcement, endemic lack of economic opportunity, and lack of corporate and governmental accountability, to a system of sustainable economic and social development, regulated by socially just institutions. Recent efforts to link environmental, public health, and labor interests on issues of clean production, "just transition" (economic support for workers and communities affected by job loss due to environmental policies), and the precautionary principle illustrate how environmental justice, public health, academic, workplace health and safety, and union interests can find common ground and forge progressive strategies (Gottlieb, 2001).

Case studies and theoretically informed studies of labor-community coalition-building tell us that there has been a rapid growth of such coalitions since the 1980s as a response to economic crisis. These coalitions have achieved important successes and brought about important new political relationships, including collaboration of different working class segments, to challenge corporations and government. But the studies also tell us that there are powerful historical conditions that prevent and challenge coalitions, including class tensions and the cultural divide between workplace and community. We need to develop a theoretical framework for a better understanding of how labor-community coalition-building is part of the process of intervening in capitalist crisis. Such a framework is vital to understanding the role of leadership, the class experience of organizations, and the particular context of industry and the state in shaping the development of coalitions.

This book uses a historical materialist framework to examine how labor-community politics arise out of the destructive character of capitalist development, and explores such collective action as part of the process of mediating and resolving capitalist crisis. The analytical framework follows the ideas of Italian political theorist Antonio Gramsci (1971), and emphasizes contradictory political and ideological arrangements that maintain capital accumulation, particularly during economic crises. It views the socially and ecologically detrimental effects of capital accumulation, and the resistance movements against those effects, as a social struggle primarily over political and ideological hegemony, and secondarily over economic hegemony. Such an approach has been criticized for not considering sufficiently the significance of economic processes.[4] In an effort to address this problem, the work presented here incorporates a structural analysis of capitalist development (Harvey, 1982, 1991; Smith, 1990) and a structural political ecological analysis (J. O'Connor, 1988). Both related approaches are deeply embedded in economic processes. From this core approach I draw heavily on approaches that are related to a Gramscian framework, particularly "regulationist" approaches.[5] Gramscian and regulationist approaches bring into focus political and ideological practice, the openness and importance of counterhegemonic strategies, particularly political strategies for collective identity formation, and consider the state as a fluid, open, and contradictory set of social institutions.

Gramsci argued that collective action comes about through an historically specific process, in which intellectual leadership observes and theorizes about specific economic relations, then educates and organizes a class or social group, and seeks to develop workable political strategies that can best confront crisis. Building in part on Gramsci, regulationist approaches address the way crisis is regulated and capital accumulation stabilized. They argue that mediation of crisis is an open and volatile process involving conflict, experimentation, and compromise. As such, social movement institutions, along with state agencies, have a role in intervening in crisis.

THE LOUISIANA PROJECT

The Louisiana Labor-Neighbor Project was an alliance of members of the Paper, Allied-Industrial, Chemical, and Energy (PACE, formerly the Oil, Chemical and Atomic Workers) union, Local 4-620[6] and a network of grassroots environmental groups in the petrochemical industrial area around Baton Rouge, Louisiana. By the time of its decline in 2002, this coalition was one of the oldest community-based coalitions in existence. While there are numerous other labor-community alliances working on production and health issues, the OCAW coalition was selected because in 1990, at the time this work was conceived, the coalition sought to institutionalize and consolidate its coalition work. The consolidation phase was deemed a crucial moment in a coalition's development by virtue of a shift from short-term tactics to longer-term strategy.

The coalition grew out of a 5-1/2 year lockout by the BASF Corporation at its Geismar, Louisiana, facility beginning in 1984. Minchin (2003) explores in great detail the emergence of labor-community collaboration during the BASF lockout. BASF locked out 370 OCAW union members of Local 4-620 over disagreements about wages and benefits. The lockout was part of a series of attempts by BASF to decertify and break unions at its facilities around the country in the early 1980s. Soon after the lockout began, the OCAW International sent several organizers to find a way to break it. The organizers built relationships with local environmentalists and began a corporate campaign that targeted not only BASF's facility in Geismar and elsewhere, but other industrial plants in the petrochemical corridor around Baton Rouge. The OCAW and its environmental allies forced the corporation to lose tens of millions of dollars by revealing environmentally destructive practices at BASF, and brought pressure to bear on the company by digging up environmental and health and safety violations at other Louisiana industrial facilities. Moreover, OCAW's corporate campaign helped bring about state regulatory policy changes, notably the creation of an "environmental scorecard," which would tie industrial property tax breaks to corporate environmental protection practices. To broaden the fight against billions of dollars in state subsidies to industry, OCAW helped launch the Louisiana Coalition for Tax Justice in 1989.

Soon after the lockout ended in December 1989, the union members agreed to fund half of a $50,000 year coalition with the National Toxics Campaign, including a full-time community/environmental organizer who would organize local community residents around health and economic issues, and would track BASF's workplace environmental, health, and safety violations. The union chose to fund the coalition as a way of returning support to the community that had supported it during the lockout. In 1990, the Louisiana Labor-Neighbor Project was formed, with an advisory board consisting of OCAW leaders and local grassroots environmental activists. Since that time, the project organized four local community organizations in Ascension Parish, which successfully demanded the creation of a public water district and water delivery system and the installation of a 24-hour air monitor of industrial pollution, both in the community of Geismar. The project was also successful in blocking the construction of an international airport in Ascension Parish, restricting hazardous materials transport on rural residential roads, and passing an Ascension Parish ordinance requiring industries and their contractors to report their job hiring records when applying for municipal bonds, in order to get local employers to hire more local labor. Further, the sister organization Louisiana Coalition for Tax Justice, by organizing an African-American community in neighboring Iberville Parish over industry's failure to alert the community during a toxic air release, helped force a federal civil rights review of industrial practices. In the late 1990s, the Labor-Neighbor Project organized a broad coalition of more than twenty religious and community organizations, called Louisiana Communities United, over a four-parish area. LCU and Labor-Neighbor were instrumental to the success of a high-profile campaign to halt the siting of plastics production facility in a low-income African-American community in St. James Parish. Altogether, the Labor-Neighbor Project became a recognized force for environmental justice advocacy and broad-based organizing in the region. In 2002, the Labor-Neighbor Project suspended operations in the wake of organizational problems.

NEW COALITIONS, NEW MOVEMENTS

Labor/grassroots environmental alliances represent a significant counter-hegemonic experiment in social movement collective action by endeavoring to overcome long-standing divisions between workplace politics and community politics in the United States. Moreover, they hold great potential for efforts to build a universal progressive political project, while balancing the politics of difference. Such alliances can potentially challenge capital at the workplace and in the community; help labor to overcome retrenchment, and communities to arrest their downward slide, experienced under economic restructuring; and aid the grassroots environmental movement by deepening its base of support and by lending it the political organizing experience and knowledge of industrial polluters that labor has. Though fraught with obstacles, both internal (such as class ideologies) and external (such as the jobs versus environment mindset), labor-environmental-community coalitions constitute a serious attempt to transcend the failures of progressive organizations in broadening their grassroots power base.

Precisely because labor-community alliances have potentially great political meaning for progressive social change, they are an important subject of research.

This study extends our understanding of the complications involved in forging a new form of identity politics between community and workplace within a specific context of global capitalism. It demonstrates how labor and the environment have dealt with material and ideological obstacles, and political opportunities and limitations. Finally, it assesses how far these alliances can realistically and potentially go in building political power and shaping environmental, occupational safety and health, and economic development policy and practice.

Critical to understanding what happened in Louisiana is Gramsci's analysis of hegemony and building a counterhegemonic politics, which is central to the discussion of labor-community politics, and its interrelationship with the politics of capitalist development. Chapter 2 examines theories and concepts relevant to creating a theory of labor-community coalitions. After examining several theories of uneven capitalist development, including geographic theories, I consider political ecology analysis, the main insight of which stresses that capitalist production perpetuates crisis by threatening and degrading the conditions of production upon which it depends—namely, labor, urban space and infrastructure, and the natural environment. This makes clear the ways in which capital redefines nature, in order to render "natural" the destructive use of nature, an important aspect of the way in which the ideological terrain is altered.

Chapter 3 considers the long history of labor-environmental collaboration and division in the United States. Common political projects between labor and community in urban industrial settings have been the exception rather than the rule throughout much of the past century, even after the onset of economic restructuring in the 1970s and 1980s. The infrequency of collaboration in the urban context is attributable to spatial and conceptual divisions between workplace and residential community. These divisions have been closely associated with capitalism since early industrialization and are widely understood to have major importance for the trajectory of class politics in this country.

As with the trench-like divisions between workplace and community, labor and environmental organizations, too, have largely been apart, and often in opposition, over the past 100 years. The split between workplace health and community health in this country is well-rooted in the pattern of segmented conceptualization of workplace and community politics since early industrialization. Despite general separation, periods of heightened collaboration between labor and community environmental groups occurred: the Progressive Era, the 1960s/early 1970s, and the 1980s and 1990s. The 1930s saw a rise in labor-community collaboration during numerous campaigns by CIO unions. The periods of greater labor-community and labor-environmental collaboration are noted for an increase in diversity of unionism and social movements, and a broadening of their political agendas. Even during periods of greater labor-community collaboration there have been tensions between insurgency and reform, between collective action based on diversity and flexibility and that based on uniformity and rigid institutionalization. Sometimes heightened labor-community collaboration is met by a backlash from corporations and government, as illustrated by the passage of the punitive Taft-Hartley Act in 1947. Taft-Hartley circumscribed labor rights, in particular by outlawing solidarity strikes, and was a response to the CIO and its successful community collaborations in the 1930s.

Chapters 4 and 5 deal with a historical geography of the Louisiana Labor-Neighbor Project. Chapter 4 examines the background and evolution of the Oil, Chemical and Atomic Worker's community collaboration through 1989. Louisiana history demonstrates precedence for labor-community collaboration, but no definitive, recurrent pattern of such cooperation. The state has a rich history of union militancy, with numerous efforts in building multiracial unions in periods of intense racial segregation. Many of these efforts drew informal, short-term tactical community solidarity. The Catholic Church was an occasional ally to workers. Antiunion corporate politics in tandem with narrow economic strategies of Louisiana labor unions, however, cut short nearly all collaborative experiments. With the passage of right-to-work legislation in 1976, Louisiana labor unions, guided by business unionist strategies focused on preserving wages and contracts at the expense of building union political power and expanding union membership across the state, were in serious trouble.

BASF's 5-1/2 year (1984-89) lockout of the Oil, Chemical and Atomic Workers took place as the company sought a flexible solution to increased competition in the petrochemical industry. The union responded with a campaign unprecedented in Louisiana, drawing on the International's experience in coalition-building and environmental and workplace health issues, and on the leadership and experience of key community and environmental activists. In the process of collaborating with, and learning from, community and environmental leaders, the union members developed an environmental consciousness. The union's local politics included efforts to apply direct and indirect pressure on BASF through issues of pollution and illegal tax exemptions. By using a particular environmental issue, and facilitated by effective long-term relationship-building with key state environmental officials, the union successfully pressured the company to end the lockout.

Chapter 5 looks at the Labor-Neighbor Project's development after 1990 and includes an examination of persisting obstacles to coalition-building. Since the end of the BASF lockout in 1989, OCAW consolidated and expanded its labor-community political project. Previously a short-term tactic oriented to ending the lockout, the union's relationship with the community became a longer-term strategy. The new project was accompanied by the development of a "coalition consciousness." The union became committed to developing a highly localized coalition politics in Ascension Parish. What began as a handful of activists in one community, developed into five local civic groups throughout Ascension Parish. More recently the project turned to linking church-based organizing with its previous base of civic groups. No longer a joint endeavor with the National Toxics Campaign, since that group's demise in 1993, the Labor-Neighbor Project continued to be a union-led endeavor. Its organizing initiatives changed the politics in Ascension Parish through the creation of a local waterworks district; efforts to include the petrochemical companies in a new municipality; and other attempts to exert popular control over local space. In the late 1990s, the Project organized a coalition of twenty religious and community organizations, Louisiana Communities United, to address economic and environmental justice problems in four river parishes. After 2001, the Labor-Neighbor Project suffered organizational setbacks due to staffing and funding problems.

Chapter 6 presents a discussion of what happened to make the Louisiana Labor-Neighbor Project develop, endure, and decline. Structure and agency in the project's development are considered while comparisons are drawn to other labor-community collaborations. The Labor-Neighbor Project is a new spatial politics structured by the spatial character of capitalist politics, mainly the petrochemical industry; the relative openness of the state; and the class experience of labor and community. Labor-community alliances are typically initiated by a dire economic situation for labor, overlapping with a community environmental crisis. The coalition agenda broadens over time from one or several issues to many issues. Significantly, for a coalition to endure and thrive, it must ultimately strengthen its coalition capacity, that is, it must build leadership skills and coalition-building skills on the part of labor and community leaders. It is experienced and skilled leadership that can maximize the use of a coalition's resources, particularly national resources, which is vital to the overall health of the organization. Over the long term a coalition must become explicitly progressive by broadening its leadership to include both working class and middle class leaders, and by challenging the state and corporations directly over economic and environmental justice issues, such as corporate welfare, pollution in working class communities, and lack of equitable economic development.

The Labor-Neighbor Project was emblematic of labor-community coalitions of the past twenty years, in that it represented a new spatial politics, addressing production and reproduction together. The project built a successful politics during the 1990s because it developed its coalition capacity—including awareness level, outside resources, and leadership skills—through a back-and-forth, discursive process among labor and community members. Such development of coalition capacity was enabled by OCAW's constant class-based intellectual leadership and the enduring organizing influence of the National Toxics Campaign and local "bridge-builders," aided by the significant multiscale resources that OCAW and the NTC legacy could bring to the effort. The Labor-Neighbor Project succeeded as long as it sustained the dynamic combination of building coalition capacity and the important provision of leadership and resources from OCAW and the NTC legacy. This dynamic prevented the project from slipping into parochial politics and buffered the coalition process against capitalist interference throughout the 1990s. The project suffered, however, when OCAW and its organizing partner could no longer provide adequate intellectual leadership and resources to the project's community leaders, which underscores the potential fragility of leadership and national resources. Gramsci's analysis of leadership in building a counterhegemonic project helps us to understand labor-community coalitions by considering how coalition intellectual leadership is rooted in the shifting political economy and how coalition politics is open and contested.

ENDNOTES

1. For instance, the Taft-Hartley Act of 1947, passed under heavy lobbying by the business community, provided legal limits to a union's base of solidarity. By outlawing secondary boycotts—the right to picket other companies and boycott products from those companies—Taft-Hartley severely circumscribed the community of labor, helping to isolate unions from one another and from communities.
2. Some of these authors employ political economic theory but do not focus on coalitions or do not consider geographical dimensions (Faber and O'Connor, 1993; Noble, 1986, 1990, 1993; Wooding, 1990). Others focus on coalitions but do not express theory within the context of global capitalism (Gottlieb, 1993; Grossman, 1985; Kazis and Grossman, 1982; Siegmann, 1985).
3. See also Hamilton's (1993) geographically-informed analysis on the importance of the people of color environmental justice movement in challenging destructive conditions set up by global capitalism.
4. Jessop (1990b) argues that Gramsci and neo-Gramscian theorists (Debray, 1973; Laclau, 1977; Poulantzas, 1978) generally underplay economic constraints rooted in the general laws of capital accumulation.
5. Regulationist approaches build on the work of the French Regulation school (Aglietta, 1979; Lipietz, 1987), expanding it to consider social movements (Hirsch, 1983; Jenson, 1989; Mayer, 1991). Other theoretical analysis informed by Gramsci are considered, including state theory (Foucault, 1980; Jessop, 1990a, 1990b; Poulantzas, 1978); poststructural political ecology (Escobar, 1995; M. O'Connor, 1993); New Social Movement theory (Habermas 1991, 1984; Melucci, 1985, 1980; Offe, 1985; Touraine, 1985); and discourse analysis (Baudrillard, 1981, 1975; Foucault, 1980; Jameson, 1984; Laclau and Mouffe, 1985; Young, 1990).
6. PACE was created in 2000 through the merger of the Oil, Chemical, and Atomic Workers (OCAW) and the International Paper Workers Union (IPWU). Throughout most of this book I will refer to OCAW rather than PACE, since the analysis focuses largely on the premerger period. PACE merged with the United Steelworkers of America (USWA) in 2005 to become the United Steel Workers (USW).

CHAPTER 2

Building a Theory of
Labor-Community Coalitions

Difficult and demanding circumstances have prompted labor and community organizations to increasingly forge alliances during the past 30 years. Successful labor-community coalition building happens because of a convergence of leadership, effective organization, and political economic circumstances. In this chapter, relevant ideas in political economic and social movement theory are examined to help explain the political and social significance of coalitions. Labor-community coalitions are part of an overall challenge from civil society to the dominance of business and industry in public policy. Political economic context is considered, including changes in capitalist development, government regulation, and related changes in the labor and environmental movements during the past thirty years. Of particular importance is the role of government in enabling civil society coalitions, providing political opportunities for collective action, while at the same time supporting capitalist development. Finally, this chapter considers the organizational capacity of collaborative projects to mobilize resources at different geographic scales, and to build solidarity by appealing to universal interests while overcoming particular interests.

HEGEMONY AND COALITION-BUILDING

The Louisiana Labor-Neighbor Project and other labor-community coalitions must be seen as part of a long-term strategy of building a counterveiling force to the dominant political economic bloc of big business and government allies. Italian social theorist Antonio Gramsci (1891-1937) provided an analysis of hegemony, or social group domination, a concept that is critical to understanding contemporary labor-community coalitions, including the dynamic of intellectual leadership in social movements and community organizations as it arises from historically specific conditions. Three aspects of Gramsci's analysis of hegemony are particularly useful: how hegemony is used by a dominant social group, and particularly how it extends beyond workplace and class material issues into a broader civic life of culture and ideology; how the counterhegemonic process operates, including the development of new political strategies and ways to intervene in crises of the capitalist system; and how hegemony is an open and conflictual process within the state. The concept of hegemony is important for understanding coalitions in both an analytical and strategic sense.

Gramsci reinterpreted how capitalism works by giving much more importance to human consciousness and action in shaping historical events. He saw the relationship between political action and economic reality as fluid and open. This fluid relationship means that people's understanding of economic crisis and political and ideological power relations is critical to creating political strategies that intervene in, or mediate, the crises of capitalist development (Femia, 1981). With his core concept of hegemony, Gramsci argued that ideology and culture were important in maintaining the rule of dominant class and other social forces. Gramsci emphasized several conflicting areas of hegemony. Hegemony meant, on the one hand, the organization of consent to a complex set of class and social forces under moral and intellectual leadership of the capitalist class, a set of forces known as a historic bloc. A ruling historic bloc consists of fluid, organically linked institutional practices of government, business, and civil society, which help to stabilize capitalist development, and a unified set of state relations. It is through dominant, or hegemonic, relations and institutions, Gramsci argued, that capitalist crises are mediated, or managed. Secondly, hegemony involves coercive practices—legal, ideological, or other forms of pressure—used by the hegemonic bloc to maintain popular support for its projects. Thirdly, hegemony refers to potential counterhegemonic projects made up of the working and middle classes and their allies, and how such projects can develop political strategies to intervene in capitalist crises.

In a current understanding of hegemony, the hegemonic bloc employs coercive strategies such as downsizing, subcontracting, plant closings, and forcing communities to compete with one another for businesses and jobs. At the same time the dominant bloc of social forces elicits consent from civil society in workplace bargaining, economic development, and policy changes such as utility or environmental deregulation, which tend to benefit the hegemonic bloc rather than the general public. The dominant bloc also builds consent through the market by creating consumer demand for products and services, reaching the point of "market triumphalism" in many aspects of everyday life (Peet and Watts, 1996). The hegemonic bloc, in effect, institutes its policies and agenda in civil society through coercive methods, using its superior economic position, and through consent, by exercising ideological, moral leadership through social institutions such as the media, education, and political parties (Boggs, 1976; Epstein, 1990). Today the hegemonic bloc promotes numerous neoliberal (or free market) solutions to social and economic problems.

Gramsci's concept of hegemony also helps us understand how the counter-hegemonic process operates. In a strategic sense, hegemony is a useful way to understand the process of building multi-class progressive alliances to hold corporations and governments accountable and advance progressive social and political reform. Gramsci's emphasis on the need for well-developed political strategy suggests that the best way to build a counterhegemonic project is through long-term strategy based on rigorous observation of events. Hegemony is a vital concept in explaining how the intellectual leadership of labor and social movement allies grasps the shifting political economic conditions that might call for new political strategies, including new alliances (Boggs, 1976; Femia, 1981).

Gramsci conceived of a counterhegemonic process in which the working-class would be a prominent force but not the only one. With the onset of Fordist[1] capitalism, an integrated system of mass production and mass consumption, in the 1920s, the working class had become far more structurally complex than in earlier capitalist development, overlapping with other classes on consumption and workplace issues (Epstein, 1990). Gramsci envisioned new leaders emerging from a changed political economic climate under Fordism. Participants in a counter-hegemonic political process would apply elements of long-term future goals, such as democratic decision making and broadening of the base of common interests. The counterhegemonic process involved a shift in the working-class struggle from a sole focus on workplace issues to include questions of culture and ideology in broader civic life. Given a broader terrain of struggle, a new long-term strategy involved coalition building, a formation of a historic bloc comprising the working class and segments of other classes (Epstein, 1990). The crisis of Fordism, beginning in the 1970s, represented for labor and social movements a shift in circumstances that challenged labor and community to reevaluate their political strategies. Intensifying neoliberalism brought an end to greater job security, as well as a backlash by corporations against government regulations and unions. The new political climate placed unions and communities in an increasingly vulnerable and weakened position and created conditions for new counter-hegemonic strategies. In this context new leaders would emerge and seek to broaden the base of common interests and build bridges between social classes, between labor and community.

A changed political economic landscape may warrant a new political strategy, a "war of position," by labor and community to counteract the hegemonic ideology of free market capitalism as well as dominant economic and political power (Epstein, 1990). The current war of position includes a universal social justice perspective (Carroll, 1989) to challenge the global neoliberal strategies of the leading political and economic powers and entities such as the World Trade Organization. The global justice movement is a decentralized, extensive network of networks of diverse civil society organizations promoting democratic institutions, fair trade, human rights, environmental justice, and sustainable development. This movement includes the active participation of many labor and environmental organizations in a direct challenge to neoliberal hegemony.

A Gramscian analysis is important for two additional, related reasons. It regards hegemony as an open and dynamic process within the state, where a set of strategic relations are in continuous conflict. Corporate interests, as well as various interests from community institutions, unions, and government officials and agencies vie to promote their proposals within an arena of often conflicting state interests, such as economic growth, consumer and environmental protection, and human rights. A Gramscian framework also views social movements as actors in a counterhegemonic process, as positioned to intervene in (or mediate) capitalist crisis. These contributions are felt through much of social theory on collective action since the 1960s and have been central to the discussion of working class social movements. The concept of hegemony helps us to understand the main points critical to labor-community coalitions: the political economic conditions conducive to labor-community coalition building; how the state enables the development of labor-community coalitions; and the organizational capacity of labor-community counterhegemony.

POLITICAL ECONOMIC CONDITIONS FOR
COALITION BUILDING

Political economic conditions are critical to understanding coalitions. Changes in the political economic landscape since the early 1970s are closely linked to the proliferation of labor-community coalitions. The changing political economy in urban and industrial production created the conditions for labor-community alliances. Within a context of intensifying neoliberal practices—deregulation, weakened environmental and labor laws, and outsourcing—labor unions lost members and were severely weakened politically. The crisis of Fordist capital accumulation forced labor to move beyond rigid thinking about purely economic issues, such as wages and working conditions, and to build alliances along broader social justice themes. Fordist production reached a crisis stage in the late 1960s, owing to intensified international competition and declining profitability. This was true for the petrochemical industry as it was across all manufacturing sectors. The shift from Fordism to post-Fordism came about because of a crisis of profitability, on the one hand, resulting from a breakdown in rigid Taylorist[2] (or scientifically managed) work organization brought on by the introduction of new technologies; and, on the other hand, due to economic destabilization resulting from intensified international competition (Harvey, 1991). In the arena of urban economic development, the Fordist crisis was expressed as a division of the urban economy into high-end production and low-wage sectors in both services and manufacturing (M. Mayer, 1991). This division intensified the competition between cities for industrial and commercial development.

The crisis of Fordist capitalism signified a need for a new form of capitalist production stabilized by a different arrangement of regulation. Regulation theorists (Aglietta, 1979; Jessop, 1990b; Lipietz, 1987; see Brenner and Glick, 1991) have argued that capitalist development is comprised of the paired coordination of regimes of accumulation (the organization of production and consumption processes) and modes of regulation (institutional forms and sets of social norms, practices, and laws). Capitalist accumulation is mediated (or regulated) through historically specific institutions, practices, and social norms. This means that capitalist production and the social-political regulatory process are specific to a given time and place. Capitalist production in the Fordist and post-Fordist periods has faced both a materials crisis, imposed by degraded environmental conditions and depleted resources, and a legitimation crisis, imposed by the political reaction to negative impacts on environmental, public, and worker health (Angel, 2000; Gibbs and Healey, 1997; Lipietz, 1992). When a regime of accumulation reaches a crisis stage, a new mode of regulation is required to establish and stabilize a new regime. Both the accumulation strategies guiding capitalist economic development and the social-political regulatory arrangements must adjust to a crisis of capitalist production. The mode of regulation includes those practices and institutions embodied in the dominant institutions and norms, such as government, as well as myriad civil society institutions and practices calling corporations and government to account. Operating in concert with a mode of regulation is a "hegemonic paradigm," which helps to order systems of values, meanings, discourse, and collective identities (Jenson, 1989). Thus regulation involves not just the ordering of production and consumption processes, and the social and political institutions that stabilize them, it entails as well the regulation of values, meaning, and discourse. In the current era, free-market values, including the valuing of individual freedom over social solidarity, must contend with contrary values of environmental consciousness and a sense of social fairness. The political and ideological struggle of such meanings and discourse results in a compromise that forms the dominant system of meaning. The regulation of capitalist society and economy, therefore, is a politically and ideologically contentious process.

The Fordist crisis led corporations and the state to shift to a regime of flexible accumulation accompanied by a new mode of regulation that sought to manage flexible production and consumption. The new mode of regulation included various free market practices and norms, such as deregulation, privatization, and outsourcing. Flexibility, a strategy introduced to serve corporate elites, operated at four levels (Harvey, 1991): flexible labor processes, such as lean production; flexible labor markets, such as subcontracting and outsourcing, which ignore Fordist job security; flexible state policy, such as deregulation and privatization of public institutions and enterprises; and the geographic mobility of capital, that is, the flexibility to move manufacturing and service facilities to lower cost environments. Flexible capital accumulation has served to keep costs down by reducing labor costs as well as capital and operating costs.

Flexible production continues capital's long-used practice of geographic isolation of workers as a method of labor control (Harvey, 1993), while decentralization of labor struggles to the local level intensifies under the new regime (Harvey, 1991; Herod, 1991). During the Fordist era corporations gained control over labor through a calculated geographic division of labor into spatially divided labor markets (Clark et al., 1986), and through the geographic dispersal of workers, particularly through the shift of industry and jobs from cities to the suburbs in the 1940s (Gordon, 1977; Walker, 1981) and from the northern industrial belt to non-union regions in the Sunbelt during industrial restructuring and decentralization since the 1950s (Clark, 1981; Davis, 1986; Peet, 1984; Walker, 1981; Young, 1986). Corporate locational shifts of industry in the 1940s and since the 1950s were sparked by surging labor militancy, unionization and working class consciousness (Davis, 1986; Storper and Walker, 1989).

The corporate and governmental embrace of flexible solutions to the Fordist crisis yielded a host of corporate practices that eroded the power and gains of unions, workers and communities. Plant closings and capital flight left workers and communities with high unemployment, abandoned factories, contaminated land, and weakened local economies. The great loss of higher wage manufacturing jobs was not met with adequate regulatory policies to restore high wage employment. Post-Fordist flexible corporate solutions, to reduce production costs and boost profitability, and accompanying neoliberal regulatory policies represent the second contradiction of capital: expanded capital accumulation and support by state governmental practices and policies serve to undermine the very conditions of production upon which capital accumulation depends, namely, workers, public and environmental health, community, land and urban space (J. O'Connor, 1988). The crisis of Fordist production and its resolution by capital (as flexible production and neoliberalism) have created an economic and environmental crisis for labor and communities.

The corporate response to the Fordist crisis has been explicitly geographic (Harvey, 1991). It represents a geographic decentralization of productive capacity, as demonstrated by the off-shoring of production facilities to lower wage, non-union economies, and the globalization of finance capital. At the same time, the corporate response entailed a centralization of corporate power through corporate mergers, increasing corporate influence over government policy, and the growth in power of explicitly neoliberal international entities such as the World Trade Organization, the World Bank and the International Monetary Fund.

The Fordist crisis and its resolution represent a struggle over the production process itself, the first contradiction of capital (J. O'Connor, 1988). The conflict over the control of the production process (including labor processes and technological changes in production) and income distribution (including wages and benefits) is the context of the BASF lockout. Corporate lockouts of unions and union decertification campaigns, plant closings, layoffs, outsourcing, and wage and benefit concessions, all represent corporate responses to the Fordist crisis. These practices are business efforts to reduce labor costs and improve profitability in an increasingly competitive industrial environment. In the on-going labor-capital conflict over control of the production process in the post-Fordist period, labor has suffered serious losses in political clout, membership, and influence over workplace decisions. Yet as unions have been at an increasing disadvantage, they have sought to build new relationships with civil society organizations to improve their overall position at the local and national scales. While the first contradiction of capital—the struggle over the labor process—is an inherent and necessary part of capitalism, labor's decline is by no means inevitable. Indeed, decisions about technological change, the production process, and economic development are social choices, shaped by the relative power and intellectual leadership of labor and its allies, corporations, and the regulatory state. Crisis and struggle are inevitable; a weakened and overwhelmed labor and community, however, are not inevitable. The conflict for labor, community, and civil society groups is one of control over the production process and economic development. Mounting a challenge for reform of capitalist development, will require the creation of a strong progressive counterhegemonic project, which can enhance the local and national power of labor and civil society organizations. Of course, the configuration of such a progressive project is itself contested and should involve the participation of a wide range of local to national organizations and alliances.

Labor studies have documented the labor movement's weakened position under post-Fordism, including its struggle for new direction under AFL-CIO president John Sweeney since 1995 to organize new members while attempting to influence electoral politics and public policy. Labor movement analysis has also examined the internal struggle going on within unions and the union movement nationally over democratic reform: the struggle between business unionism and social movement unionism (Bronfenbrenner, 2001; Early, 1998; Moody, 1988, 1997, 2001). Unions have increasingly used strategies such as community coalitions and corporate campaigns in response to corporate political practices that address the Fordist crisis.

At the same time, the shift to post-Fordist corporate flexible practices has forced progressive movements to address their own internal political fragmentation (Harvey, 1991). Since the 1960s social movement politics had become increasingly single-issue oriented, a trend that complicates the creation of durable labor-community coalitions. Nevertheless, the shift to post-Fordist flexible capitalism has forced labor and community to unite against policies and practices that undermine workers, the environment, and communities, that is, against the second contradiction of capital. Real and perceived corporate attacks on unions and communities have prompted some community organizations and labor unions to broaden their agendas and become explicitly social justice organizations as a way to maintain ongoing collaboration.

In summary, the shift to flexible capitalist production and neoliberal economics brings a host of anti-labor, anti-community practices by corporations and government. For the past thirty years the hegemonic bloc has employed practices and policies that weaken unions and community institutions. Such practices are part of the second contradiction of capital, that is, capital practices that unintentionally undermine the conditions of production, including workers' rights, worker and environmental health, and the economic viability of communities. The second contradiction of capital has ultimately triggered the emergence of labor-community coalitions and the beginnings of a coherent counterhegemonic project.

HOW THE STATE ENABLES COALITIONS

Labor-community coalitions need to avail themselves of political opportunities to advance their agenda and build popular support. Understanding the dynamics of the state, therefore, is important. This study follows the Gramscian notion that the state is not monolithic, but rather is a set of open, fluid, strategic relations, an ensemble of contested projects within the hegemonic bloc (Jessop, 1990a; Poulantzas, 1978). The state has separate projects for economic development, environmental protection, civil rights protections, and community development, and each of these projects is contested. Labor has a certain degree of influence in several, but not all, state projects, while environmental organizations and community also have a varying degree of influence. At any given moment, labor-community and labor-environmental coalitions have an opportunity to exercise civic power in certain state projects. Within any given state project having strategically positioned allies, such as legislators or agency officials, is vital to the overall ability of labor-community coalitions to exert influence.

The state enables coalition-building by providing opportunities for counterhegemonic efforts to confront the hegemonic bloc within certain state projects. For instance, labor and environmental organizations can join forces to promote new environmental, health and safety legislation, or local municipal ordinances about environmental protection or public works. State projects such as social welfare policies may sometimes seem to contradict overall goals of the hegemonic bloc, such as advancing economic growth and the accumulation of capital. Protecting worker, community and environmental health, as well as promoting human and civil rights, are also goals of some state projects, and provide opportunities for labor-community and labor-environmental collaboration. Because of the tendency of capital accumulation to undermine the conditions of capitalist production, state projects are vital arenas for labor, community, and social movement organizations to collaborate to seek improved protections of human rights and greater economic and social resources for communities and civil society organizations. The balance of forces in state projects is dynamic and in constant flux, with political opportunities for social movements to influence state projects shifting between local, state, and national levels. The experience of labor-social movement collaboration during the past forty years demonstrates that collaborative pressure can be effectively applied at all levels, from the successful campaign to create the federal Occupational Safety and Health Act, to numerous labor-community campaigns to win municipal support for a living wage. Local labor-community coalitions may take advantage of a permeable local state, that is a government with potential strategic allies within important, conflicting state projects. Conflicting state projects, such as one for environmental protection and another for generous public financial support of corporate development, provide major political opportunities for unions and community organizations to organize against destructive practices in corporate-dominated projects. State projects have faced political challenges to their own legitimacy during the past thirty years, as an emergent mode of regulation seeks to resolve the production and consumption crises under Fordist and post-Fordist flexible capitalism. Such legitimation crises provide opportunities for social movement coalitions to form, promote corporate and governmental accountability, and put forth an alternative democratic vision of economic development.

THE ORGANIZATIONAL CAPACITY OF LABOR-COMMUNITY COUNTERHEGEMONY

Social movement and labor studies have consistently argued that social movement efforts succeed when they fulfill the capacity of movement organizations to mobilize people and other resources, and take advantage of the political opportunities, including those in the state. Fulfilling organizational capacity is critical to building power and having a political impact. Organizational capacity depends upon the experience and strength of community, movement, and union leaders to organize, understand and exploit political openings, and develop counterhegemonic strategy. To effectively build power and make a political impact depends upon how well leaders understand political economic trends and exploit political openings in the state. The ability of leaders to identify and mobilize multi-scale financial and organizing resources and to become coalition builders is critical. All of these factors define organizational capacity.

Organizational capacity depends upon an organization's structure and resources as well as external political conditions. "Resource mobilization" theorists contend that movement organizations succeed when they access and mobilize resources, particularly through organizational networks, and when they build organizational structures that foster democratic participation and effective use of skill, financial, other resources (Jenkins and Perrow, 1977; McCarthy and Zald, 1977; Oberschall, 1973; see B. Miller, 2000). "Political process" theorists argue that movements mobilize not only because of organizational resources, but because of their capacity to take advantage of shifting political opportunity structures (McAdam,

1982; Tarrow, 1983; Tilly, 1978; see B. Miller, 2000). Indeed, organizations must have necessary internal capacity, such as shared interests, or a common agenda (Tilly, 1978); a readiness to mobilize, including having access to networks, the presence of skilled leaders, and motives for solidarity (McAdam, 1982; Tilly, 1978); as well as an emerging consciousness demanding social change. But there must also be weak political alignments combined with allies located in strategic positions (Tarrow, 1983). External mid-level politics cannot be underestimated. On the one hand, unfavorable political opportunity structures can prevent organizations from mobilizing, even if they have sufficient resources and grievances; on the other, if political opportunity structures are favorable, community and movement organizations can successfully mobilize if they have sufficient resources and grievances (B. Miller, 2000). Labor and community organizations forge coalitions, in part, to build stronger organizational capacity to mobilize people and resources and act on political opportunities.

The labor-community collaborative process, therefore, depends on the consciousness and intellectual capacity of leaders and their organizations to organize, finance, and sustain a coalition, while recognizing political opportunities and cultivating relationships with strategically positioned allies. Leaders and organizations with previous coalition-building experience bring a greater awareness to a new situation calling for labor-community collaboration. Leaders with an awareness of the destructive tendency of capitalist economic growth, the second contradiction of capital, are at an advantage in recognizing the need for building common ground. That leaders are aware of shifting political economic conditions and the need for new organizing strategies is an important step in recognizing the need for coalition-building. When labor leaders acknowledge that working class struggle is no longer just about workplace issues but also about broader community issues, including environmental health and community development, they are in a position to assist in the coalition process. Union and community leaders with this awareness are potential bridgebuilders who may ultimately regard labor and community as partners in challenging destructive production and economic growth.

The new awareness by labor-community leaders of the importance of collaboration stands in stark contrast to the parochial, divided political awareness of labor and community leaders in the immediate post-World War II period. The post-World War II capital-labor accord, together with the divided, issue-oriented progressive politics beginning in the 1960s, form the baseline from which new labor-community strategies rose. Some labor and social movement leaders were ahead of the curve, drawing from labor-community collaboration traditions from the 1930s and earlier. Several unions had a tradition of coalition-builders, particular in health and safety. Yet by and large labor-community collaboration was a rediscovered or altogether new practice for unions, social movement organizations, and communities.

The political economic backdrop for the new labor-community counter-hegemony is comprised of several significant factors: new assaults on the conditions of production brought on by the shift to "flexible" capitalism and neoliberal, free-market regulatory policies; the fragmentation of progressive politics along issue lines since the 1960s Great Society (Harvey, 1991); the broken capital-labor accord, brought on by corporations' shift to flexible production; and the ongoing divided agendas of labor and community organizations. Against the backdrop of failed protections for civil society and fragmented movements has emerged not only a wave of labor-community experiments, but the rise of many new civil society organizations in general. The failure of the hegemonic bloc to protect human rights (workers' rights, civil rights, environmental rights), has helped to fuel a growth in civil society organizations since the 1960s. Facilitating the growth of civil society organizations and the emergence of citizen leaders has been the communications revolution, making possible far-flung networks of social justice organizations and intensified "community building" on a wide range of social justice and ecological issues (Lappé, 2005).

Labor and community organizations have different experiences, organizational structures, and goals that may foster or hinder coalition building. The capacity of labor and community leaders to recognize opportunities, develop strategies, and mobilize critical resources to build coalitions depends upon a number of factors, among which are coalition building experience of the organizations and leaders, on the one hand, and a sense of urgency or crisis among the organizations' members, on the other. The capacity of organizations to form coalitions—call it intellectual leadership attentive to the real issues and concerns of union and community members—faces numerous challenges that have long confronted labor and community organizations. Those challenges include: longstanding divisions between labor and community, between production-based and consumption-oriented organizations and movements, and the related tendency toward isolation among unions and community organizations; racial and ethnic divisions within unions and communities; and the fragmentation of progressive politics into issue-oriented politics. But the divisions can be bridged, as demonstrated by the re-emergence of coalition-building after the dissolution of the post World War II capital-labor accord, which had undermined the urgency of coalitions.

Bolstering organizational capacity to confront the larger challenges of isolation, parochialism, and fragmentation, requires an understanding of class and power, particularly as they relate to the hegemonic bloc of corporations and certain segments of government. By employing a class-power analysis of corporations and the state, labor-community coalitions may better understand free-market ideology in its many forms and how the moral leadership of corporations and the state uses both coercive and consensus-based strategies. Labor-community leaders may then begin to develop progressive strategies, based on a common agenda that joins production and consumption struggles, community and labor interests. This is a significant challenge, but one that is essential for constructing a durable collaboration.

BUILDING A COMMON AGENDA: LEARNING FROM SOCIAL MOVEMENT ANALYSIS

Social movement analysis and labor studies have made important observations that are pertinent to social movement coalition-building. The major point is that for movements to have a more powerful and lasting impact they need to transcend the limitations of "old" and "new" movements and build new institutions with a common agenda. Such new collaborative institutions must then face the challenge of balancing consensus building with a diversity of interests. Social movement analysis makes the following points.

Rigidity and Fragmentation

Traditional ("old") movements and new social movements have been limited by rigid and fragmented strategies and organizational structures (Plotke, 1990). In the case of the labor movement, considered an old or traditional movement, while it had periods of coalition-building in its heyday of the 1930s and 1940s, it experienced a long period of narrow strategies and rigid organization from the 1950s until the 1980s. While new social movements (environmental, peace, women's rights, gay rights) have achieved much through raising national consciousness and shaping social policies, their commonly single-issue orientation has served to keep them isolated from other movements.

For decades "business unionism" in organized labor has kept the focus on collective bargaining and servicing members rather than on building political strength through coalition building, organizing new members, and strengthening union democracy (Moody, 1988, 1990, 1997, 2001). While there has been a significant shift in the AFL-CIO since the mid-1990s to strengthen labor support for elected officials and put more resources into organizing, the service orientation of business unionism has persisted, from national unions to union locals. Despite the departure from the AFL-CIO of the "Change to Win" coalition of five national unions in 2005, with a call for extensive organizing of new members, national unions continue to be plagued by business unionism. Numerous union locals and central labor councils, however, have engaged increasingly in social movement unionism, joining Jobs with Justice or other local community coalitions in order to build local power (Early 1998; Fine, 1998). Arguably such local experimentation in social movement unionism on the fringes (Fine, 1998) may have had some influence on the shake-up in the leadership and direction of the AFL-CIO in the mid-1990s and again in 2005. National AFL-CIO leaders have acknowledged that the service model of unionism was unable to stop or offset the significant loss of union membership. To build union strength leaders chose to invest in new member organizing and electoral political action. The labor movement is experiencing dynamic change, while clinging to old practices of top-down business unionism. Neoliberal economic globalization has severely weakened the labor movement, draining members and exacting significant contract concessions, while the movement has been unable to respond entirely effectively. Unions have waged numerous successful campaigns against individual companies. Moreover, labor's shift to service sector organizing has been widely successful. The overall trend of declining union density, however, is alarming. In response, labor has developed flexible organizing targets, approaches, and strategies.

The environmental movement, for its part, suffered from a narrow issue focus and a narrow membership base into the 1980s, at which point environmental justice and anti-toxics activism forced the mainstream environmental organizations to broaden their environmental strategies to include a more aggressive critique of consumption and production in a capitalist economy. In contrast to mainstream organizations, anti-toxics and environmental justice activism helped to bring greater class and race awareness to environmental issues, and they frequently employed more confrontational tactics toward corporations and government. Environmental organizations became increasingly networked regionally and nationally. Yet despite such networking and collaboration, the narrow range of issues taken up by environmental groups often hindered collaboration with labor and other social movements. Such narrow issue focus of anti-toxics organizations and other environmental organizations has been characteristic of many new social movement organizations (B. Miller, 2000).

New social movement theory demonstrates the potential for conflicting identities between old and new social movement organizations, as well as the importance of forging broader agendas out of narrow ones. The Louisiana Labor-Neighbor Project and other labor-community alliances represent efforts to forge collective identity, and create a new sense of community, out of two or more sometimes conflicting movement identities. Unions are characterized by a slower, more deliberative process, generally based on majority rules in decision making and with a formal organizational structure. New social movements are characterized by a quicker decision making process based on consensus, and often have a more informal structure. New movement analysts and activists alike have regarded the need for building broader agendas, surmounting organizations' tendency to be single-issue focused, fragmented from each other, and defensive in posture. Both old and new movements continue to experience, and contribute to, fragmented progressive politics. Much of the fragmentation has to do with class barriers between old and new movement organizations, a weak class analysis, and weak class-based instruments, such as political parties (Epstein, 1990; Foley, 1992; Harvey, 1991; Navarro, 1991). Without a coherent and effective political party to represent their interests, labor and social movements have generally operated in political isolation from one another. Progressive politics have suffered from a lack of incisive class analysis and debate, at all levels, and thus have not sufficiently grasped the overwhelming reach and power of neoliberal capitalism.

Progressive political organizations lack effective class instruments, such as rigorous labor laws—ensuring the right to organize and the right of the secondary, or solidarity, strike—and more aggressive enforcement of environmental, health, and safety laws. The rigidity and fragmentation of labor and progressive politics demonstrate the need for new forms of organizing and new and strengthened relationships among various movement and community organizations.

Increasing Diversity of Actors and Activism

Both old and new social movements have been often characterized by increasing diversity. The increasing diversity of labor and environmental movements, in particular, indicates that collective action is at once about class relations, ideology, culture, race, and gender. Demographic shifts in the U.S. workforce have helped to transform the labor movement, despite the persistence of a largely white male union leadership at the national level. Organized labor has responded to the diversity of the American workforce through organizing campaigns on behalf of immigrant workers of color, such as the Service Employees International Union's "Justice for Janitors" campaigns.

The environmental movement, for its part, has also become increasingly diverse during the past 30 years, with the rise of anti-toxics and environmental justice activism. What was once largely a movement mainly of white middle and upper class activists, was transformed by local struggles of white working class communities and communities of color (Bullard, 1993; Heiman, 1989). Decades of toxic dumping and polluting facilities, in tandem with the existence of an inadequate environmental regulatory structure, helped give rise to community mobilization against polluters and contamination of poor and working class residential communities. The growth of environmental justice activism in working class and poor communities of color represents a shift of environmental concerns to include human rights. While working class and people of color environmental activism certainly broadened modern environmentalism, such class and racially diverse environmentalism has forerunners in the urban worker health activism of the late 1800s and the farm worker health mobilization of the 1940s (Gottlieb, 1993).

Despite such important changes in the constitution of labor and environmental movements, there is still much progress to be made by inclusion of grassroots leaders from communities of color, working class communities, and union locals in decision making of national organizations and networks. Indeed the process of democratization of labor and environmental movements has a long way to go.

Limitations and Potential of Geographic Scale

Urban social movements have been limited too often by their local geographic scale, and ineffective at building links to regional or national organizations and resources. The parochial tendency of urban social movement organizations has prevented them from benefitting from or contributing to a larger progressive project. The challenge is to access national social movements, such as labor and environment, and use multi-scale resources. Linking with international allies is sometimes an appropriate strategy. This applies particularly to American labor unions, which, with exception, have generally not engaged in international solidarity networks. One factor in the recent crisis at the AFL-CIO has been the labor federation's general lack of active solidarity with unions and rank-and-file workers in other regions of the world. Geographic isolation can severely hamper the building of a national and international counterhegemonic progressive project. Multi-scale solidarity and networking can help to overcome such isolation and parochial tendencies in urban social movements and organized labor. For locally-based movement organizations, mobilizing financial, skill, and technical assistance resources at multiple scales can help counteract local isolation and narrow agendas, and can lead to engagement in national and international solidarity with other movement organizations.

Social movement analysts have observed the tendency of movement organizations to remain locally-based and not organize sufficiently at a broader scale (Castells, 1983; Fainstein and Fainstein, 1985; B. Miller, 2000). Local organizations rely on place-based relations without attempting to build a large-scale organization needed to challenge the corporatization of community life, or "colonization of lifeworld" as argued by Habermas (Habermas, 1984; B. Miller, 2000). The increasing colonization of civic or community life by the rational market-orientation of neoliberal capitalism affects many facets of social and political life: schools, religion, the media, political discourse, cultural expressions, work organization, leisure time, and family relations. However, commodification of community life could foster resistance movements that could potentially create powerful counterhegemonic political projects that operate at multiple scales (Harvey, 1996; Heiman, 1990; B. Miller, 2000; Young, 1990).

A critical factor in local resistance to destructive or degrading practices of capitalism and ineffective governance is the existence of a strong geographic sense of place. The geographic scale of sense of place helps shape the construction of identity as well as social movement strategy, for instance, whether an organization or movement should mobilize on local or national issues (B. Miller, 2000). Resistance that draws from a sense of place has been most effective when linking local organizations and communities to larger-scale organizations, however, such resistance must avoid the trap of parochial or exclusionary action (B. Miller, 2000; Young, 1990). Organizations engaged in local resistance to developers, corporations, or government readily focus on a narrow range of issues in one place, at the expense of collaborating with other organizations, locally or beyond. Such isolated action, without coordinated effort with other organizations and movements, may ultimately undermine efforts to build political power of movement organizations. Urban activism against destructive development and environmentally damaging industrial practices have been prone to such isolated impact.

Yet such local struggles against destructive economic growth and expansive capitalist development have served a vital role in forcing a degree of accountability on developers, corporations, and governments. Numerous urban and rural land use struggles have sought to halt or limit urban and industrial development deemed incompatible with neighboring communities or overall regional development. Such land use struggles demonstrate an expansion/exclusion relationship, whereby the expansion of capital-led economic development, such as shopping mall and big box construction, faces challenges from community organizations seeking to exclude that activity at a particular location (Plotkin, 1984). Despite the tendency of community and regional civic organizations to become isolated in their struggles, community and social movement organizations could form regional or national networks in opposition to certain types of capital expansion. The current national campaign involving unions and local community organizations to slow the expansion of Wal-Mart stores is one such example, as are countless efforts to promote smart growth—involving a mixture of dense commercial, office, and residential development and green space preservation—over big box development. Community organizations and coalitions engaged in land use struggles can be regarded as part of ecological movements challenging the destruction of production conditions (public and environmental health, worker health and safety, urban and rural space and infrastructure) by expanding capital accumulation (O'Connor, 1988, 1994), such as industrial facilities, waste sites, highway projects, and shopping malls. Local opposition to such capital projects has been significant, though rarely coordinated. In a broader sense, countless local struggles in the United States and throughout the developing world over employment and economic livelihood, a clean environment, and health care are in reality ecological struggles, or liberation ecologies, pitted against the destructive practices of capitalist development and inadequate regulation (Peet and Watts, 1996). Such ecological struggles are against the destructiveness of capitalist growth, or rather "accumulation by dispossession," the process of depriving people of their health, environment, and economic livelihood through capital accumulation (Harvey, 2003). These struggles tend to remain isolated from one another, although there is great potential for them to link together through national and global social movement networks.

In addition to the tendency toward fragmentation of local community struggles, there has been a strong tendency for division between workplace struggles and community-based struggles (Castells, 1983; Katznelson, 1981). Such "city trenches" have accompanied the growth of U.S. cities over the past 150 years (Katznelson, 1981). Expansion of production facilities from urban to suburban settings in the early 1900s was in part an effort by management to weaken community solidarity for plant workers. Of equal importance to the spatial isolation of work and home is the conceptual separation of workplace struggles from community struggles, which is driven by the difficulty in forging class collaboration while balancing identity politics based on racial, ethnic, and cultural differences (Katznelson, 1981). The recent rise in labor-community collaboration, however, indicates that the conceptual and geographic separation of workplace from community struggles can be bridged in many situations.

Thus there is a history of locally-based mobilization, most of it isolated and oriented toward one particular struggle in one place, some of it coordinated regionally or nationally in campaigns against one corporation, yet with a potential for more effective multi-scale resistance. Multi-scale resistance contains the potential for forging connections between labor, other social movements and community organizations over the defense of living space (Heiman, 1990; Katznelson, 1981; Plotkin, 1984; Preteceille and Terrail, 1985). The challenge in working through tendencies for separation of locally-based or single-issue struggles, is to cultivate a larger sense of place that transcends the local. Harvey (1993) argues for the creation of a broader sense of community that transcends and brings together local struggles in an interconnected counterhegemonic project. Such a project builds upon the local sense of place in each local struggle but creates a broader sense of place, connected by universal principles and values of social justice.

Class Conscious Environmental Justice Activism

Challenging corporations and government can unite labor and community in a potentially class-explicit way. Numerous urban social movements focusing on capital expansion effectively challenge corporations, developers and governments over the use of land and resources. The essence of environmental justice struggles is a challenge to corporations' right to harm communities through destructive industrial production, while emphasizing communities' right to health. Ecological movement struggles provide opportunities for coalition-building between community-based and production struggles. The anti-toxics and environmental justice movements since the mid-1980s have frequently made the link between the changes in production necessary to reduce contamination of the environment and neighboring communities (Bullard, 1993; Faber, 1998; Faber and O'Connor, 1993; Hamilton, 1993). The anti-toxics and environmental justice movements effectively transcended community "consumption-based" struggles by restricting the flow of toxic wastes from production facilities to waste disposal sites, such as incinerators, landfills, and dumpsites (Heiman, 1990). The success of these movements in slowing the flow of waste owes much to their working class roots and ability to mobilize multi-class, multi-scale resources in their local campaigns.

Environmental justice and anti-toxics organizations have challenged corporations not only over the physical degradation of public health and the environment, but as well over ideologies and symbols of the environment (M. O'Connor, 1993). Ecological struggles may face a capitalist ideology that seeks to undermine and divide community and environmental forces (Dowie, 1995). Such capitalist ideological strategies include "jobs versus environment" rhetoric, promises by the American Chemistry Council of "responsible care" among chemical manufacturers, and the use of corporate science and risk assessment to discredit non-corporate, public science. Environmental justice organizations often confront such corporate ideological strategies employed to win consent among a broader public, using moral leadership, while challenging corporations' use of legally or illegally coercive tactics to undermine movement leaders and organizations. Ecological movement struggles demonstrate the interconnection of production (work), reproduction (community), and nature, while capitalist ideology—such as jobs versus environment rhetoric—seeks to divide movements and collaborations.

Environmental justice struggles do not necessarily result in labor-community collaboration, but they do provide the basis for a class analysis of production and community problems which may lead to later coalition-building. Environmental justice activists and scholars have recognized that the capitalist system has placed environmental burdens inordinately on communities of color. Corporations often target weak communities, often communities of color, for hazardous facility siting. This is the basis for a class/race analysis of corporate environmental behavior. Environmental justice activism has been characterized by some as a struggle against capitalist relations (Bullard, 1993; Faber, 1998; Harvey, 1996) and against institutional practices in government and corporations which are biased against communities of color (Bullard, 1993). Indeed, environmental justice struggles are regarded as being at once against class exploitation and racial discrimination (Bullard, 1993).

While such a class/race analysis may provide a good understanding of the problem, and may help environmental justice organizations to challenge corporations and government, it does not necessarily lead to a coherent counterhegemonic strategy of coalition-building. Many environmental justice activists in communities of color and white working class communities, however, have made the conceptual leap to see workers inside production facilities, and their unions, as allies or potential allies. Collaboration between unions and community residents has been the exception, not the rule. Because of intimidation by employers, racial divisions, and lack of effective leadership, collaboration often does not occur between workers in a controversial industrial facility and neighboring community activists. However, when bridge-builders do emerge and successfully forge collaboration between production workers and community residents, those actions become a positive example, a "demonstration effect" (Wills, 1998) that can then inspire leaders and organizations in other settings. Labor-community bridge building as a strategy has clearly spread during the past several decades. The basis for each successful coalition has been the challenge by unions, communities, and movement organizations to corporations and government: demanding corporate and governmental accountability; better regulation and enforcement; and fair and just social and economic policies.

Unions, for their part, have often lacked the class analysis useful in collaborating with community and social movement organizations (Bronfenbrenner, 2001; Moody, 2001). Most union leaders and activists recognize that corporate influence on governmental regulation and economic policy, as illustrated by corporate economic globalization, present a huge problem for democracy and economic security of working people. Yet by and large the day-to-day practice of unions has not been building an effective counterhegemonic project, in part because many union leaders do not apply an effective class analysis to understand that multi-class political alliances among social movement organizations are an important component of building a counterhegemonic force. Despite the recent focus by the AFL-CIO on organizing new members as a way of building union strength, as well as supporting political candidates, business unionism, with its emphasis on wages and contracts, still guides most unions. Much of organized labor has not fully understood the importance of social movement unionism, and thus has not adequately supported on-going coalition-building at the local and national levels. Social movement unionism, nonetheless, has taken root at the fringes of the labor movement, building coalitions with community and other social movements (Fine, 1998). The split in the AFL-CIO in 2005 was significant for its general lack of class analysis. As Fletcher (2005) points out, missing from the debate over keeping the AFL-CIO intact or allowing a major split in the federation was a discussion about building a counterhegemonic project to challenge corporations and their government allies. In other words, what is needed is a class analysis of global capitalism if labor is to arrest its decline and build political strength again. Labor cannot be saved simply by building up its membership base and supporting elected officials and political candidates. Rather, it must build political strength by creating community and social movement alliances at many geographic levels. Many steps must occur simultaneously: building up membership; fostering union democracy and leadership development; building multi-class bridges to community and other social movements; mobilizing the membership base and allies to win the support of political officials; waging corporate and governmental accountability campaigns; and pressuring for progressive reform of the Democratic Party, while encouraging the development of labor and social movement friendly third parties. Linking the previous actions together is an effective class/race/cultural analysis that keenly understands how global capitalism will continue down a destructive path if not challenged by an effective, progressive counterhegemony calling for a new system of social regulation, a new social contract.

Observers of economic globalization and civil society have argued that civil society organizations must place their particular agendas—single-issue or otherwise narrowly based—in the context of globalization and develop a class-explicit behavior in order to effectively challenge the global hegemonic bloc (Harvey, 2003; Roy, 2004). Such broadening of organizational agendas has occurred particularly among participating organizations in global justice events, including the World Social Forum conferences, held yearly since 2001 (in Porto Alegre, Brazil, and in several other cities) as an alternative to the hegemonic World Economic Forum in Davos, Switzerland, and alternative conferences to the World Trade Organization, such as the Seattle conference and protests in 1999. Despite the important interaction of international social movements, much can still be improved by increasing the participation of more unions, environmental and social justice organizations in campaigns calling for a new democratic system of social regulation.

FOSTERING COMMON GROUND: A COOPERATION/DIVERSITY PROCESS

Given the tendency of movements to become rigid and fragmented in practice, a "cooperation/diversity" process can strengthen movements by bringing them into collaboration (Brecher and Costello, 1990). This process has three vital components: the bridge builders, the creation of new institutions through a class-oriented strategy, and multi-scale strategies. The bridge builders help mobilize resources. Together with organizers, bridge builders employ, explicitly or not, a class-oriented strategy to build multi-class alliances. The class-oriented process aspires to create new institutions by balancing shared interests with the particular interests of the collaborating groups. The new institutions apply multi-scale strategies to ensure continuing resources and support.

Supporting Bridge Builders

Bridge builders are leaders often with interests in several camps (Rose, 2000), such as a trade unionist engaged in community affairs or progressive political issues. Generally they are leaders with a strong sense of social justice who can empathize with those beyond their own organizations and social class. For instance, a middle-class professional engaged in environmental activism can follow a sense of social justice and engage in solidarity for working-class trade unionists. Collaboration is common sense for bridge builders, despite any potential personal and political risk involved for the leader. Leaders that initiate the bridge building process identify and enlist the engagement of counterparts in the potential allied organizations. Early bridge builders from the partner organizations begin to mobilize the necessary financial, organizational, and skill resources to create and deepen a collective project. Bridge builders have access to resources at different scales, since they may work at different scales already. They can help bring a national thrust to a local collaborative effort.

What motivates leaders, particularly within labor, to foster coalitions is the recognition that circumstances are difficult for their organization, indeed may have worsened, and that their organization could benefit from collaboration with an organization and movement of a very different structure and operating style.

Such leaders generally understand national and local political and economic conditions sufficiently to value the importance of collaboration between very different organizations. Bridge builders provide the intellectual leadership to convince others of this strategy. Bridge builders bring an understanding of class, a class capacity, as well as important moral and intellectual leadership, to a collective endeavor. Their understanding of class and the importance of multi-class alliances may be grounded in their organization, which may have a history of participation in coalitions. Alternatively the bridge builder may represent an organization with no coalition experience and thus may take bold and risky steps to promote coalition building.

While the active engagement of bridge builders is essential to launching a collaborative project, their involvement is vital to on-going operations as well, steering coalitions through difficult periods, such as during staffing changes or funding shortages. Indeed bridge builders may be called on frequently to mobilize resources, tap into national networks for advice and solidarity, and reinfuse the coalition with its historical mission.

Bridge builders between labor and environmental organizations have often been health and safety activists, local and national labor leaders or workplace safety advocates with experience in improving workplace health and safety. Being a health and safety activist is not a prerequisite, yet health and safety leaders do occupy a unique location astride environmental and occupational health, with overlapping interests in protecting workers and the general public. They are thus uniquely positioned to engage environmental organizations and workers in a dialogue about protecting workers' health and economic well-being and environmental health at the same time.

Creating New Institutions Through Multi-Class, Multi-Racial Organizing

The essential aspect of building coalitions is the creation of a new institutional arrangement by building common ground while balancing the particular interests of the collaborating groups. Negotiating the common ground is greatly facilitated by class-explicit, multi-class organizing. Collaborating across the working class/ middle class divide, or between labor and working class community organizations, involves understanding your own class position vis a vis the class position of adversaries, such as corporations. Trade union activism in recent decades has been generally framed by a populist solidarity consciousness rather than class consciousness (Moody, 1988, 2001). The same can be said for much of social movement activism. Nevertheless, forging common ground between social movements, between labor and community, requires a degree of class conscious organizing on the part of bridge builders and leaders. If labor-community allies are fighting a company shutdown of a facility, they understand the class basis of the struggle: workers and community versus company ownership.

Coalitions become new institutions based on the practice of multi-class negotiation of common ground. Formation of a new institutional arrangement is what separates coalitions from networks of organizations. While networks involve participating organizations' ad-hoc endorsement of policies and positions, coalitions engage in longer term investment of time and energy in the direction of a coalition.

Cooperation/diversity, then, is about building new institutions, by building common ground, by balancing the particular interests of the collaborating groups. The common ground is comprised of universal interests, such as protecting the rights of workers and community members to a healthy environment, or supporting workers that have been unjustly prevented from continuing their jobs (through layoffs or a company lockout) or are involved in a strike over issues that the broader community can identify with. It is essential that universal interests be negotiated (Young, 1990). Coalition participants negotiate universal notions of social justice and political direction based on similar, but not the same, political or ideological position (Harvey, 1993). Negotiating common ground, and creating a broad cooperative project, involves a strategy of making broad social justice appeals, avoiding narrow, parochial interests, but at the same time preserving the diversity of specific group interests, including identity politics (Harvey, 1993; Young, 1990). The negotiation of universal interests among the particular interests of labor, community, and social movement group positions is a profoundly important practice in building progressive movement alliances.

Universal interests must be understood to be multi-class interests, transcending the working and middle classes. The theme of protecting public health and the environment, while promoting economic development that benefits the broader public, can be viewed in class terms as improving the condition of the working and middle classes. This theme can be viewed as well in a populist sense as protecting health and the environment and building a strong economy that supports all Americans with a decent standard of living. Coalition building creates several types of new institutions: not only the emerging and continuing coalitions themselves, including their organizational structure and governing process; but as well the creation of new projects and programs within the community to promote social solidarity and the well-being of a broader society, including the fostering of governmental and corporate responsibility for social solidarity.

Coalition parties recognize shared universal interests through developing a community of solidarity in a particular struggle. Just as struggle is a necessary precondition for the development of class behavior (Calhoun, 1988; Cumbler, 1974; Fantasia, 1988; Navarro, 1991), struggle, or crisis, is a necessary step for the development of a community of solidarity, which recognizes shared universal interests. Unions and communities engaged in a struggle over universal issues—such as public health, economic development, and living-wage jobs—understand the importance of the fight about such issues in forging solidarity between groups. Indeed, instilling class interests and class behavior in the labor and community participants of such struggles is essential to building a counterhegemonic project (Navarro, 1991). In order to thrive, a community of solidarity must establish institutions that continue to organize on issues of great relevance to people, beyond the original crisis for labor and community.

Multi-Scale Strategies

Local communities of solidarity by themselves may not be enough to sustain local coalition work. It is often up to regional and national organizations and networks to support local coalitions. Local coalitions face huge odds of maintaining capacity, particularly given parochial tendencies and disappearing resources. Higher-scale resources, including progressive organizations, can assist local initiatives to endure, expand, and survive.

The new institutional arrangement of building common ground goes beyond local labor-community coalition partnerships to include building common ground on multiple scales—locally, nationally, internationally. Building common ground against corporate and governmental power that would endanger public health and opportunities for local sustainable development would involve a multi-scale solidarity project. While it is difficult to sustain a community of solidarity on multiple scales, maintaining a network of common (multi-class) interests on multiple scales is essential, particularly if the coalition requires assistance in facing the weakness of social movements and the challenges set forth by corporations and the state. Harvey (1993) notes the failure of social movements, including labor, to mobilize in support of workers killed in a 1991 fire at a Hamlet, North Carolina, poultry processing plant. What should have been a seminal moment uniting labor and other social movements in national outrage over the poultry company, the consequences of an anti-union climate, and the failure of health and safety regulation, failed to materialize. That a multi-scale community of solidarity never arose points to an inability of organized labor to launch a strong solidarity campaign, and the continuing fragmentation of progressive forces in the United States. The divisive ideological forces of corporations and government, as well as a general lack of solidarity among civil society organizations, as evidenced by the Hamlet aftermath, can be effectively challenged through a broad counterhegemonic project, employing universal themes, such as safe, living wage jobs, effective government safety regulation, and the right to organize for better wages and working conditions. Hamlet demonstrated the need for broad-based social movement alliances to address social injustices and demand social policy changes.

More recently, the reconstruction of New Orleans and the Gulf Coast after Hurricane Katrina in 2005 demonstrates the importance of broad-based, multi-scale social movement alliances in demanding social justice in reconstruction efforts. New Orleans labor-community coalitions have sought to overcome common fragmentation of labor and community to demand protection of the prevailing wage and participation in reconstruction planning.

Building common ground involves the development of new institutional networks of organizations that mirror the geographic reach of corporations. What was lacking in the Hamlet, North Carolina, case, and what will necessarily help provide for successful labor-community participation in the New Orleans reconstruction, is the mobilization of resources at the local and national scales. While it is difficult to sustain a community of solidarity on multiple scales, maintaining a network of multi-scaled common interests is vital to a coalition's ability to resolve problems and obtain assistance. Mirroring the spatial strategies of corporations (Smith, 1990) is a vital tool for waging international campaigns, or as a way to access national resources and social movement networks for strength. Mirroring the geographic reach of capital becomes a way for communities and unions to overcome geographic isolation and corporations' pitting of communities against one another.

The cooperation/diversity process is spatially complex; there is no multi-scale formula for success (Brecher and Costello, 1990). Local coalitions are largely driven at the grassroots level; while they may be framed by national networks and parent organizations, they tend to draw their strength and direction from grassroots initiative. National level collaboration are typically informed by local initiatives. The interlacing multi-class movements of the global justice movement involve participation of organizations of varying spatial reach, from local to international organizations.

Ultimately, the cooperation/diversity process—with its ability to build bridges, draw on multi-scale resources, and develop new institutions and networks—will face the fragmenting ideological forces of corporations and government, as well as the general lack of solidarity from civil society organizations. Yet it is the cooperation/diversity process itself that seeks to build a universalizing counter-hegemonic project through social movement and labor-community political alliances that can bring about progressive social change.

CONCLUSION

Labor-community coalitions and other social movement alliances are pieces of a larger counterhegemonic project. Such coalitions represent a challenge to current social and political regulation, where governance has failed, market relations are expanding into all aspects of everyday life, and the broad middle and working classes are suffering the destructive effects of Fordist capitalism and post-Fordist corporate practices and social and economic policies. Environmental justice activism and labor-community alliances are struggles against accumulation by dispossession (Harvey, 2003), the gradual erosion of human rights to health and economic and social well-being. Moreover, social movement collaboration and local labor-community partnerships are as much a response to previous weaknesses of social movements—particularly their fragmentation and narrow agendas—as they are to the shifting political economic circumstances.

The failure of social and political regulation to protect the health and economic livelihood of the broader public demands more active intervention by progressive political organizations including labor-community coalitions. Building a counterhegmonic project entails building organizational coalition capacity, taking advantage of political opportunities, particularly in the state, and effectively challenging the strategies and policies of the dominant political-economic bloc. In building movement capacity, there is a need for a well-developed political strategy based on a sound understanding of changing political economic events, including strategies and practices of corporations and government. Labor-community coalitions are part of an alternative set of institutions helping to shape regulation of economic, environmental, and public health policy and practices, in part by introducing and expanding a discourse of corporate and governmental accountability. They represent a force for democratization of social and political regulation. Democratic regulation holds the hope of stabilizing capital accumulation and regulating crises of capitalist development by instituting more effective checks by civil society to the dominant corporate and state powers.

The challenges for building counterhegmonic projects are numerous. Coalition-builders emerge and must be sustained by social movement and community organizations. Coalitions are fragile institutional arrangements that can easily collapse. If the intent of the collaboration is beyond an ad-hoc partnership, the partner organizations must find ways to ensure that the coalition can weather the vicissitudes of organizational leadership and resource availability. The commitment of larger scale organizations, such as union internationals and national environmental organizations, or assistance from experienced coalitions in other places, can help local labor-community coalitions get started and survive organizational crises. Building a sustained counterhegemony may entail effective mobilization of multi-scale financial and skill resources and the application of multi-scale strategies. Applying the appropriate political strategy and mobilizing the necessary resources implies that social movement and community leaders have a practical understanding of strategies in the current political economy. Ultimately, coalitions arise and succeed because of.effective leadership with the capacity to adapt to new political economic circumstances, mobilize resources at multiple scales, and build new alliances and institutions. Coalition leaders invariably face the reality of building on universal themes and a common discourse that transcend separate agendas and identity politics, while developing multi-class, multi-racial institutions that reflect the broader populations that they represent. Finally, coalitions and their leadership are about developing stronger relationships in the state, civil society, and the business community to build a more democratic society.

ENDNOTES

1. Fordism, a term developed by Gramsci, referred to the new arrangement of production and consumption, regulated by a new set of social institutions, practices and norms. Gramsci (1971) argued that Fordism was created as a way to turn workers in a mass production society into mass consumers. Fordism is comprised of mass production and a broader consumption of produced goods. A new structure of society was called into being, based on Ford's vision, consisting of modernist, populist democracy, mass consumption, a new system of labor reproduction, and a new psychology from the state, to the family, to individual morality. The goal of the new society was to ensure that mass consumption matched mass production (Harvey, 1989).
2. Taylorism, or scientific management of production, involved the subdivision of the labor process into discrete tasks, and a highly organized hierarchy of tasks from management to the production line. Originating several decades before the inception of Fordism, Taylorism enabled the routinized, highly structured Fordist mass production process.

CHAPTER 3

Labor-Environmental History: From Collaboration to Division and Back Again

The Louisiana Labor-Neighbor Project is part of a long, but uneven history of labor, community, and environmental collaboration in the United States. For most of the history of organized labor, collaboration with community was frequent. There were, however, important periods when collaboration declined. This chapter illustrates the ebb and flow of collaboration as a response to constraints and opportunities for collective action and social reform presented by historical shifts in capitalist development and social regulation. Figure 1 gives an overview of the historical periods of collaboration and division.

Labor-community collaboration has occurred most notably during the major social reform periods: the Progressive Era, the New Deal, and, to a lesser degree, the 1960s Civil Rights and Great Society period. The most recent phase of labor-community alliances—from the 1980s to the present—differs significantly from the previous collaborative periods in being a time when social reforms were under broad assault from neo-liberal forces in business and government. Indeed, the 1980s resurgence of labor-community collaboration coincides with the crisis of Fordist capitalism, the demise of the postwar capital-labor compact, and the onset of industrial restructuring. As labor became weaker and the economy globalized since the early 1970s, labor-community collaboration returned. The Fordist and post-Fordist capitalist crisis, then, spurred labor to gradually readopt a social unionism it had practiced in previous periods.

Labor-environmental relations experienced high points during the Progressive Era, the late 1960s and early 1970s, and the period since the mid-1980s. Greater collaboration coincided with mounting urban environmental problems related to increasing destructiveness of capitalist production. In each of these periods, some unions collaborated with environmentalists and public health advocates on environmental issues because union members suffered deleterious economic and public health consequences of poorly regulated industrial production. During all

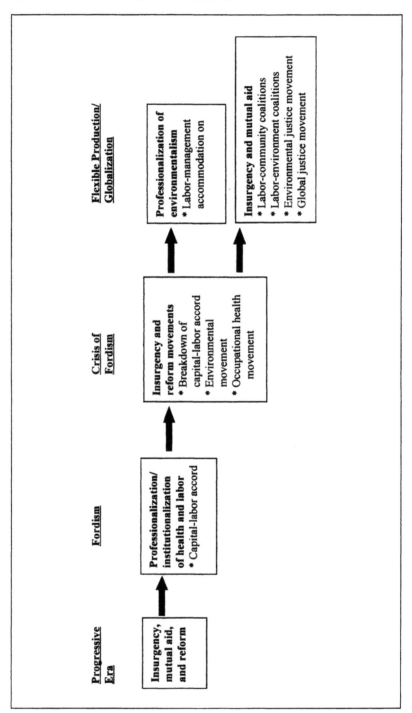

Figure 1. Labor and environment: Historical periods of collaboration and division.

of these periods, labor, community, and environmental cooperation entailed efforts by all parties to be inclusive and oriented toward social justice ideals.

Collective action historically involved a tension between rigid and open organizational form and strategy. During periods of labor and social movement cooptation and reduced collective action there was a rigidity within and between organizations, while periods of greater collective action involved openness and flexibility in strategy and organizational form. The relationship among labor, community-based, and social advocacy groups, was the result of experimentation in institutional forms and strategies to intervene in capitalist crises. Each of these periods, as well as the years between surges of collective action, are now explored in detail.

LABOR-COMMUNITY DURING EXTENSIVE INDUSTRIALIZATION: 1840s-1880s

Widespread industrialization, urbanization, and immigration from the 1840s to the 1880s, represented the rise to dominance of industrial capitalism in the United States. The destructive effects of industrialization, however, together with a lack of government regulation, fostered the growth of the labor movement and social reform movements. While most workplaces from colonial times through this period had been structured along craft lines, as industrial capitalism developed by the 1870s and 1880s, new worker organizations emerged, namely, protoindustrial unions and broader social unions. Reform movements developing during this period also reflected changes in capitalism.

Urban industrialization beginning in the 1840s exacted an enormous toll on workers, urban residents, and the environment. Poor water and air quality, mounting sewage and waste generation, inadequate sanitation and disposal, and an abundance of industrial workplace diseases and public health hazards, including epidemics such as cholera and tuberculosis, posed serious environmental problems (Gottlieb, 1993). Compounding these problems was the dominant thinking of industry and government, which defined environmental degradation as a result of poor individual habits of the poor and working class.[1] Industry and government took insufficient steps to control or reduce pollution. Local governments believed that doing so would undercut the urban economic base. Environmental degradation on such an extensive scale had obvious class underpinnings, burdening industrial workers and the poor to a far greater degree than the wealthy.

Labor-community collaboration occurred during this period of industrialization despite divisions between the two. While the linking of labor and community met its greatest challenges in rapidly growing larger cities, it occurred more readily in small cities and towns. Workplace and community were largely separated, both spatially and conceptually, since the industrialization of the 1840s, a separation coinciding with strong ideological divisions in residential community based on class, race, and ethnicity in the United States (Katznelson, 1981). During this period of industrialization a split consciousness was developed: class-based at work, ethnicity- and territory-based in the community. This split consciousness—rooted in class, race, and ethnic divisions in the residential community—helped make fragile the links between the two spheres. While urban neighborhoods often fostered the growth of political parties and unions, only rarely was class struggle broad-based, connecting the struggles of workers where they worked and where they lived (Katznelson, 1981). A split consciousness during early industrialization inhibited broad-based class politics, in the European tradition of class-based political parties and incorporating workplace and community struggles, during later industrial periods.

Despite the divisions, the early labor movement often collaborated with social reform movements. Middle-class social reformers, together with farmers, often provided crucial support to local labor-based political organizations (Brecher and Costello, 1990). There were many instances of tightly integrated workplaces and residential communities in the mid 1800s, although they were much less frequent after the Civil War, as larger cities grew rapidly. Company mill towns and mining communities, with a strong sense of community and close linkage between workplaces and residential community, persisted into the 1900s but through urbanization became much less common. Small towns and cities generally provided a greater structure of solidarity for labor during the Guilded Age (1865-1890) than did large cities (Gutman, 1963). In the larger cities, under growing class divisions, urban isolation and anonymity, the middle and upper classes, and their institutions—including the press—showed little support for labor and the working class. Despite often-greater corporate control over housing and stores in small cities and towns, a strong sense of community tended to support the working class and unions. Segments of the local middle class, including small businessmen and shopkeepers, lawyers, professionals, the press, and local officials, often came to the aid of labor during industrial conflicts (Calhoun, 1988; Fantasia, 1988).

Mutual aid organizations, such as fraternal organizations and benefit societies, were instrumental to the survival of unions during the economic depressions and attacks by business and government during this era (Bacharach et al., 2001). They helped to sustain a communalism among workers from before the American Revolution and were vital to the growth of unions and the labor movement. Mutual aid organizations of the eighteenth and nineteenth centuries provided workers with critical support outside the workplace: taking care of sick members and members with drinking problems; helping workers and family members to find work. They served as a link between workers in the workplace to family and worker support networks in the community. The mutual aid logic—that workers take care of each other in difficult times—or communalism, therefore, is indeed an important component of labor-community collaboration.

Despite these forms of labor-community solidarity, the gender division of labor, established during the industrial revolution, helped to divide workplace and community politics by weakening the working class and strengthening the male ruling class (Cockburn, 1984). During this period and well into the 20th century women were systematically excluded from an active role in workplace politics through their exclusion from wage-labor altogether, or from occupations that offered opportunity for collective action, or, at the very least, from union membership or union leadership (Sayer and Walker, 1992). This strengthened the divisions between community and workplace politics by preventing women from building solidarity with each other and with men. Community support for workers was very often facilitated by women assuming an active role in building solidarity, thereby overcoming the false division of work and home (Faue, 1991; Frank, 1991). Women proved to be active bridge builders.

PROGRESSIVE ERA SOCIAL UNIONISM AND LABOR-ENVIRONMENTAL SOLIDARITY: 1880s-1920s

The Progressive Era signified the onset of a new, broader, more hazardous phase of capitalism that lacked social regulation to protect workers and the public. New social movements emerged to challenge degraded environments, public health, and work conditions. New forms of collaboration—between unions, professionals, and community institutions—emerged to intervene in the regulatory process. Industry became increasingly mechanized, the division of labor more elaborate, with increasing government intervention in labor-management relations. Manufacturing followed increasingly Taylorist scientific management practices.[2] Significant restructuring of major industries took place, such as in the foundry industry, which from 1900 to 1920 experienced the introduction of new hazardous technologies, deskilling of the workforce, and a major increase in the proportion of its workforce which were African-American and immigrants (Gottlieb, 1993). Accelerated pollution associated with Taylorist production facilities exacerbated already discriminatory class and race segmentation in the division of labor and urban residential structure.

Against a backdrop of Taylorist production, rapid urbanization, and degradation of environmental health, social unionism developed, addressing many workplace and community issues, while linking labor and community activists and professionals. Despite its name, the Progressive Era was largely repressive for labor. Brutal crackdowns by companies and their security forces overpowered numerous incidents of working class militancy. The courts were hostile as well, frequently using injunctions against labor that protected property and property owners (Merkel, 1983).

Seeking to mobilize its ranks, the working class experimented with many organizational forms, an effort that had an important impact on labor's relation to community and other potential allies. In the 1880s, the Knights of Labor undertook broadly inclusive campaigns which involved not only a mixture of craft, general, and industrial unions, but cooperation with middle-class reformers and farmers as well.[3] They were the first labor organization to base their campaigns on principles of grassroots democracy, equal rights and universal justice. The American Federation of Labor, dominant in the labor movement since the 1890s, rejected such an inclusive social unionist tradition and propelled the movement down a path of "separation of labor" along skill lines. Built primarily on craft-based unions of skilled workers, the AFL kept different organizations of craft workers apart and attempted to block union solidarity with potential community allies and the rest of the workforce (Brecher and Costello, 1990).[4] Matching the broad social unionism of the Knights of Labor was a multitude of social reform movements: agrarian, public health, temperance, women's suffrage, charity organization, industrial education, civic reform, prohibition, settlement, housing, city planning, and African-American advancement.[5]

While clear divisions between workplace and residential community politics were the trend in major U.S. industrialized and commercial cities, there were exceptions. In the late 1800s and early 1900s, the union workforces at textile mills and steel plants in smaller industrial cities of New England, such as Lynn and Fall River, Massachusetts, fought for and won better wages and working conditions only because of broader community support (Cumbler, 1974, 1979). Labor was embedded in residential communities and derived much of its strength from family, religious and social advocacy institutions. Working-class communities created their institutions, both formal and informal, which supported workers during workplace conflicts. Besides the union itself, there were fraternal orders, benefit societies, as well as child care arrangements, eating and drinking establishments for social activities, and job information arrangements. These mutual aid institutions served primarily the community of workers. During strikes, the small business community came to support the union workers.

Women played a key role in overcoming workplace/community divisions during the Progressive Era. Social reform provided professionally-oriented women, largely excluded from appropriate wage labor, with tasks conducive to their skills, as volunteers in reform movements (Geiser, 1977). Women previously confined to household work found engagement in consumer activism, which provided solidarity with labor militancy. In Seattle in the early 1920s, for example, women defined their central organizing role in consumer boycotts and producer and consumer cooperatives as integral to the labor movement (Frank, 1991). In certain instances middle-class and working-class women activists created new ways of thinking, which attempted to remove, if only briefly, the ideological barriers between workplace and residence.

Urban Health Reform:
First Wave Of Labor And Environment

Urban environmentalism came into its own during the Progressive Era to combat a severe public health and environmental crisis and health and safety problems resulting from urbanization and extensive industrial production (Gottlieb, 1993). This activism was the first wave of labor and environmental collaboration, involving middle-class professionals, working-class communities, and unions. Women's, often class-conscious, intellectual leadership forged many of the links. The hard-fought success of such reform activism, however, was ultimately compromised by the professionalization of public health, which eventually took control of the debate.

Struggles over health and environment in this era were initially community-oriented, framed by a social justice perspective, and facilitated by activists with access to regional and national legal and scientific assistance. These multiscaled environmental networks faced powerful companies with national financial, legal, and organizational resources, as well as the absence of effective state intervention in urban environmental and social problems. Activists such as health researcher Alice Hamilton, the founder of modern community and occupational health, and workers in the settlement movement, successfully linked concerns about workplace hazards with concerns about public health and the community environment.[6] They succeeded because they defined workplace environmental and community health problems as socially created and therefore resolvable through worker empowerment and social reform. Hamilton's activism grew out of the settlement movement, led largely by middle- and upper-class women who sought to improve urban neighborhoods and the urban industrial environment, focusing on housing, sanitation, and public health (Gottlieb, 1993). Settlement workers helped start the earliest women's labor unions in the United States and were leading advocates for women's protection against workplace environmental hazards.

Beginning in the 1890s, unions and worker advocacy groups promoted worker health and safety in western mines, and in foundries, textile mills, and garment sweatshops in the industrial belt.[7] These organizations pushed for social reform and regarded industrial hazards as a public health issue, important to both workers and community residents. Even the AFL-CIO urged resolution of workplace health and safety problems, given the rising incidence of tuberculosis in its membership (Wooding, 1989). Two prominent organizations addressing workplace environmental health during the Progressive Era were the National Consumers League and the Workers Health Bureau (WHB), both led by women. Primarily an environmental and consumer organization, the National Consumers League sought to protect a growing number of women and children in the industrial workplace from hazards. The Workers Health Bureau, organized in 1921 by women reform activists based in the labor and consumer movements, provided support on health and safety to the union movement and promoted workplace environmental conditions. The WHB believed that improvement of workplace and community environmental health could occur only when labor challenged corporate control of the production process (Gottlieb, 1993).

Workplace and environmental health reform advocates of this period defined health and illness as a class issue, where industrial disease oppressed workers just as much as exploitation by capital, and was as equally important as wages and other working conditions (Gottlieb, 1993). Such an analysis resonated broadly in working class communities hit hard by pollution, industrial accidents and worker exploitation. The arena for grassroots urban environmentalism was, therefore, large and inviting. Public health reformers, espousing the ideology of Progressive Era movements, demanded government and industry intervention to improve working conditions as a way of ameliorating class conflict (Rosner and Markowitz, 1989).

The federal government did little to improve working conditions before the turn of the century, when the Bureau of Labor supported the investigative work of reform advocates like Alice Hamilton. Yet not until World War I did the government become an ally of health reformers, owing to health and safety concerns about wartime production of weapons and the increasing use of hazardous chemicals, and due to increasing government intervention in the organization of production (Rosner and Markowitz, 1989; Wooding, 1989).

Parallel to the public health reform movement of this period was the growth of professionalization of public health. Under Taylorist scientific management of production, workplace health and safety and environmental health became professionalized, guided by scientific principles and defined by professional associations and state institutions heavily influenced by industry. Public health advocates—comprised of various professionals, reformers and radical labor activists, largely outside the medical profession—campaigned for the establishment of boards of health, environmental agencies, and sanitation and disease prevention programs. Physician groups, on the other hand, while having a socially oriented advocacy, were part of the growing professionalization of public health focused on individual health care. Professionalization forced a shift in policy focus from workplace and environmental issues and social reform to a case-by-case diagnosis and treatment, oriented toward identifying bacterial causes of diseases. While the social reform approach was community-based and socially-oriented, comprising both professionals and constituent groups in the sanitarian movements, the institutional approach was controlled by physicians and other specialists who sought to apply bacteriology and epidemiology to confront public health problems (Gottlieb, 1993).

At the same time, professional associations, mainly industrial engineers, employed Taylorist scientific management approaches to pollution and sanitation problems. They sought to rationalize the production system while reforming a corrupt system of urban infrastructure maintenance. Rather than focus on transforming the production process, the professional health movement focused on controlling pollution, a paradigm which has remained dominant ever since.

The labor and health reform movements' protest over the damaging effects of industrial capital to human health and the environment helped build strong public opinion, which forced a reluctant government to intervene in the regulation of production and the economy. The politics of "protest and regulate" (Szasz, 1991) in workplace and environmental health issues became an accepted social practice during the Progressive Era. The formation of these early state regulatory structures set the context for continuing struggles in later periods (Hays, 1959).

In summary, the Progressive period was one of increasingly hazardous industrialization and urbanization within the context of the emergence of monopoly capitalism and a restructuring of major industries. While the state took an increasingly active role in regulating capitalist competition and in quelling labor unrest, its role in addressing urban social and environmental problems was at first largely absent. As workplace and urban social problems raged on, there was a broad terrain upon which counterhegemonic movements could operate, in that the hegemonic bloc of civic and state leaders and industry was not organized well enough to completely hinder movements for broad reform. The public health and settlement movements, with their mix of middle-class activism, involving professionals and women leaders, and working class insurgency, allowed broad experimentation in counterhegemonic institution-building. Moreover, business unionism of the American Federation of Labor was only in its early stages of development, and numerous experiments in inclusive social unionism, including collaborative efforts with community organizations and social movements, had room to flourish despite capital's often brutal suppression of labor insurgency. Social movement and reform movement mobilization created the necessary pressure for emerging regulation of workplace and environmental health, creating a state institutional framework for future movement struggles. Professionalized public health, however, with its emphasis on Taylorized scientific management of public health, took control of policymaking by the 1920s.

INSTITUTIONALIZATION AND RESISTANCE DURING THE TRANSITION TO FORDISM: 1920s-1930s

The 1920s and 1930s represented the transition to the Fordist mass production economy, as a response to a crisis of Taylorist overproduction and a crisis of competitive regulation (Lipietz, 1988).[8] Fordism emerged to replace shortcomings of Taylorism by linking mass production with mass consumption, and entailed major shifts in labor power, politics of labor control, and political life of society. Working-class resistance to both Fordism and Taylorism, however, presented a hurdle to the introduction of Fordist production into many industries in the 1920s (Harvey, 1989). Moreover, the severity of the 1930s Depression, with its lack of effective demand for consumer products, forced a search for appropriate state intervention to restore economic and social stability, which resulted ultimately in the application of Keynesian scientific-management strategies, involving a range of nonrepressive government powers.

The reform agenda, vigorously advocated by the settlement movement and community oriented public health movement, ultimately became institutionalized and professionalized with the creation of state regulatory and social welfare institutional bodies in the 1910s. The movements became victims of their own success, by creating new levels of organization that co-opted and depoliticized radical approaches. The new dominance by technical rationalization and professional groups in public health discourse hampered social reform by narrowing environmental quality from an issue of production and municipal regulation to an issue of treatment and environmental control.[9]

The formation of the workers' compensation-safety apparatus, along with the institution of the company doctor and industry-groups like the Industrial Hygiene Foundation, gave industry control over occupational health and safety discussions, which kept public and workplace health distinct (Berman, 1979). Both industry and the health reform movements promoted government intervention in workers' compensation, but for entirely different reasons. The movements hoped for a systematic, regulated improvement in working conditions. Industry, on the other hand, sought to discourage massive legal claims by workers and to transcend capital's profit-mongering image, thereby redefining health and safety from a point-of-production issue to an administrative and consumption issue (Navarro, 1983; Wooding, 1989).

Institutionalization of reform, together with political repression linked to a climate of anticommunism, as well as economic decline in the 1920s, helped narrow the agendas of unions and social movements, away from community-oriented social justice activism. In the 1920s all that remained from the health and safety reform movement were workers' compensation laws, albeit an important achievement; the industry-dominated National Safety Council, which proceeded to reintroduce an ideology blaming workers for workplace disease and accidents (Wooding, 1989); and the short-lived Workers Health Bureau. Successful professionalization of the settlement and workplace health movements kept the movements apart.

Moreover, business unionism at the national level, embodied by the American Federation of Labor and characterized by a narrow range of strategies (Moody, 1988; Navarro, 1991), reached a new height with its political alliance with Woodrow Wilson. Business unionist labor leadership withdrew its support for health and safety advocacy, in part by reasserting male control over health and safety discussions. Urged on by big business, the AFL pressured many union locals to stop supporting the Workers Health Bureau, effectively terminating it after eight years of existence. For the AFL and organized labor, wages and employment issues came to outweigh all other demands, including health and safety.

The Depression and New Deal politics deepened the existing tensions within the urban reform movements, between empowerment-oriented activism and institutionalization. As with health and safety activism, social justice activism was ultimately overwhelmed by structural co-optation of critical ideas and activist energy and leadership. In some cases, critique advanced by reform movements, such as radical demands for urban restructuring through public works programs, was incorporated by New Deal government agencies, thereby tempering the critique with narrower goals of job creation and welfare provision. In other cases, activists accommodated social-justice goals such as renewed community democracy by shifting their focus toward issues of economic redistribution within a reformed capitalist city (Gottlieb, 1993). In general, the professional associations, industry and national union bureaucracies—all male-dominated and representing the institutionalization of reform—tended to regard workplace and community health as separate issues, which effectively stifled the perspectives of women and grassroots labor and overwhelmed endeavors to forge grassroots labor-environmental collaboration.

Women's Labor-Community Bridge Building

The rise of business unionism in the 1920s and the institutionalization of social reforms in the 1910s and 1920s gave rise to two waves of labor militancy that bridged the gulf between workplace and community politics brought on by the early 1920s consumer activism in Seattle to support labor militancy (Frank, 1991), and again during the 1930s labor militancy, owing in large part to efforts to establish gender equality (Faue, 1991). In both cases, women were the primary bridge builders, as the gender division of labor favored labor-community collaboration. During the Seattle consumer activism, domestically based women became politically active in the labor movement by taking central roles in consumer boycotts and producer and consumer cooperatives. Women's leadership blurred the distinction between consumption and production and redefined them as a key part of the labor movement. In the community-based militancy of the 1930s, women activists were regarded as vital to the success of the union movement. The resilience of the labor movement during the 1930s owed much to the work of women activists—at the grassroots and in the public interest arena—to build community support for working class struggles. Gender-egalitarian discourse was prevalent in much of the labor-community collaboration during this period. Much as during the Progressive Era, professionally oriented middle-class women, significantly shut out of appropriate wage labor by structural gender divisions, were an important part of liberal public interest advocacy efforts that worked closely with grassroots labor during the New Deal.

The 1930s labor movement drew support from broad communities of solidarity, of which women activists were a part. Labor's outreach strategy to other constituencies was not new during this period, but rather was retrieved from previous practices of the late 1800s. Like community solidarity of the late 1800s in the industrial Northeast, working people from various workplaces, small businesspeople, church members, and social advocacy activists provided substantial support to workers engaged in strikes, lockouts, and organizing drives (Epstein, 1990). Workplace-community divisions were overcome in part because of clear divisions between communities of solidarity, on the one hand, and capital and its allies, on the other; and because of formation of a working-class collective identity forged during workplace conflict (Fantasia, 1988). Notable examples included strikes of the early CIO, involving huge community mobilizations and coalitions with other groups: Farmers rallied in support of Minneapolis Teamsters in 1934; unemployed workers assisted UAW strikers in Toledo in 1934; Detroit's African-American community helped organize at Ford in the late 1930s; and GM workers in Flint, Michigan, rallied the broad working class community to support a sit-down strike in 1936-1937 (Moody, 1988). Although the CIO had been a militant force seeking to overcome the "separation of labor" by organizing a broad range of industrial workers, by the end of the 1930s it had lost its militancy. The CIO leadership discouraged independent political action among its own member unions after achieving legitimacy with the Democratic Party and allying itself with it (Brecher and Costello, 1990).

As during previous periods, communities of solidarity during the 1930s were generally workplace-oriented. One notable exception was the Back of the Yards campaign in late 1930s Chicago. In this campaign, the CIO and the Packing Workers Organizing Committee of Chicago were part of a community organizing effort led by Saul Alinsky in the Back of the Yards neighborhoods (Horwitt, 1992). The Back of the Yards Council was a mutually sustaining coalition of churches, small businesses, and the CIO. The packing workers used the Back of the Yards Council as a base of support for organizing nonunion meatpacking facilities and for a looming strike by the Packing Workers, while the council gained the support of the workers in promoting better living conditions in a depressed section of the city. Neighborhood support was less for CIO organizing efforts than it was for the council's agenda of housing and child welfare and health. Alinsky successfully brought together the distinct interests in a groundbreaking endeavor to get churches, particularly certain Catholic Church leaders, as well as businesses and social clubs to support the Packing Workers (and implicitly the CIO). That a Catholic bishop threw his support behind the Packing Workers by applying the papal encyclical was a seminal event for the country at that time.[10]

Despite successful efforts to overcome divisions between labor and community in the 1920s and 1930s, the base of the labor movement largely shifted from community to the workplace by the end of the 1930s. This shift coincided with the resumption of women's marginalized position within unions. As the community base of women activists dwindled, labor-community divisions reemerged.

Health and Safety in Submission

Although public health institutionalization stifled much of health reform activism, it did not, of course, completely disappear, because the destructive tendencies of Taylorist and Fordist production continued and intensified. Alice Hamilton continued her important work into the 1930s and 1940s. CIO politics retained some concerns over health and safety issues during the New Deal. Nevertheless, the high unemployment of the Depression and the CIO's focus on organizing workers and challenging the AFL through union militancy in the 1930s, diverted any serious attention away from health and safety questions in the workplace and community. The economic reality of job loss and poverty rendered health a luxury issue, not of immediate material relevance. Rank-and-file mobilization on health and safety during the 1930s and 1940s was rare.[11] As such, the base of urban environmental activism dwindled. Yet no degree of professionalization could put a halt to increasing workplace disease and accidents during this period, as epitomized by the Gauley Bridge, West Virginia, disaster in 1930-31, where 764 workers, mostly African-American, died from silicosis contracted from silica dust inhaled during construction of a hydroelectric tunnel.[12] While the tragedy generated grievances by survivors and families, settled in and out of court with serious underpayments, no movement mobilization ever resulted. Interest quickly faded, despite efforts of isolated worker advocates to publicize the racist and class exploitative nature of the disaster. Both the issues of silicosis and risk discrimination for African-Americans were ultimately dropped by policy makers and reform advocates.[13] As activists attempted to connect the tragedy at Gauley Bridge with other social justice struggles, the separate agendas of labor and other social movements, in tandem with the significant racial divide in collective action, prevented the formation of significant campaigns. Finding common ground on social justice issues across divisions of race and between workplace and community movements, even without interference from capital and the state, was extremely difficult.

There were no serious challenges to industry over health and safety conditions for most of the period from 1930 to 1960. As asbestos production surged during this period, posing increased hazards to workers and community, industry successfully controlled discourse by manipulating and covering up government and industry research on asbestos hazards until the early 1960s. Only in the 1950s did unions become active again in any significant way on health and safety.

In summary, the institutionalization of reform in the 1910s and 1920s, together with science-based discourse and management of health, overwhelmed the radical activism, led mainly by women, in the public health and settlement movements. Institutionalization only strengthened male control over governmental and corporate discourse. Legitimation of reform turned public health and workplace health and safety into issues of state command-and-control, removing them from the arena of production questions. At the same time, union insurgency and radical reform tendencies withered in the face of political repression, economic decline, and the rise of business unionism. Innovative social unionism, including collaboration with the public health movement and community organizations, as a more open terrain of counter-hegemonic resistance during the Progressive Era, was substantially circumscribed, leaving radical reformers and social unionists isolated. Labor-community collaboration, in the early 1920s and the 1930s, was generally workplace-oriented and more successful when women working-class activists and middle-class reformers found ways to provide solidarity to the labor movement and when women unionists developed a greater voice within unions. Renewed cooperation during the 1930s came as a result of unions' need to seek out broader community solidarity while they successfully defined the ideological divisions between labor-community, and capital and its allies. Community-driven collaboration, such as Saul Alinsky's organizing in the Back of the Yards, was made possible by skillful cultivation of labor and religious leadership. The issue of health and safety was merely secondary, as the dominant New Deal discourse focused largely on economic redistribution under reformed capitalism.

LABOR AND ENVIRONMENT UNDER FORDISM:
1940s–EARLY 1970s

Fordist capitalism brought a tremendous growth of the middle class, production and consumption of consumer goods, as well as a significant rise in union membership. On the other hand, its social regulation allowed for severe degradation of the environment, coopted union leadership and hindered union militancy, including coalition building with community and social movements.

Fordist capitalism represented a shift to mass production of a vast array of new industrial and consumer products.[14] Fordism brought with it a rapid, large-scale introduction of new products, chemical substances, and technologies, many of which were hazardous to human health and the environment, into many areas of production, notably petrochemicals and agriculture. This helped to undermine production conditions, particularly worker and environmental health, in far more spatially extensive ways than previous regimes.

Unions came under intense attack in the postwar years. A resurgent militancy in the mid-1940s, together with the huge rise in union membership during and immediately after the war, brought increasing pressure from business and the federal government during the late 1940s and early 1950s to root out radical activists and leaders under the pretext of anticommunism. Capital's counterattack culminated with passage of the Taft-Hartley Act in 1947, which, in tandem with the Wagner Act of 1935, served to discipline labor, in part by decentralizing and fragmenting union struggles (Herod, 1991). Labor bureaucracies assumed greater power to cooperate with Fordist production techniques, ensuring discipline of the rank-and-file in return for stable and increased wages (Burawoy, 1985).[15]

Labor and community collaboration waned after the Second World War, owing to the capital-labor accord and suburbanization, both of which undermined labor militancy and the need for labor to draw strength and support from communities of solidarity, as in the 1930s. Despite worker discontent with the pressures of Fordist production, the labor-capital accord obviated unions' need for community allies. Business unionism at the local and national levels gained the upper hand over grassroots innovation, removing obvious incentives for workers and union locals to collaborate with community organizations. Suburbanization, with its attendant rise of mass homeownership within the working class (Walker, 1981), helped to deepen the conceptual divisions between workplace and community. This made difficult the formation of working class identity within the residential community or identification with union labor on the part of the nonunion community. To the extent that suburbanization fostered the fragmentation of working-class communities during the 1940s and 1950s, new strategies for building collaboration with community and other social organizations had to be devised.

Under Fordism, the modern labor-community coalition, requiring a variety of strategies and forms, was born. Prior to mature Fordism, communities of solidarity had emerged much more readily (see Moody, 1990); only coalition-building with the African-American community required a distinct, well-articulated strategy, due to the long history of separation between black and white workers (Moody, 1990). During the war years, the formal egalitarianism of the CIO brought African-Americans and women into unions, which then put pressure on the Confederation toward a formal commitment to equality in hiring and pay (Moody, 1988). While racism and sexism prevailed in practice, in principle the CIO was oriented toward providing opportunity for and recognizing rights of blacks and women in union employment. Through pressure from the black community on the CIO to follow through on its formal egalitarianism, the CIO leadership was brought into political alliance with the NAACP and other black leaders (Meier and Rudwick, 1979), a groundbreaking establishment for organized labor which strengthened its overall position (Moody, 1988).

Yet the need for labor-community collaboration in the post-war period remained strong, given the increasing deterioration in environmental health. In the 1940s and 1950s, urbanization, industrial pollution, and military research and development had widespread effects on public health and the environment. Yet there was only isolated local opposition by labor and community mounted against urban pollution and rapid suburbanization. Absent social movement mobilization over the destructiveness of Fordist production, the federal government took very little legislative interest in health and safety and environmental health questions during this period.

Characterizing this period were major industrial accidents, such as the deadly toxic cloud released over Donora, Pennsylvania, in 1948, and government-supervised radioactive contamination of western mountain communities, particularly Native American lands, through production and testing of nuclear weapons. Pesticide contamination of farm workers and wildlife, and major contamination of urban air and water became common problems. One exception to labor's lack of environmental activism was the strong reaction by the United Steelworkers of America to the Donora disaster, which prompted a congressional investigation of the incident and a report of the investigation published by the Steelworkers (Kazis and Grossman, 1982). Another exception was a campaign led by the United Auto Workers, and joined by the United Electrical Workers and United Paperworkers in the late 1950s to stop construction by Detroit Edison of an experimental fast-breeder reactor in Detroit. More generally, the first organized protest against the dangers of postwar technology was the antinuclear movement of the 1950s and early 1960s, led primarily by a network of scientists familiar with the dangers of nuclear power and supported by union leaders such as Tony Mazzocchi of the Oil, Chemical, and Atomic Workers.

In summary, the capital-labor accord and material abundance characterizing the postwar era help to explain the general lack of activism, particularly within the labor movement, to community and workplace pollution during this period. Labor's lack of critical interest in health and safety and environmental protection was compounded by Cold War purges of leftist trade unionists, on the one hand, and the overall success of the capital-labor accord, which ruled out major challenges over workplace conditions, on the other. The red scare ravaged environmentally conscious unions like the Mine, Mill, and Smelter Workers; while the capital-labor accord meant that many industrial unions agreed to the introduction of hazardous new technologies. Most unions, with several notable exceptions, never raised questions of health and safety until the late 1960s.

Opposition movements in the 1950s—namely, the civil rights, anti-nuclear, and anti-materialist lifestyle (beat) movements—while common in their concern about capitalist destruction of people's well-being, did not specifically address urban environmental health hazards. These movements, however, would ultimately come to play an important role in defining identities and issues of grassroots environmentalism after the late 1960s.

1960s RETURN OF COLLABORATION:
CIVIL RIGHTS AND HEALTH AND SAFETY

Labor-community and labor-environment returned in the 1960s on the wave of social movements, but in a limited way, specifically in mobilizations for civil rights and health and safety. Coalition-building was employed as a tactic in a few cases, but still faced the intransigence of business unionism and the capital-labor accord. The huge surge in urban protest movements in the 1960s was largely about systemic denial of access to the purported benefits of Fordist mass production and mass consumption: better jobs, equal rights and opportunity, and a higher quality of life. Most of the efforts in community-based, social and labor movements, however, were unable to bridge the divisions between workplace and community concerns. Many urban protest organizations—while crafted along the lines of Saul Alinsky's populist style of confrontational organizing, articulated as the "haves" versus the "have-nots"—generally failed to replicate the late 1930s Back of the Yards model of workplace-community coalition building.

Despite the great social movements of the 1960s—civil rights and anti-war—broad progressive politics began to fragment late in the decade. This resulted from several factors: Great Society reforms which brought about a shift from universal programs, characteristic of the New Deal, to group-specific programs which divided the working-class into interest-groups; and entrenched business unionism with its singular focus on collective bargaining (Harvey, 1993). The 1960s neighborhood and community protest movements, which helped pave the way for Great Society reforms, collapsed through their institutionalization by the state, which coopted movement leaders through public policy responses. Similar institutionalization put an end to militant and progressive workplace-community collaboration in the 1920s, and helped undercut the insurgency of the 1930s labor movement. Out of this fragmentation of progressive politics arose new social movements. Fragmented reform politics continued into the 1970s with the passage of interest-group oriented reforms—on environmental, consumer, and worker protection. Thus, the narrow agenda of various reform movements combined with the new tendency in state intervention to address public welfare less universally and more separately, creating for pluralist yet issue-based progressive politics.

The civil rights movement was a significant exception to the 1960s workplace-community political divisions, by merging civil rights concerns in the workplace and community. Like the 1930s labor movement, communities provided important strength to the civil rights movement. The AFL-CIO and organized labor generally shunned explicit, formal support of the civil rights movement.[16] The civil rights and Black Power movements were essentially working-class and poor people's movements (Marable, 1983). The urban ghetto uprisings of the mid-1960s represented the biggest expression of working-class anger since the militancy of the unemployed and workers of the early 1930s. Yet few labor leaders responded.[17] The civil rights movement made workplace issues the focus of certain campaigns, such as the march on Memphis in 1968 to support the rights of African-American sanitation workers.

The 1960s was a watershed decade for workplace and community environmental mobilization, propelled by destruction of health and the environment in communities of color, the workplace, and white middle-class communities. Despite the important return of environmental activism, labor-environmental coalition-building was largely limited to occupational safety and health. Organized labor's commitment to the capital-labor accord continued to inhibit social unionist support for environmental health protection. Communities of color led opposition to pesticide contamination and lead poisoning, with assistance from health and environmental professionals. The rapid surge in pesticide use in the 1950s and 1960s put farm workers at serious risk. The United Farm Workers made farm-worker exposure to pesticides an important issue in its organizing drives. In California they formed a tactical alliance with the mainstream Environmental Defense Fund[18] and California Rural Legal Assistance in

1968 over a lawsuit on DDT exposure; the alliance was short-lived because it made no effort to redefine the pesticide issue (Gottlieb, 1993). Community-based initiatives on lead paint poisoning began in inner-city Chicago in 1965 and then developed in communities of color in numerous other cities. Both lead and pesticide campaigns by people of color were supported by progressive groups of legal and health professionals. Campaigns against lead, pesticides, and uranium contamination on native American lands, however, failed to sustain ongoing collaboration with parallel white middle-class environmental initiatives, in that the white mainstream groups did not link social justice to environment.

By 1960, unions and health professionals had begun to collaborate to challenge corporations' decades-long control of information on industrial disease. The United Mine Workers had been increasingly active throughout the 1950s over the increasing incidence of black lung brought on by widespread introduction of continuous mining machines in the 1940s, which increased the amount of coal dust inhaled by miners (Kazis and Grossman, 1982). The United Rubber Workers in the early 1960s challenged the rubber industry for causing increased respiratory illnesses resulting from a new vulcanizing process.

Job blackmail was successful in the postwar period to the extent that industry controlled information derived from corporate-oriented science (Kazis and Grossman, 1982). Environmental health researchers in the 1950s and 1960s were responsible for exposing government and industry cover-ups of health risks (Kazis and Grossman, 1982). Most prominently, the action-oriented investigative research on asbestos and asbestosis by Irving Selikoff seriously challenged decades-long manipulation and suppression of evidence on asbestos-caused industrial diseases. Selikoff's work inspired a generation of occupational health advocates and helped pave the way for important workplace-community environmental health linkages in the late 1960s. Other activist-driven reporting of chemical contamination raised public awareness throughout the 1960s; in particular, Rachel Carson's *Silent Spring* on effects of DDT, and the PCB research of the late 1960s, which overturned thirty years of government and industry inaction on known health dangers for workers. By the late 1960s, substantial health and pollution information was reaching the public as never before, catalyzing local and national collective action.

Into the 1960s the labor movement had not taken a prominent role in advocating health and safety regulation, although labor did respond to rank-and-file unrest over hazardous working conditions in dangerous industries. Public health activists, activists in victim organizations, and certain national level union health and safety activists were the active bridge builders. The United Mine Workers, for instance, had long been active on health and safety. But much of the innovative organizing on health and safety in the 1960s and 1970s came from outside formal union structures, largely because of previous union inaction (Kazis and Grossman, 1982). Unions eventually integrated health and safety into their demands, but only after grassroots initiatives mobilized thousands and achieved some success. The surge in wildcat strikes between 1965-1967 by auto, chemical and mineworkers was often over unsafe or unhealthy workplaces (Donnelly, 1982). The black lung movement originated at the grassroots level in West Virginia through an ad hoc coalition of retired miners, VISTA volunteers, public health physicians, and union activists. The black lung movement, in particular, and the occupational safety and health movement, generally, were aided significantly by the catastrophic explosion at a Farmington, West Virginia, coal mine in 1968, which killed seventy-eight miners, triggering national public outrage over health and safety problems. Victims' organizations, like the Black Lung Association, Brown Lung Association, and White Lung Association, grew out of Selikoff's asbestos research and related evidence on cotton dust and lung problems (Wooding, 1989). These organizations helped forge links between workers and community activists, raising public awareness about the hazards of dust and chemicals to workers health, and urging unions to pressure the federal government for legislative protection for workers (Judkins, 1986).

The United Mine Workers and other unions eventually joined the collective efforts promoting health and safety, due to the work of victims' organizations as well as key union activists who succeeded in pressuring union leadership to join the health and safety efforts.[19] Although the emergent 1960s health and safety movement, which was grassroots in origin and leadership, helped to mobilize unions, the impetus for change within government and industry came largely from the federal government, not from the grassroots or labor (Wooding, 1989).[20] The federal government's lead in the creation of OSHA was possible only because the capitalist class was divided over the importance of government-backed social programs; international capital in favor, domestic capital opposed (Wooding, 1989). As Wooding argues, the passage of the OSH Act was the outcome of working-class action on health and safety, in tandem with divisions within capital and capital's capacity to influence policy, all within a climate of general social reform.

The "outside" environmental movement, which became a suburban middle class phenomenon in the 1960s, was not a party to labor-environmental collaboration because it did not consider social justice issues, much less take any stance against the hegemony of production decision making. Although the new middle-class environmental movement moved beyond traditional issues of wilderness preservation and resource conservation to oppose rapid suburbanization for its degradation of urban air, water, and quality of life, its agenda was limited only to what would work and was accepted by state structures, namely, legislation pressure groups, and legal action to increase enforcement and interpretation of laws (FitzSimmons et al., 1991).

Yet progressive activists in the middle-class environmental movement, those focused on public health and environmental quality, combined with a fledgling consumer protection movement and intensified labor struggle in the late 1960s, helped forge the connection of the labor and environmental movements into ad hoc coalitions. What would develop in the 1970s into separate but over-lapping movements related to industrial production, was an endeavor to relink the community and workplace environments. The initial struggle that forged this link was the campaign to pass the Occupational Safety and Health Act in 1970, led by activists Tony Mazzocchi of the Oil, Chemical & Atomic Workers, Frank Wallick of the United Auto Workers, and Ralph Nader, with active involvement of the Sierra Club, Friends of the Earth, and Environmental Action, consumer groups, and religious organizations (Kazis and Grossman, 1982; Gottlieb, 1993). Mazzocchi and Wallick, for their part, were progressive activists from progressive unions. The campaign was successful despite the absence of active involvement of most union national leadership and most nature preserva-tion and conservation organizations.[21]

In summary, under Fordism, labor-community collaboration was initially hampered by political repression, the capital-labor accord, the fragmentation of working class communities through suburbanization, and attendant increasing political conservatism within the working class. Whereas communities of solidarity once developed more readily, they now had to be cultivated more strategically. Civil rights activism led the way in forging labor-community col-laboration, from within the labor movement and into the African-American community in the early 1940s, and from within the broader African-American community into several unions in the 1960s. Racial diversification of the labor movement was intimately linked to the movement's orientation toward broader community outreach.

The 1960s social movement mobilization against the limits of Fordist capitalism—failed access to purported social benefits and general degradation of public health and the environment—stimulated labor-community collaborative experiments on many fronts, including community and workplace health. Fordism represented an increasing ideological incorporation of nature into the capitalist system, nature which had previously been exploited as an external source of wealth. Even the household, once external to operations of capital, became internalized as human capital through the growth of mass consumerism. The postwar period brought the widespread use of systems-oriented management, which entered environmental regulation in the 1960s. The 1960s movements posed the strongest challenge since the Progressive Era to the destructiveness of industrial capital to health and the environment. As in the previous era, the new environmentalism took two distinct forms: technocratic/managerialist and grassroots/socially oriented. The technocratic environmental mainstream mobilized around regulation and control issues, staying away from thorny questions of production decisions; while grassroots and progressive impulses addressed more directly the public and worker health depradations brought on by capitalist production.

The environmental crisis evident in the 1960s, which both these movement streams helped illuminate, presented a major problem of legitimacy for capital, based in the economic supply crisis of environmental resources and in the social resistance to environmental degradation by capital. Capital's response was to treat nature as an internal stock of capital (M. O'Connor, 1993). This new hegemonic paradigm of capitalizing nature became codified in the command-and-control, "self-management" environmental regulatory paradigm of the 1960s, which has remained in place ever since. The mainstream environmental movement, through its participation in liberal state legislative and regulatory arenas, was enlisted to support this hegemonic bloc. In contrast, the workplace health and progressive environmental movements, both independently and in ad hoc coalition with one another, challenged capitalist discourse that attempted to explain health and environmental problems as an accepted cost of doing business.

FORDIST CRISIS AND RESOLUTION: 1970s–EARLY 1980s

Fordism broke down in the early 1970s largely because of a profitability crisis, rooted in increasing international competition and the rigidity of the Fordist system to respond.[22] Flexible accumulation became the resolution to this crisis. Capitalist elites introduced a regime oriented toward flexibility, involving globalization and decentralization of production. It entailed deregulation to help capital keep all production costs down. Deregulation served to undermine the enforcement of environmental and workplace safety and health laws passed in the early 1970s and was made possible by capital reorganizing itself, overcoming previous divisions between segments of capital.

The crisis of Fordism and onset of flexible accumulation accelerated the already existing decline of American trade unions, primarily by undermining labor's principal defense strategy, pattern bargaining, and replacing it with concessionary, decentralized, and competitive bargaining. Decentralization also included a shift to flexible labor markets and increasing pressures on towns and cities to compete for investment capital. Such decentralization measures were facilitated by the federal government's efforts to transcend the rigidity of the postwar capital-labor accords, and by political assaults on unions by proponents of neoliberal economic policy (Jonas, 1998). Decentralization represented a deliberate strategy to politically fragment, or "localize" labor (Peck, 1996). With the globalization of capital, management became much more hostile in bargaining. Bureaucratized business unionism, which monopolized the bargaining process while demobilizing the rank-and-file of industrial unions, was incapable of withstanding capital's challenge, as the mounting history of failed strikes attest. Indeed, business unionism proved to be disastrous for labor, as unions were fully unprepared for corporate industrial restructuring. In the face of deindustrialization and political decentralization, unions and communities found themselves caught in a "local-global paradox" (Jonas, 1998), where economic relationships have become increasingly global and political responses to globalization increasingly localized; that is, globalization breaks down national and regional boundaries, while places become increasingly competitive for jobs, capital, and economic development. Yet many local unions and several international unions quickly began applying new strategies and tactics, most based on reaching out to other constituencies besides labor.

Whereas in the 1960s capital was unable to effectively confront OSHA and other social reforms (such as environmental protection and consumer safety), in the 1970s capital forged unified class-oriented organizations that permitted a successful challenge of OSHA (Noble, 1986; Wooding, 1989). This challenge was at once ideological in that capital redefined its interests as being based on a fundamental link between an individual company's profits and a societal need for economic growth (Noble, 1986). At the same time, American liberalism shifted again, away from a regulated social welfare system, as during the New Deal and Great Society, during which the state mediated the interests between capital and labor; and into a neoliberal role of crisis manager in the 1980s, ensuring the maintenance of capital's interests, within a climate of political neoconservatism (Wooding, 1989). Ultimately, OSHA was severely weakened by the lack of public authority in capital investment and other production decisions, and by the lack of worker and community participation to ensure enforcement (Noble, 1986). The same can be said of environmental regulation during this period. OSHA's command-and-control regulation, by not actively involving worker and community input, was unable to build the political support for public officials necessary to withstand capital's assault on regulation.

LABOR-ENVIRONMENT RESPONSE
IN THE 1970s

In the 1970s, the domain of the conflict over health, safety, and the environment was largely at the government level, because of the belief by labor and nongovernmental organizations in state regulation to solve problems. Labor-environment collaboration tended to be on the national level, ad hoc in nature, and focused on passing national environmental legislation. Worker-environment coalitions achieved some success, owing to the initiative of the OCAW, Steelworkers, and national and local level health and safety and environmental activists. Grassroots collaboration, in support of local struggles, took on greater importance toward the end of the decade.

The OSHA campaign and its aftermath brought the creation of organizations and networks that were the basis of a new occupational health movement. Ralph Nader's efforts continued, with the formation of the Health Research Group of the recently founded Public Interest Research Group. Health professionals came together to form scientist and physician networks with a focus on workplace and community environmental health, while community-based activists and professionals began linking up to form Committees on Occupational Safety and

Health. COSHs developed in numerous states in the 1970s, and together with the health networks paralleled the Workers Health Bureau of 1920s with their goal of worker empowerment through the struggle for workplace health and safety. Set up outside traditional union structures, the COSH groups had a clear worker support function, bringing together union and community actitivists and health professionals for education and training (Kazis and Grossman, 1982). Most COSHs made links successfully to local unions despite the opposition of some union leaders. The COSHs, together with the OCAW and Steelworkers, formed the backbone of the progressive health and safety movement.

The OCAW, through the activist leadership of Tony Mazzocchi, continued to be a leading alliance-builder. In 1973 the OCAW drew support from the public interest and mainstream environmental communities for a five-month strike against Shell Oil at facilities in four states, over health and safety conditions, and a boycott of Shell products. The Shell strike, a seminal event for labor-environmental collaboration, resulted from multiscale organizing by OCAW, including years of relationship building with national environmental organizations by Mazzocchi and efforts by the union to win support first from local environmental groups, which drew the backing of six mainstream national environmental organizations.

The Urban Environment Conference was the first to take on corporate job blackmail, which was effectively used against mainstream environmental groups and union officials and became more potent with the 1973 recession. The conference, established in 1971 by Congressman Philip Hart (D-MI) and financed and supported by the UAW and the Steelworkers, also set up a clean air task force, which later gave rise to the National Clean Air Coalition, involving union support for the Clean Air Act. Union support for both the Clean Air Act and Clean Water Act was strong due largely to the job-creating potential in environmental protection.

Environmental and energy organizations created Environmentalists for Full Employment (EFFE) in 1976, which confronted directly the issue of job loss and called for development of alternative energy sources as a way of creating more jobs. The oil shock of 1973-74 provided industry with an opportunity to lash out at energy and environmental organizations for allegedly seeking to inhibit economic growth and eliminate jobs. Many unions, particularly the building trades, supported their employers. Together with the Labor Committee for Full Employment, EFFE promoted full employment and labor-law reform and worked to build alliances between labor and environmental groups during the late 1970s.[23]

The AFL-CIO and many unions had worked for passage of the Safe Drinking Water Act of 1974 and the Toxic Substances Control Act of 1976, while environmental groups lobbied for passage of mine safety legislation and improved regulation of workplace health and safety, and together with antinuclear groups lobbied for labor-law reform and supported the 1979 United Mine Workers' strike to refuse dangerous work (Kazis and Grossman, 1982). Despite the mutual support by labor and environmentalists to back key legislation in the 1970s, the tension between the two movements remained great, particularly at the local level.

At the national policy level, cooperation between organized labor and some environmental groups continued to broaden. National-level collaboration, however, was rife with pitfalls. EFFE's efforts to establish an ongoing national labor-environment coalition ultimately failed because of the unwillingness by environmental leaders to take on a social justice agenda, union leaders' fear of aligning with environmentalists in an increasingly hostile political environment, and the lack of involvement of grassroots union and environmental leaders. Yet EFFE's work in creating labor-environmental cooperative role models, which focused on a range of job, energy, and environmental issues, helped break down the single issue perception that unions and environmental groups had of themselves and of each other.[24]

Environmentalism in the 1970s was highly successful, largely due to innovative confrontational strategies and tactics learned from the 1960s movements, as well as to the increasing diversity of its constituent base and in its range of issues. A wider range of environmental struggles was waged by people of color and working-class organizations, as environmentalism gradually was redefined to include the survival of communities in the face of urbanization and urban environmental problems.

THE REVIVAL OF LABOR-COMMUNITY
SINCE 1980

Grassroots labor-community collaboration staged a significant comeback in the 1980s because of the crisis of Fordism, the demise of the labor-capital compact, and a growing disillusionment in the federal government's ability to solve problems. The revival was really a return to the labor-community links of the period before business unionism and co-optation had undermined democratic impulses in trade unions. Labor and community faced interrelated crises: downsizing, plant closings, declining tax bases for communities, and declining employment. Crisis increasingly forced them to seek each other out for help.

In the 1980s, organized labor suffered its most precipitous drop in membership since the 1920s, a 20 percent drop from 1979 to 1989 (Moody, 1990). Matching its loss in membership was its real loss in organizational clout, manifested by a mounting history of failed strikes. Responsible for the decline were the conservative leadership and strategies inadequate to match global economic restructuring. Grassroots union activism stepped in to provide alternative strategies and practices. Younger union members, who did not have the comfortable wages and benefits of the postwar generation of workers, were generally more open to coalitions with community organizations and social movements in the 1980s and 1990s (Rose, 2000).

Radical neighborhood politics staged a resurgence in the late 1970s and early 1980s, this time with a more comprehensive understanding of the links between urban crises and capitalist development (Boyte, 1980; Katznelson, 1981). The focus of collective action was again the residential community, not the workplace, as activists considered workplace economic issues secondary. Yet despite a better understanding of broad economic processes, movement activists and leaders generally sustained the separate practice of workplace and community politics.

Until the 1980s, unions rarely sought to win support from community leaders and institutions in their struggles against companies, choosing instead to battle companies solely in the workplace, where companies' ownership of property gave them an overwhelming legal advantage (M. Miller, 1980). In the early 1980s, however, there was a noticeable shift in the practice of some unions and community organizations to collaborate. A combination of job loss, factory shutdowns, and loss of public services for unions and communities, and a better structural analysis of urban crises and capitalist development among activists and organizers, set the stage for new experiments at bridging the traditional trenches.

In the early 1970s unions began redefining the community as their territory and not the companies', although many unionists recognized that corporations were quite capable of undercutting community support for unions (M. Miller, 1980). In the New South, for example, many companies saw community support of unions as a clear threat to them, and thus worked to eliminate community support of workers by bringing in workers from well outside of the area, and even from other states (M. Miller, 1980). Yet the number of successful attempts by unions to enlist the support of other community institutions grew rapidly in a highly unstable period of globalization of capital and economic restructuring, as ever more unions and community organizations encountered the limitations of not reaching out to one another (Brecher and Costello, 1990).

Labor's "community coalitions" became an increasingly frequent strategy, first emerging outside of the national AFL-CIO framework, at the local level and in alternative labor networks. Jobs with Justice, founded in 1987, from the start developed communities of solidarity at the local level, which included other unions and community organizations, to lend support to unions or workers engaged in workplace struggle. Numerous local coalitions arose out of plant closings, or threatened plant closings. Indeed, some of the more durable labor-community coalitions to emerge in the 1980s—the Labor/Community Strategy Center in Los Angeles, the Calumet Project in northwest Indiana, and the Naugatuck Valley Project in central Connecticut—developed out of plant closings characteristic of restructuring in heavy industry.

More recently, unions and community organizations have conducted living-wage campaigns in more than seventy-five cities, as the ranks of poorly paid, largely nonunion service workers has grown. Beginning with the Baltimore living-wage campaign in 1994, a collaborative project of BUILD (Baltimoreans United in Leadership Development, an affiliate of the Industrial

Areas Foundation) and AFSCME, local living wage campaigns won commitments from many city governments to ensure adequate wages for employees of companies with municipal contracts.

LABOR AND ENVIRONMENTAL JUSTICE

The post-Fordist era of industrialization, downsizing, and globalization brought new opportunities for labor and environmental collaboration. Out of 1960s movement struggles grew new streams of environmentalism that took on social issues, in particular those led by communities of color and the working class against pollution and the failures of government regulation, as well as progressive occupational health and safety networks. Working class antitoxics environmentalism and environmental justice activism intersected with unions and workers, which were increasingly under siege from a hostile corporate climate in the late 1970s and 1980s and which sowed further mistrust between labor and environmentalists. During the early Reagan years, in particular, unions were under attack and OSHA programs eviscerated. Even unions like the United Steel Workers, previously active on health, safety, and environmental matters, could not devote energy to them. Despite the difficult economic circumstances, this broader environmentalism led to a complex yet promising process of collaboration between labor, environmental justice, and antitoxics organizations, each having separate origins. Three strategies—right-to-know, environmental justice, and pollution prevention—provided potential common ground for labor, health and safety, and environmental organizations.

Working class antitoxics activism began in early 1970s in the aftermath of the 1960s' rise in environmental consciousness among the general public and as a response to a recognized hazardous waste crisis and the failure of hazardous waste regulation. Beginning with scattered local struggles over hazardous waste dumping, it acquired national legitimacy with Love Canal in 1978. Thousands of community-based antitoxics groups formed to fight hazardous waste dumps, incinerators, and polluting production facilities. Many of the groups were in low-income communities of color targeted for hazardous facility siting. Grassroots mobilization diversified traditional environmentalism and conceptions of health and environment, thereby allowing a place for labor and workplace, and underscored the working class and racial basis of the new environmentalism. This broadened environmentalism beyond a narrow focus on issues not pertaining to production decisions to a focus on reducing the flow of hazardous waste. The success of "policy Luddism" (Szasz, 1991), which used democratic procedural provisions to upset the siting of hazardous waste facilities, was due in part to the contribution that women, people of color, and the working class brought to environmentalism.

Environmental justice activism grew out of civil rights concerns about degraded public health in low-income urban and rural neighborhoods, and demonstrated that the hazardous waste crisis had a disproportionately greater impact on low-income communities of color, especially in the rural South and large urban areas. Local struggles against such hazardous facility sitings, made most noticeable by a 1983 struggle over the siting of a hazardous waste dump in Warren, North Carolina, prompted a national analysis by middle-class advocates, resulting in the landmark 1987 report by the United Church of Christ's Commission for Racial Justice, *Toxic Waste and Race*. Since that report, environmental justice leaders have demonstrated consistently that communities of color have been targets for toxic facility siting because of their lack of economic and political power, and because of institutional racism. The struggle against environmental discrimination, environmental justice activists contend, is both a subset and catalyst of a broader civil rights struggle for social and economic justice. Environmental justice activism brought the language of civil rights and social justice to environmental practice. In the early 1990s it challenged the national mainstream organizations to diversify their staffs and boards and broaden their focus to social and economic justice. It turned environmental justice into an effective political strategy to stop hazardous facility siting and brought social justice concerns into the national environmental regulatory process. To do this, however, some national environmental justice leaders employed identity politics, strategically defining the environmental justice movement as "people of color" to mobilize and solidify their base against a hostile opposition (Pulido, 1995). In the short term, this complicated efforts to collaborate with unions on the national level. However, at the grassroots level, environmental justice organizations built successful collaborations with local unions. With experience, the people of color environmental justice movement has moved beyond a focus on environmental racism to consider issues of power, production, and the universal human right to live in a sustainable world.[25] This has made collaboration with unions easier, as exemplified by the collaboration of environmental justice and progressive labor organizations on the Just Transition campaign.

Antitoxics activism, environmental justice, and workplace health and safety, though seemingly distinct streams of environmentalism, worked together on occasion. In the late 1970s and early 1980s there was considerable collaboration between antitoxics and worker health and safety activists, as labor, health, and safety, led in part by COSH groups, and environmental organizations campaigned for passage of state and federal right-to-know legislation (Slatin, 1999). OCAW health and safety advocates assisted Love Canal activist Lois Gibbs' coalition-building with labor in late 1970s. The Coalition for Black Trade Unionists brought an environmental justice perspective to early 1970s' right-to-know activism (Slatin, 1999). The growth of the antitoxics movement, together with health and safety network activism, helped build substantial local participation in the right-to-know campaign. The campaign had been previously dominated by the OSHA-Environmental Network, formed in 1981 and consisting of national-level labor and environmental activists, and did not have much connection to either local labor or community grassroots efforts.[26]

Out of local antitoxics organizing arose two highly influential national antitoxics networks, the Citizens Clearinghouse on Hazardous Waste (now the Center for Health, Environment and Justice), founded in 1982 by Love Canal activist Lois Gibbs, and the National Toxics Campaign, founded in 1984. The National Toxics Campaign, a network of local groups plus a national policy arm, was a particularly strong force behind the grassroots campaign to gain passage of the Superfund Amendments and Reauthorization Act (SARA) in 1986, which included right-to-know laws. NTC was an active bridge builder between unions and community organizations in several parts of the country. Both NTC and CHEJ worked to build links between local working class antitoxics and environmental justice groups.

The working-class environmentalism of antitoxics and environmental justice activists did not mean ready collaboration with unions and workers. A shared sense of place was significant in forging links between workers and community activists, as was the case at Love Canal. Shared local space helps explain why community groups in communities of color have worked with local unions and white working class community groups to take on polluting facilities and broader urban pollution.

Right-to-know was one strategy that yielded labor-environmental collaboration at the local and national levels. Yet right-to-know needed to be more closely linked with questions about production itself, the lack of community and worker participation in production decisions, and economic development issues. Another environmental strategy offering potential for cooperation was pollution prevention, which grew out of the right-to-know campaign. The pollution prevention concept focused on intervention in the generation of toxic waste at the front end of production through input substitutions, process design changes, and product changes. Pollution prevention paralleled Barry Commoner's call for "social governance of production decisions" (Commoner, 1990), and focused the environmental debate on how many current policies ignored the impact of toxic substances on workplace health and the shifting of pollution from one medium to another. Progressive community-based networks like NTC and the Silicon Valley Toxics Coalition had raised critical questions about systemic hazards of production and waste generation and about the dislocation of workers. OCAW activist Tony Mazzocchi introduced the concept of Superfund for Workers (now called Just Transition) to confront concerns about worker dislocation due to changes at the front end of production.[27] This concept was adopted by environmentalists and the occupational safety and health community during the right-to-know campaign. By the late 1980s pollution prevention had become a major policy alternative and organizing strategy for alternative antitoxics groups because of the potential it held for radical industrial conversion. Emboldened by victories in federal right-to-know and Superfund reauthorization campaigns, activists in

Massachusetts and New Jersey helped push through the country's only toxics use reduction laws. The federal government responded to pressures to move beyond waste minimization regulations with the pollution prevention act of 1990, although the federal measure was voluntary, focusing on technical assistance and lacking the necessary enforcement to move industry toward broad reductions in toxics use. Much of industry has been slow to adopt pollution prevention or outright opposes its implementation. Moreover, many community-based environmental groups were slow to focus on pollution prevention and questions of production in their struggles against specific facilities.

Pollution prevention provided a basis for labor-environmental collaboration, by suggesting a common focus for organizing on health hazards. It offered a strategy for workers and communities to influence production decisions in manufacturing, service, and public sector workplaces. Beyond right-to-know, it offered initial steps in the right-to-act to promote cleaner production. This presented an opportunity for labor-environment collaboration. At first, pollution prevention was not a good coalition-building strategy because it did not address the question of economic security of possibly displaced workers and disrupted communities. After a broader discussion of Just Transition, led by the Oil, Chemical and Atomic Workers and its ally the Labor Institute, an integrated pollution prevention and Just Transition strategy becomes a more understandable strategy to workers and community organizations. Pollution prevention without a Just Transition for displaced industrial workers will continue to face the divide between workplace and environmental groups; coupled the two concepts may be the basis for social movement strategies on economic conversion, community and worker empowerment, and the reconceptualization of work, environment, and the relationship between the two. However, designing an organizing strategy around integrated notions of pollution prevention and Just Transition has been hindered by ideological barriers between workers and environmentalists, primarily differences in how work is defined.[28]

Despite this potential, the barriers to labor-environmental collaboration remain substantial, the largest of which are the real and perceived impacts on work and jobs through implementation of pollution prevention practices. The divisions between workers and environmental organizations have become legendary through the conflicts over the cutting of old-growth forests in the Pacific Northwest in the late 1980s and 1990s. There the labor-environment divisions were both class (Rose, 2000) and geographic (Obach, 2001), where outside middle-class environmentalists were pitted against local working-class timber workers and their communities. Surmounting such deep divisions has proved impossible without effective bridge builders and discussions about a Just Transition strategy. But there have been a number of labor-environmental successes, on a state and regional level, in particular the annual New York Labor-Environment Conference, the New Jersey Work Environment Council, and the Los Angeles Labor-Community Strategy Center. At a minimum they have drawn together leaders and activists for ongoing dialogue about jobs and the environment issues, worker and community health.

The right-to-know campaigns of the 1980s, and their successor campaigns on environmental justice and clean production, have developed a prevention outlook, demanding that industry and government prevent the creation of toxic waste. While national mainstream environmental organizations were initially generally supportive of this approach, they adopted an approach to environmental problems based on hazard controls and risk assessment as a compromise for promised access to the Clinton Administration. This accommodation hindered coalition-building efforts between the Washington-based mainstream environmental groups and national unions in the 1990s, particularly because of mainstream environmental support for the North American Free Trade Agreement. Realization by some national mainstream environmental organizations of the flaws of NAFTA, however, prompted them to join with labor and human rights organizations in blocking the passage of free trade fast track in 1997. National campaigns on fair trade provided opportunities to transcend the divisive "jobs versus environment" conflicts such as the logging versus forest preservation controversies in the Pacific Northwest. Such conflicts continue to demonstrate that arguments in favor of pollution prevention and natural resource protection, absent explicit demands for economic security for workers and communities, tend to feed anti-environmental sentiment and undermine the capacity to build a broader progressive project. The apparent success of the 1999 Seattle coalition between labor, environmental, and human rights organizations, while inspiring in its images of multiclass, blue-green coalition building, was an important step in challenging labor-environment conflict. But it was not followed by important campaigns to build national collaboration. Nevertheless, efforts by national organizations in Washington, D.C., to collaborate on labor-environment have developed since the late 1990s. The Blue-Green Working Group, facilitated by the AFL-CIO and comprising numerous national unions and environmental organizations, has taken on difficult challenges such as global warming, alternative energy, and Just Transition. Blue-Green collaboration led to several significant reports and a national alternative energy initiative, the Apollo Project.

RESURGENT SOCIAL UNIONISM AND
NATIONAL LEADERSHIP CHANGE

The crisis for labor—represented by declining membership resulting from downsizing, contracting out, automation, and loss of jobs to Southern countries— had reached such a level by the mid-1990s, that a new leadership was voted in at the national AFL-CIO. With the election of John Sweeney and a reform slate in 1995, the new leadership sought to challenge the limitations of fifty years of business unionism and reinvigorate labor through new-member organizing and social unionism. New-member organizing was given high priority and resources at the AFL-CIO and numerous member national unions. At the same time, the AFL-CIO set the tone on building vital relationships with other social movements to shape a national progressive political strategy. National unions had learned from the spirited but unsuccessful fight to stop the passage of the North American Free Trade Agreement in 1993, that despite collaboration with some social movement organizations, they had to strengthen their political position by deepening and broadening relationships with other social movements.[29] Adopting a social unionist model paid off quickly, with the decisive defeat in 1997 of President Clinton's fast-tracking of the expansion of NAFTA to the broader western hemisphere. Here a counterhegemonic "fair trade" coalition of labor, environmental, and public interest organizations roundly blocked the legislation in its tracks. The new social unionism reached the national popular consciousness in late 1999 with the protests in Seattle against the World Trade Organization, where unions and various movement organizations converged to challenge capitalist-directed globalization of the economy, and specifically the existence and policies of the World Trade Organization. "Teamsters and turtles" became a symbol of this convergence, although it inaccurately conveyed that labor-environment was something entirely new and that it was somehow led by one union (the latecomers-to-environmentalism Teamsters) and one type of environmentalist (preservationists). Seattle represented less a formal collaboration of counterhegemonic forces than a convergence of discrete movement organizations.

Despite the AFL-CIOs shift to organizing and coalition building with progressive partners, it continued to operate within a business unionist framework by continuing to seek cooperation with management despite the crisis for workers in the transition to lean production. The federation continued to focus on wages and benefits, rather than issues of speed-up, downsizing, lengthening work time, subcontracting, and outsourcing (Moody, 1997). While the AFL-CIO has employed tactics of social movements, particularly civil rights and immigrant rights, in its efforts to build membership, it has not engaged enough in self-reflection and building democratic union organizations to counter the overall decline in unions (Bronfenbrenner, 2001). Moreover, the lack of democracy within many unions, combined with a lack of a class analysis by the AFL-CIO and many unions leaders, has prevented the building of effective strategic coalitions with community and progressive movements. As Moody states,

> What is needed in the United States is not simply bigger unions and improved techniques but a labor movement with dynamic unions at its core drawing on many kinds of working-class organizations and communities. To get from here to there requires open debate within the unions. It demands a class identity that recognizes difference, but defines what we hold in common in society and who the enemy is. (Moody, 2001)

Labor-community coalitions became widespread in the 1990s, due in part to national networks with local mobilizing efforts, such as Jobs with Justice, living-wage campaigns, and SEIUs Justice for Janitors campaign. Since 1987, Jobs with Justice has successfully built coalitions in forty cities in twenty-nine states because it operated outside of a traditional union framework to include unions and community groups in a looser framework of solidarity. It drew funding from organization dues and foundations (Early, 1998). Coalitions such as Jobs with Justice and the original living-wage campaign in Baltimore, led by the congregation-based Baltimoreans United in Leadership Development and the American Federation of State, County and Municipal Employees, have moved progressive organizing ideas "from the margins to the center" of labor and community organizing (Fine, 1998). Such coalitions demonstrate the strong return of social unionism as a way of building social justice links between politically weakened labor, community, and environmental organizations.

In summary, the period of corporate globalization and flexible accumulation from the 1970s to the present has witnessed growing labor-community and uneven labor-environmental collaboration in the face of industrial restructuring, corporate downsizing, loss of higher-paid manufacturing jobs and the establishment of neoliberal government policies, beginning with the Reagan administration. Capital responded to a crisis of overproduction and to increased regulation of workplace and community environments by organizing itself as a class, subsequently undermining reforms won by unions and social movements in the 1960s and 1970s by using aggressive tactics such as union decertification campaigns and job blackmail against unions in all sectors. Beginning particularly with the Reagan administration, neoliberal policies protecting aggressive corporate practices and eroding welfare state protections helped to weaken an already weak labor movement and erode public confidence in government to solve social and economic problems.

Within this context of weakened government protections for working people and communities, there were numerous opportunities for collaboration among unions, communities, and environmentalists. The increasingly dire situation for unions—specifically, declining membership and reduced power at the bargaining table—stimulated new experiments by unions to confront internal problems, particularly their isolation from other constituencies and their increasing conservatism. While national union bureaucracies continued to abide by "pure and simple unionism," despite forging ad hoc alliances with national environmental groups, union locals and militant union leaders made outreach into the broader community an increasingly common strategy, particularly since the late 1970s. Lacking the protections of a capital-labor accord, unions needed all the allies they could find and found them in churches, local social justice organizations, and various labor-community solidarity networks.

Issue-based interest groups and Alinsky-style community organizing, born out of the 1960s new social movements and fragmented progressive politics, expanded in the 1970s and 1980s. But their narrow range of issues limited their relative political power and made coalition building with other organizations, including labor, often necessary. Urban and rural communities suffered decline in political power, as capital centralized its control; thus community organizations increasingly sought collaboration with unions to challenge capital flight and job layoffs. The fragmentation of reform politics, then, in tandem with a fragmented governmental response to social problems, have made labor-community and social movement coalitions essential to building power and shaping public policy.

Environmentalism was transformed through greater public awareness of environmental problems and the emergence of clear race, class, and gender dimensions to environmentalism itself. Widespread pollution and hazardous waste siting, legacies of Fordist production, awakened environmental activism in working-class communities and communities of color. A new generation of labor rank-and-file grew up with the heightened environmental awareness created by the 1960s environmental and occupational health movements, which enabled unions, from locals to internationals, to more readily collaborate with environmentalists (Rose, 2000). In general, gender and racial diversity in unions and environmentalism, together with growth of working-class environmentalism, have fostered labor-environmental collaboration.

CONCLUSION

Over the past hundred years labor-community and labor-environmental collaboration intervened in crises that capitalist development had helped create. The high points of collaboration—the Progressive Era, the 1930s, and the period since the 1960s—are characterized by increasing diversity of unions and social movements, including environmentalism, and the attendant broadening of agendas and more inclusiveness. Unions such as the Knights of Labor, as well as community institutions, engaged in a higher degree of mutual aid in times of crisis. This contrasts with the general isolation and division characteristic of unions and community during all historical periods, and most specifically during the post-World War II period to the 1960s. Collaboration occurred as an attempt to overcome previous isolation and fragmentation of counterhegemonic politics. Indeed, more recent experiments have sought to bridge the fragmented progressive politics existent since the Great Society reforms initiated separate interest group politics. Business unionism, or the servicing model of unionism, a participant in hegemonic blocs over much of this century, facilitated the demise of progressive collaborative organizations, such as the Workers Health Bureau in the 1920s, union health and safety efforts in the 1950s, and Environmentalists for Full Employment in the early 1980s.

In the current period of capitalist-led globalization, as well as historically, coalition experiments between labor and community have been riven with tensions between working the system from within, militant confrontation with the power holders, and building independent institutions (see Brecher and Costello, 1990). In the dialectic between insurgency and reform there is constant danger that progressive collaboration gives way to institutionalized coalitions that merely service the coalition partners without active participation of the rank and file. Divergent class cultures (Rose, 2000)—working class versus middle class—and the differing legal and political structures—federally supervised worker organizations versus variously structured, voluntary social movement organizations (Obach, 2001)—have interrupted or outright prevented collaboration. Yet bridge builders have compensated tensions between classes and between different organizational structures by creating and implementing effect-I've campaigns that build trust between union members and community and movement members.

The political and ideological position of the working class has shifted significantly over the past 100 years, demanding of counterhegemonic movements that they develop new strategies and new forms of organization to advance popular-democratic and class struggles. This trend continues to illustrate Gramsci's argument that intellectual and moral leadership of working class organizations and social movements must understand changing political-economic conditions and devise new political strategies accordingly. As unions became more conservative and locked into tighter control by business unionism by the 1970s, it became imperative for their own survival that they forge broader counterhegemonic alliances, in which they were equal partners with other constituencies. As corporations have gained increasing control over spaces in recent decades, labor and social movements have begun structuring their war of position around a broad and inclusive social justice perspective and strategy.

Government has provided avenues for collaboration victories by labor and social movements, particularly during reform periods. Once reforms were institutionalized, however, alliances generally fell apart for lack of an organizational structure durable enough to withstand a strong backlash from the business community, such as in the 1920s, 1970s, and 1980s. Despite its involvement in the erosion of working class and union political power, the American liberal state has provided labor and grassroots environmentalism with procedural channels to intervene in the production process. The history of labor-community-environmental collaboration tends to support the notion of government as an open, contradictory, contested, and emergent strategic process.

The politics of labor, community and social movement collaboration have a strong gender and racial component. The Progressive Era alliances between unions and social and health reformers achieved important reforms for the working class because of the energy and insight of middle- and upper-class women activists working together with working-class men and women. Widespread community solidarity for labor militancy during the 1930s was facilitated greatly by women activists and leaders in both unions and communities. Since the 1970s, labor-community collaboration, particularly around environmental and job preservation issues, has succeeded because of important leadership by women in community organizations. Intervention by African-Americans within the labor movement and by the African-American community has stimulated union outreach into broader communities, as well as the racial diversification of unions themselves. This was particularly true in the mid-1940s and during the 1960s civil rights mobilization.

Counterhegemonic alliances are clearly only one form of resistance politics. Many different types of race, gender, and class resistance never make it into organizational alliances. As Frank (1995) noted, beyond the visible social and labor movement struggles are daily confrontations by women and people of color over equality at home, in the community and in the workplace, struggles which may never be manifested in organized counterhegemonic politics. It is important to recognize the rich background of microsites of resistance, out of which a rare number of political alliances emerge.

The history of labor-community and labor-environment collaboration has a geographic message as well. The rise and fall of labor-community and labor-environment efforts reflects the ability of such politics to work at different geographic scales—national, regional, and grassroots simultaneously. Successful coalitions have drawn on national resources (skills, financial support, and ideas) and local diverse leadership, issues, and initiative. Such projects might spread their innovative strategies around, providing a "demonstration effect" (Wills, 1998) to unions and communities in need of workable organizing strategies. Without the ability to work at different scales, coalitions can grind to a halt, as during the 1940s and 1950s, when the capital-labor accord undermined local labor-community collaboration. In recent years, labor-community networks such as Jobs With Justice have built local coalitions in many places, spreading successful strategies around. Such coalitions demonstrate that successful coalitions are consciously multiscale and provide one possible map of where labor-community politics are headed.

ENDNOTES

1. This rhetoric has its modern counterpart in governmental and corporate victimization of the consumer and the mass-consumption lifestyle as the primary culprit in urban pollution and the global ecological crisis.
2. Taylorism was characterized by scientific management of work relations, which structured work organization into work teams. It tended to accelerate the production process, fill gaps in the working day, and put workers under greater control to ensure increased output. Taylorism involved the separation and specialization of production tasks to challenge workers' relative autonomy and control over working conditions (see Aglietta, 1979). Both Taylorist scientific management and Fordist mass production, first introduced in 1914, built on the profound expansion of modern corporate organization, particularly advanced by the surge in corporate mergers around the turn of the century (Harvey, 1989).
3. The Farmers Alliance, representing 100,000 farmers fighting dislocation due to skyrocketing costs of mechanized farming, supported the Knights of Labor on numerous occasions (Foner, 1974). The Knights of Labor, however, were plagued by internal

practices of racial discrimination, particularly against Chinese-Americans, owing in part to the racist positions of some of their leaders (Foner, 1974). Subsequently, the Industrial Workers of the World and the early CIO would organize along broad social justice themes as well (Moody, 1988).

4. AFL chief Samuel Gompers' pronouncement of "pure and simple unionism" disallowed union participation in social reform or political parties (Moody, 1990).

5. The period of the 1880s to the 1920s was actually comprised of two separate waves of social reform: populism, in the 1880s and 1890s; and progressivism, from 1900 to the 1920s (Geiser, 1977).

6. Alice Hamilton investigated and advocated on occupational and community health risks that focused specifically on the hazards posed by the introduction of new technologies and new substances, such as petrochemicals, into the workplace. She warned workers that they were being used as guinea pigs to such exposures. She identified class, race, and gender factors in workplace exposure.

7. Militant unions such as the Western Federation of Miners and the Industrial Workers of the World, arose from the industrialization of hard-rock mining in the West with its attendant highly hazardous, environmentally unsafe working conditions (Gottlieb 1993; Rosner and Markowitz, 1991). New drilling technologies increased silica and lead dust poisoning. The WFM, in particular, campaigned against degraded working and environmental conditions. Industrial-belt mills and sweatshops had become far more dangerous through overcrowding, the introduction of toxic dyes, and hazardous vapors emitted from stoves (Gersuny, 1981; Gottlieb, 1993).

8. Competitive social regulation, conducive to the period of rapid expansion of capitalist production in the late 1800s, did not work well with intensive Taylorist production relations. The expansion of Taylorist scientific management of production relations by 1920, involving the reorganization of work and further incorporation of labor into the needs of capital, created such large gains in productivity that competitive regulation could not provide enough demand to keep up with the production gains, resulting in an overproduction crisis in the 1930s (Lipietz, 1988).

9. This development demonstrates the tenuousness of social reform strategy, shifting between confrontation and legitimation. The danger of professionalization of social reform movements is addressed by Piven and Cloward (1977), who argue that too much organization is a bad thing in that it leads to co-optation of leaders by moderating, establishment forces.

10. This campaign serves as a precedent for the recent wave of labor-community alliances focused on a broader social and economic agenda, particularly those led by community and congregation broad-based organizations, such as those currently affiliated with the Industrial Areas Foundation, founded in 1940 by Saul Alinsky.

11. One exception was a lawsuit filed against U.S. Steel by 108 black steelworkers over lung diseases in 1935.

12. The owning company, Union Carbide, and its contractor knew beforehand of the hazards of tunneling through the silica rock.

13. It was only in the 1970s and 1980s, with the reemergence of the occupational safety and health movement and the emergence of the people of color environmental justice movement that Gauley Bridge was recognized as a tragic milestone in the history of hazardous working conditions and environmental racism (Gottlieb, 1993; see also, Lee, 1990; Page and O'Brien, 1972; Rosner and Markowitz, 1991).

14. Fordism was a response to a crisis of overproduction in the previous economic regime (Lipietz, 1987), where corporate profits had been constrained by lack of consumer income and by working-class mobilization for a living wage and better working conditions. Fordism developed into its mature phase mainly after World War II, after the major shift in the structure of production from basic industry to mass production (Lipietz, 1987), the development of appropriate forms of state intervention (Harvey, 1989), and only with the institution of labor control and compromise after the defeat of the resurgent labor militancy of the immediate postwar period. Like Taylorism, Fordism was an intensive regime characterized by dynamic changes in the production process through incorporation of workers' know-how into increasingly automated production; intensified separation of conceptual work from unskilled labor; and rising productivity of labor and of volume of fixed capital per capita (Lipietz, 1988). The mature Fordist regime was accompanied by a monopolistic mode of regulation involving constant adaptation of mass consumption to gains in productivity, maintained by increased state intervention in the economy (Lipietz, 1988). It included raising workers' wages and benefits and subsequent growth of consumer industries, suburbanization and the welfare state. The state would intervene in capital-labor conflict through collective bargaining, and assumed an increasing role in market planning and regulation.

15. The capital-labor agreement of collective bargaining in return for industrial peace helped to ensure the full functioning of Fordist accumulation. But business unionism's collaboration with management and government during the Cold War ultimately proved to be a false partnership and disastrous for labor. Despite labor's adaptation to collective bargaining, rank-and-file discontent with the hardships of routinized Fordist production brewed beneath the surface (Braverman, 1974; Harvey, 1989).

16. The African-American-led Trade Union Leadership Council and the Negro American Labor Council forced the AFL-CIO to adopt policies of nondiscrimination, and to support civil rights legislation. Yet the AFL-CIO followed, never led, and would not go as far as the civil rights movement did. The federation failed to support a "Jobs for Negroes" program, a forerunner to affirmative action. While the NALC's and TULC's militancy in the early 1960s helped phase out the worst discrimination within the AFL-CIO, it was unable to end racial discrimination within the labor movement in general, largely because its best-known leaders and voices of protest were assimilated by the federation's bureaucratic business unionism (Moody, 1988).

17. Cleveland Robinson, an African-American secretary-treasurer of UAW District 65, was an exception but drew no support from the AFL-CIO leadership (Moody, 1988).

18. The Environmental Defense Fund, inspired by Rachel Carson's warning in *Silent Spring,* had led the campaign to ban DDT due to its impact on wildlife.

19. Union activists George Taylor of the AFL-CIO, Tony Mazzocchi of the Oil, Chemical and Atomic Workers, John Sheenan of the United Steel Workers, and Frank Wallick of the UAW were instrumental in promoting health and safety reform and were familiar with or well-connected to Washington politics.

20. The Johnson Administration acted on health and safety as part of a broad "quality of life" reform agenda, not in response to grassroots or labor pressure. Clearly, the health and safety movement was rooted in a larger flourishing of social movements fostered by a transformation of American liberalism during the Great Society era. The

American liberalism of the New Deal, with its coalition of capital and banks, actually encouraged the development of social programs confronting urban social unrest, as part of a plan for Keynesian stimulus solutions for the economy (Ferguson and Rogers, 1986). The Great Society programs, however, met stiff opposition from domestic capital and small business, thereby forcing state mediation, which provided an arena for social movement mobilization on health and safety.

21. Two big exceptions to the lack of national union leadership were the Oil, Chemical and Atomic Workers, which had several hundred thousand members working in highly dangerous workplaces and worked actively to develop local links with health professionals and activists, and the United Auto Workers, which broke away from labor's mainstream by opposing the Vietnam War and subsequently withdrawing from the AFL-CIO in 1969 over the war.

22. Numerous factors contributed in reducing profitability. Taylorist production methods failed with the introduction of new technologies. Increasing international competition destabilized the regulation of production and society (Lipietz, 1992). Rigidity in production investments, labor contracts and allocation, unrestrained growth of the Welfare State, and the tight relations between the government, business, and organized labor, combined to seriously weaken the Fordist system (Harvey, 1989, 1991). The mode of regulation, involving the monopolistic regulation of wages, reached a crisis where reductions in consumer buying power would lead to recession, while increased buying power would lower the rate of profit (Lipietz, 1988).

23. Beginning with a labor-environment summit on jobs and the environment held at Black Lake, Michigan, in 1976, EFFE was part of an effort that linked antinuclear and alternative energy groups with unions not represented in the top AFL-CIO leadership and with those construction trade unions that understood best the need for alternative energy development. In 1979 EFFE and a number of Washington-based antinuclear and progressive environmental groups formed a striker support group for 1,600 OCAW members who had been on strike for seven months at a DOE uranium enrichment plant in Piketon, Ohio (Kazis and Grossman, 1982). The OCAW members had struck over economic, health and safety issues at the plant, which was operated by Goodyear Atomic. Despite the attempt by federal legislators to split the coalition by portraying the antinuclear organizations as out to destroy the workers' jobs, heavy lobbying efforts by the strikers' support group and the OCAW built the necessary pressure to get the company to meet the strikers demands.

24. EFFE's active presence in building bridges allowed mainstream environmental groups to escape responsibility for involvement in that task, leaving it up to EFFE instead. EFFE failed to elicit an ongoing deeper commitment from the environmental mainstream because the latter did not want to make social justice a part of its agenda and developed only peripheral links to labor. Moreover, industrial restructuring was eroding labor's membership base and political power. The corporate attack on OSHA, begun already during the Carter Administration, combined with the loss of health and safety leader and coalition-builder Tony Mazzocchi in his bid for the presidency of the OCAW, all worked to seriously undercut efforts to build national labor and environmental coalitions. EFFE's efforts suffered from working with national union and environmental leaders instead of spending several years organizing environmental grassroots, union rank-and-file and local union leaders. EFFE closed down because it believed that national leadership-dominated coalitions for progressive causes would

ultimately fail because they did not function democratically, ignoring their rank-and-file membership (Grossman, 1985).

25. Environmental justice analysis and activism have tended to be two separate but interrelated spheres of activity. Much environmental justice analysis since the 1980s has focused on "distributive justice" (hazards disproportionately impacting communities of color) and a limited form of "procedural justice" (communities of color have been shut out of hazardous waste siting decisions), while not addressing production decisions (Lake, 1996). However, more recent analysis has taken a broader of view of justice (Ferris and Hahn-Baker, 1995), beyond a focus on the discriminatory siting of facilities, to address the lack of political power on the part of communities of color to affect decision making (Bullard, 1993), as well as important production questions such as capital investment and choices about production technologies and relationships (Faber, 1998; see Gottlieb, 2001, for a good overview of these arguments). The environmental justice grassroots (regional and local), for its part, has continued to have an increasingly broad approach to justice, looking beyond the civil rights concerns of discriminatory siting of facilities, while building multiethnic coalitions and examining production questions, such as choices about production and transportation technologies, including pollution prevention methods.

26. Grossman (1985) asserts that the AFL-CIO's Industrial Union Department took control of the OSHA-Environmental Network, precluding grassroots and rank-and-file participation.

27. Modeled after the G.I. Bill, Just Transition calls for up to four years' full income support and education support for workers displaced from workplaces for environmental cleanup reasons. The Just Transition concept is an attempt to support dislocated workers while new, safer forms of work are developed. Some argue it must be extended to include all workers (and communities) displaced by post-Cold War defense cutbacks in order to be effective.

28. See Chary (1997) and Merrill (1997) for a discussion of labor and environmentalist positions and responsibilities in making toxics use reduction and Superfund for Workers work.

29. Many of the mainstream national environmental organizations, such as the National Resources Defense Council, the Environmental Defense Fund, and the National Wildlife Federation accommodated to President Clinton's promise of a "seat at the table" and supported NAFTA. This later proved costly, as Clinton abandoned many of his environmental promises.

CHAPTER 4

The BASF Lockout and the Origins of the Louisiana Labor-Neighbor Project

This chapter and the next focus on the relation between labor politics and capital politics as the context for the development of the Louisiana Labor-Neighbor Project in the 1980s and 1990s.[1] This chapter explores Louisiana history for particular clues indicating a tendency for labor politics to develop labor-community institutions as a way of confronting capitalist crises. It also examines the creation of the Oil, Chemical and Atomic Workers' politics of collective identity as it was shaped by the politics of the BASF Corporation and the Louisiana petrochemical industry. The next chapter looks at the ideological and political transformation of OCAW's labor-community project after the union's tactical victory over BASF.

The Louisiana Labor-Neighbor Project is a grassroots community-labor coalition that grew out of a 5-1/2 year lockout of members of OCAW Local 4-620 at the BASF chemical facility in Geismar, Louisiana. Figures 1 and 2 show the petrochemical corridor and study area. Both the Labor-Neighbor Project and its sister organization, the Louisiana Coalition for Tax Justice, were creations of OCAW Local 4-620 and community activists. As of 2002, the Labor-Neighbor Project continued to draw its financial support from member dues of the 650 members of PACE (formerly OCAW) Local 4-620 and from foundation grants. The project represented the PACE local and several community groups it helped to create in Ascension Parish. Until 2002, the project had an eleven-member board of directors representing the community, public health advocates, and PACE Local 4-620.

Soon after OCAW Local 4-620 successfully forced the BASF Corporation to end the 5-1/2 year lockout on December 15, 1989, Leonard and Nauth (1990) analyzed the union's victory (see Minchin (2003) for another detailed analysis of coalition building and the BASF lockout.). Leonard and Nauth attributed the union's success to five factors: the stamina and solidarity of the union local's

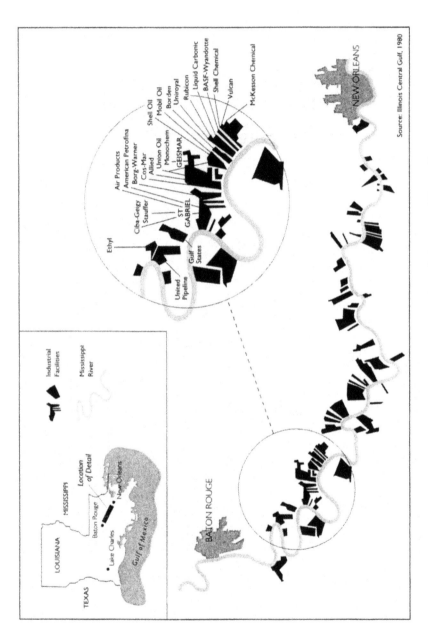

Figure 1. The industrial corridor between New Orleans and Baton Rouge.

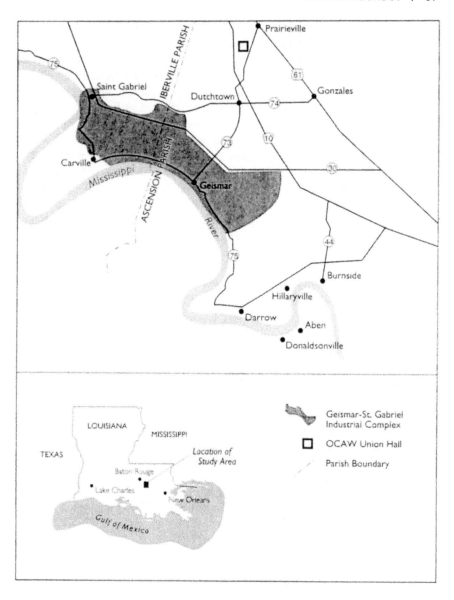

Figure 2. Study area: Ascension Parish and the
Geismar–St. Gabriel Petrochemical Complex.

members; the solidarity provided by Louisiana's grassroots environmental network; superb, inexhaustible leadership by the union local and its international representatives; access to a large quantity of company documents; and unflagging solidarity from the OCAW International Union. While these factors undoubtedly were central to the union's success, they do not provide a complete explanation for the union's victory. In this chapter the five factors identified by Leonard and Nauth are developed by situating them in the historical context of labor politics as shaped by capital politics and state institutional relations in Louisiana. OCAW's politics are explained as being shaped by the politics of the Louisiana petrochemical industry and BASF. That union politics are shaped by corporate politics and state relations is directly related to the particular history of collective action by the OCAW International and to new forms of industrial unionism in the 1970s and 1980s. In other words, to understand OCAW's success against a petrochemical giant we need to consider closely the historical context of the players involved: petrochemical capital; the state and political leadership; and labor and civil society forces.

OCAW's collaboration with community in Louisiana emerged within the context of the crisis of Fordism and capital's response of economic restructuring. Labor-community solidarity, however, is better understood in reference to Louisiana's particular history of labor politics, capitalist politics, and political opportunities provided by the state. In this chapter, I argue that OCAW's success in building a labor-community coalition that would break the BASF lockout was due to the following factors: the experience of OCAW International in health, safety, and coalition-building; the strong history of industrial unionism and labor militancy in Louisiana, in particular New Orleans; a porous neoliberal state, rooted in bourbon elitism, with corrupt and reformist tendencies; community bridge builders, steeped in civil rights activism; the crisis of Fordist production, demonstrated by continued underdevelopment, decades-old environmental devastation, and a persistent antiunion regulatory environment; a growing antitoxics network in Louisiana, with key environmental bridge builders; a relatively immobile and vulnerable petrochemical industry; and a national right-to-know movement at its peak.

OCAW's RICH EXPERIENCE IN HEALTH, SAFETY, AND COALITION BUILDING

The Oil, Chemical and Atomic Workers Union brought a rich history of advocacy, militancy, and coalition building to its role in the BASF lockout. The union's intellectual leadership had informed numerous local struggles over several decades and was critical to the union's ability to survive and break the lockout. The creation of the Oil, Chemical and Atomic Workers Union in 1957 was influenced heavily by the hazardous nature of heavy industrial production, which helped give the union a deeper awareness about workplace health and safety. Formed out of the merger of the Oil Workers International Union and the Chemical Workers Union, the union's democratic structure was strongly shaped by the western insurgent heritage of the OWIU and its affiliation with the CIO. Since the early 1960s, the union was actively engaged in promoting occupational safety and health regulation and was a key player in the campaign for the passage of the OSH Act in 1969 and 1970.

Throughout the 1970s the OCAW International was a leader in struggles over workplace health and safety and a coalition builder with environmental organizations. Its premier struggle of that decade, the 1973 strike against Shell Oil, was largely over health and safety and forged an ad hoc alliance of unions and environmental groups. Although the union had some pro-environmental leaders, most notably health and safety activist and one-time International vice president Tony Mazzocchi, the International was still greatly concerned about tensions between environmental protection and job preservation. Mazzocchi's bid for the presidency in 1980, in part based on the strategic link between workplace and environmental health, was halted by fears generated by his opponent over Mazzocchi's position calling for the development of alternative energy, which the opponent claimed would cost the union thousands of jobs in the nuclear industry. Despite this setback within the national leadership, the union continued to be an active watchdog on worker health and safety.

OCAW, both at the local and International levels, was democratically structured. One of OCAW's predecessors, the Oil Workers International Union (OWIU), introduced in the 1930s a unique governance structure of direct election by union locals of members of a national executive council, which had oversight powers over international union officers. Local unions elected their own officers, officers of their district council, and executive council members by referendum. Prior to this, all nominations and elections had been run by international union conventions (Green, 1986). Thus, the OCAW's leadership capacity on health and safety and alliance-building with environmental organizations arose from the union's base in hazardous industries and the democratic union structure to emerge from that.

A STRONG HISTORY OF INDUSTRIAL UNIONISM IN LOUISIANA

Despite being a part of the "right-to-work" South, where union militancy has been less frequent than in other regions, Louisiana is not simply a right-to-work state. Louisiana's rich industrial union heritage, punctuated by important moments of militancy, mainly in New Orleans but also in smaller towns and rural areas, helped shape the capacity of union leaders in some industrial unions in New Orleans, including OCAW. OCAW's success at building a lasting labor-community coalition must be seen in context of Louisiana's strong history of industrial unionism, though sporadic, and history of social unionism and labor-community solidarity. OCAW's savvy union local leadership and regional leadership must be seen as a link to a longer tradition of industrial union militancy in the New Orleans region.

Table 1 provides an overview of the shifting political-economic context for working-class mobilization from the mid-19th century to the crisis of Fordism in the 1970s and 1980s. Louisiana's labor institutions and strategies historically gravitated between inclusion and diversity, on the one hand, and exclusion and narrowness, on the other. Louisiana unions often sought to address crises of working conditions by diversifying their constituency and building broad industrial unions. These efforts, however, were consistently challenged by the narrowness of the dominant craft union elite and by capital's divisive tactics.

Unions emerged in the late nineteenth century as a response to a crisis of working conditions at the intersection of a Northern-directed wage labor system, plantation capitalism, and an emergent New South industrialism. New Orleans set Louisiana apart from the rest of the South, because of its position as the state's primary trade link to the North and significant source of capital to the plantation economy. As a crossroads of different economic systems, New Orleans became an important arena for local struggles and a conduit for militant and reform impulses coming from other regions. Bourbon politics of white supremacy and export-led development created the conditions for major social unrest and a rich experimentation in union building, particularly in New Orleans. The city's multiskilled workforce, including high-demand skilled workers, formed part of the foundation for organizing along inclusive industrial union lines, which often included significant community solidarity. Divisive strategies by businesses and craft unionism—dividing workers along skill and racial lines—consistently challenged and undermined these industrial union experiments.

But divisions were occasionally bridged. African-American workers' rights activism was one such bridge. With opportunities for political and civil rights activism severely constrained, African-American activists found workers' rights to be a more fruitful struggle. African-American unionists militated against entrenched segregationism and successfully pushed for inclusion in broad-based industrial unions, putting New Orleans at the forefront of inclusive, industrial unionism. In contrast, mobilization of African-American plantation workers largely failed because the dominant craft union leadership would not provide the solidarity necessary for the difficult task of organizing nonskilled workers in the face of powerful planters, preventing effective organizing until the 1940s (Becnel, 1980; Hair, 1969; Hofstadter and Wallace, 1971). Despite these setbacks, African-American social unionism was important in its impetus toward inclusive, industrial unionism and in the occasional solidarity it gained from some Catholic priests (Fairclough, 1995).

Another effort to bridge skill and racial divisions was the New Orleans industrial union movement, with leaders such as the Brewery Workers Union, the Dock and Cotton Council (an alliance of several waterfront unions), and the

Table 1. Capitalist Development and Collective Resistance in Louisiana, 1850-Present

	Pre-Fordism: 1830s-1920s	Fordism: 1920s-1973	Post-Fordism: 1973-present
Economic Regime	• Plantation capitalism combined with northern-directed wage labor system. • Ascendancy of New South industrialism after 1900. • Largely low-wage working class. • Higher wage skilled workers in New Orleans. • After 1890, increasing modernization of urban social infrastructure.	• Rise of oil, gas, petrochemical-based economy. • Emergence of Longist welfare state and post-war social programs, financed by industry excise taxes.	• Crisis of Fordism delayed by expanded oil, petrochemical production in 1970s, due to OPEC oil embargo. • Boosted revenues to state treasury, social services. • After 1980, slowed economic growth, rising unemployment, declining revenues from industry, crisis for "tooth fairyism." • Petrochemical restructuring: consolidation; over-production; replacement of workers through modernization; greater use of poorly-trained contract labor.
Political Leadership	• Bourbon oligarchy: alliance of planters, merchants, native capitalists. • After 1900, rise of New South modernizationists, progressive urban reformers.	• Longist neo-populism supplants modernization elites and Bourbons. • Creation of Fordist state, bi-factional political system. • Rise of corporate open-shop (right-to-work) offensive. • Longist populism alternating with periods of moderate and conservative reform.	• Edwards neo-populism, alternating with moderate reform. Based on multi-racial electoral alliances. • Passage of right-to-work (open shop), stepped-up attack on labor. • Persistence of racial prejudice in government and corporate institutions. • Deregulation of workplace health and safety. • State legitimation crisis in environmental protection, followed by environmental policy reform, followed by decline of reform, lack of environmental leadership.
Collective Resistance	• New Orleans-based labor movement is fertile ground for industrial union experimentation, but divided by dominance of craft unions. • African-American workplace struggles are important, after white supremacism limits political opportunities and civil rights activism.	• Weak and divided labor movement, undermined by anti-communism, open-shop movement, business unionism in 1920s, 1950s. • Spread of industrial unionism across state in 1930s-1940s. • Growth of African-American union and civil rights leadership. • Frequent support of labor by Catholic Church.	• Anti-toxics movement emerges in response to massive environmental degradation by petrochemical industry. • Labor hampered in building effective political power, and in challenging open-shop and anti-union forces. Due to dominance of business unionism and lack of labor grassroots mobilization. • Labor-community politics as response to petrochemical restructuring and environmental degradation.

Central Trades and Labor Assembly (representing thirty industrial and mechanical trades), the Knights of Labor, and the Industrial Workers of the World. Despite these efforts, the craft union leadership consistently excluded African-American workers from white unions, as the AFL and the Louisiana Federation of Labor often undercut broad-based, multiracial unionism to preserve the dominance of certain crafts.[2] Nevertheless, industrial union militancy, with its attempts at building inclusive solidarity, had a lasting impact in challenging white supremacy and set a precedent for later industrial and social unionist experiments.

New Orleans' experiments at industrial unionism helped generate similar efforts in other cities and in rural areas. While some of these were successful, most failed to summon sufficient broad labor solidarity to confront powerful industrial and plantation capitalist forces. The rise in production brought on by World War I defense needs initiated a huge surge in union militancy—despite opposition by the State Federation of Labor—and a rise in union membership. By the 1920s, however, collective action had reached an impasse, as even the craft unions were thrown on the defensive by a growing anti-union climate, manifested by a flourishing anticommunism and the beginnings of the corporate-led open-shop movement. Decades of internal divisions and betrayal by the craft-union elite left the labor movement in disarray.

Agrarian populism, a recurring movement in Louisiana since the 1830s, was another front for inclusive working-class organizing. Based in the northern upland parishes, and initially a predominantly white movement, populism united African-American and white populists to challenge the Bourbons politically over worsening agricultural conditions and constitutional restrictions on black suffrage (Hair, 1988). The agrarian populist base of the 1890s movement was a direct result of the dispossession of farmers and squatters by northern- and British-based lumber and railroad syndicates in the 1870s and 1880s. Once the movement shifted to an electoral agenda, however, with the formation of the People's Party in the 1890s, it was destroyed by the Bourbon Democrats. Yet, the populist sentiment in the northern uplands persisted because of continued difficult living and working conditions of the rural working class. A hybrid of socialist radicalism and rural political populism arose in the northern uplands in the first decade of the 1900s, actively supported by the Socialist Party and the IWW. It manifested itself in the Brotherhood of Timber Workers, forging a multi-racial industrial unionism of white farmers and squatters and African-American sharecroppers. Timber barons destroyed the union in 1913, for lack of effective statewide solidarity due to opposition from the state AFL (Cook and Watson, 1984; McWhinney, 1988).

Industrial unionism found a frequent community partner in the Catholic Church, beginning with support for the Knights of Labor's agricultural workers' campaign in the 1880s and the papal encyclical of 1891, which called for a social justice that both ensured the working class a living wage and protected private property. Both events inspired church and lay leaders to accept the importance of unions for their efforts in promoting social justice for the working class through unions' efforts to win arbitration and the living wage (Becnel, 1980). Church priests tended to focus their solidarity on lesser-skilled workers, particularly African-Americans. They assisted in the Knights of Labor's organizing efforts with black sugar cane field workers in the 1880s, and in multiracial industrial union organizing in New Orleans (Cook and Watson, 1984). Beyond the Catholic Church, the numerous union struggles in New Orleans were grounded in cultures of solidarity involving community institutions such as African-American churches and families, while rural populist struggles were supported by solidarity between farmers and timber workers.

The shift to New South industrialism provided openings for inclusive industrial unionism by weakening the Bourbon's political dominance while at the same time stimulating the growth of multiskill workplaces. National labor organizations, such as the Knights of Labor and the Catholic Church, were important influences in broadening labor organizations beyond a narrow craft-unionist, largely white constituency. New Orleans' leadership in creating a broad-based, inclusive unionism that drew heavily on community solidarity was short-lived. Social unionist experiments outside New Orleans, such as the agrarian radicalism in northern Louisiana, were similarly brief.

Labor's efforts to build an inclusive unionism in Louisiana were only slightly more successful during the Fordist period than the previous period. While industrial unionism became more established during the 1930s and 1940s, attempts at building broader union institutions were neutralized by the narrow politics of business unionism, as embodied in the post-World War II capital-labor accord, and by direct antiunion campaigns. Community solidarity with labor, while important particularly in the militant unionism of the 1930s and early 1940s, was brief and never institutionalized. More importantly, unions' focus on wage and employment questions, to the exclusion of broader economic development issues, limited the development of institutional collaboration between labor and community.

As in the rest of the South, the labor movement in Louisiana was weak and divided during the Fordist period, with only 18 percent of the nonagricultural work force unionized in 1946 in contrast to 30 percent nationally (Cook and Watson, 1984). Initially savaged by anticommunist business campaigns and an incipient industry-led open-shop movement in the 1920s, labor also continued to be undermined by internal conflict between industrial and craft unionism. These internal divisions in Louisiana labor became more pronounced with national level conflicts between the AFL and the newly formed CIO in the 1930s. Throughout the Fordist period, and particularly during Huey Long's tenure, the state AFL, and subsequently the state CIO, lacked vision and bought into notions of industrial "partnership" and in-house state appointments for AFL officials. As such, labor was well-contained by Louisiana businesses and the state.

The national wave of industrial union militancy in the 1930s brought unionism to numerous towns and cities in Louisiana. In step with the rapid development of the oil and petrochemical industries in the 1930s and 1940s, CIO-affiliated unions organized many oil and chemical workers in the state. Despite labor's craft/industrial divisions, African-American workers' rights activism thrived within the labor movement in the 1930s and 1940s, stimulated by the political openness of the Longist New Deal. Militant CIO unions in New Orleans fostered development of a new generation of black leaders and provided important support to developing civil rights organization.[3]

The Cold War fueled both anticommunism and white supremacism in Louisiana, stifling the New Deal era political ferment for labor and civil rights.[4] AFL business unionism overwhelmed the militant impulses of industrial unionism, abandoning nonskilled and lesser skilled workers, and thereby preventing the AFL from building sufficient political clout to stop the Right-to-Work campaign of 1946. The AFL's narrow accommodationist position led it to abandon agricultural workers in their struggle against sugar producers in the 1950s.[5]

The Catholic Church played an active role in the campaigns to stop right-to-work legislation and in some labor organizing campaigns. Jesuit priests were central to the organizing efforts by the National Agricultural Workers Union to organize sugar cane and other agricultural workers during the 1940s and 1950s, although these organizing drives were ultimately crushed by the AFL's abandonment of agricultural workers and the overwhelming power of the sugar establishment (Becnel, 1980; Cook and Watson, 1984).

In summary, the Fordist period in Louisiana was characterized by more aggressive antiunion capital politics and increased political space for labor and community politics, yet missed opportunities for building a broader labor-community politics. Industry conducted an open-shop campaign in the 1920s, resuming it in the 1940s. The 1930s Depression gave rise to Longist New Deal programs to mediate crisis, and provided unusual political space for union organizing. Labor's institutional experiments included militant industrial unionism, often with informal community support. Labor and its community solidarity, however, were largely focused on production questions, that is, issues of wages and working conditions. Labor-community collaborative efforts passed up golden opportunities to address questions of economic development, particularly the issue of equity and the ten-year industrial exemption. The low tax burden on the middle and working classes—"tooth fairyism"—helped to divert public resentment away from the state and industry. Moreover, the Fordist ideology of mass consumption linked with mass production in the postwar era militated against popular challenges to economic development policy. As such, despite the enlarged political space for working class organizations, there were no serious efforts by labor to address economic development during the Fordist period. While labor's productionist focus under Fordism limited its collaboration with community, African-American unionism successfully developed labor-community ties that transcended a narrow production focus. By promoting racial integration of Louisiana unions in the late 1930s, the 1940s, and the 1960s, African-American trade unionists were an important force in the civil rights movement. Efforts to develop a more inclusive labor politics were stifled again by the Cold War collaboration of capital and business unionism. Impetus for labor-community political collaboration was largely absent in the 1960s, except within the African-American community.

By the 1970s Louisiana labor was again under assault by a corporate right-to-work campaign, which successfully gained the passage of a right-to-work law in 1976. Moreover, with fraying of the post-war capital-labor accord, numerous Louisiana companies attempted to institute antiunion measures, which were often resisted. Rationalization within the petrochemical industry in an increasingly competitive global context put labor on the defensive, meaning that traditional institutional forms of unionism would no longer work as before. Decades of accommodation by narrow craft-unionism—with its exclusionary business unionist philosophy—had rendered the labor movement more vulnerable to the open-shop, antiunion onslaught. Labor's elite-driven craft unionism had indeed won economic gains for union workers in the 1950s and 1960s, and its racially liberal leadership promoted integration. Victor Bussie, the labor federation's head since 1956, through tireless lobbying won higher benefits for the workers of Louisiana than in any other Southern state, and was a staunch supporter of integration. Yet Bussie's efforts were constrained by the state AFL-CIO's lack of inclusive, grassroots unionism, and by its long history of accommodation to segregationism.[6]

Beginning in the 1970s with the institutionalization of desegregation and civil rights mandates, the civil rights movement fragmented into smaller initiatives. School desegregation campaigns, access to public services, housing and jobs, and black electoral campaigns defined African-American activism in Louisiana in the post-Fordist era, and became the training ground for a new generation of black leaders and activists. Some of these activists assumed leading roles in incipient environmental justice activism in African-American communities.

A POROUS NEO-LIBERAL GOVERNMENT, WITH REFORMIST AND CORRUPT TENDENCIES

Louisiana's porous neo-liberal government has a tradition of catering to the needs of industry, often in corrupt fashion. But since the 1920s, it also has had a tradition of social and political reform, providing avenues for political action by public interest and community organizations. Louisiana's reputation of a corrupt political elite closely allied with business interests has its origins in Bourbonism, an oligarchy of native capitalists, merchants, and planters that governed Louisiana from the 1830s to the early 1900s. Over the past century there has been a constant tension between bourbonist oligarchical control and reformism, in the form of modernization, social welfarism, and the expansion of government. Bourbonism and modernization forces were challenged by active trade unionism, based largely in New Orleans, which helped create political openings for reform-minded leaders such as Huey Long, who introduced social welfare ideas, brought in from outside Louisiana.

The Bourbons' centralized power facilitated not only the reintroduction of white supremacy after Reconstruction, but the continuation of a corrupt, elitist state leadership, and an extraction-based, export-led economy.[7] Louisiana's economy was largely extraction-based, first with sugar and cotton, subsequently wood products, and then oil and gas. This extraction economy was significantly controlled by Northern and foreign capital, and as such, wealth was largely removed rather than reinvested in the diversification of production or in social infrastructure. By dramatically lowering reconstruction taxes and putting constitutional limits on property taxes, the Bourbons did little to build up the state's manufacturing base and social infrastructure, and train a diversified workforce. The Bourbons maintained their power against an increasingly mobilized citizenry through electoral fraud and a white supremacist ideology that portrayed African-Americans as the enemy of the working class, thereby hiding the real class tensions of New Orleans-based trade and plantation systems (Prothro, 1988), and depriving African-Americans of political suffrage and economic opportunity. This rigid cast system dominated until Huey Long came to power in 1928 (Fairclough, 1995).

After 1900 the Bourbon hegemony was gradually supplanted by New South modernization-oriented reform politics, promoted mainly by urban progressives,[8] which helped transform Louisiana politics and the orientation of the state's production system. The reform and modernization forces took away the Bourbons' political base of African-American plantation workers and tenant farmers by legislating suffrage restrictions, and brought about the demise of the New Orleans machine, which had a large working-class base, by promoting the cleanup of corruption, the restoration of social order, and the modernization of the city. When progressive elites assumed state power in 1920, they instituted a severance tax on the export of natural resources, based on "gentlemen's agreements" with oil, gas, and timber companies. These developments provided a basis for the rise to state power in 1928 of Huey Long (Jeansomme, 1990).

Modernization and the rise of Fordist production in Louisiana represented new crises and political opportunities for labor, community and social movements. Both the neopopulism introduced by Huey Long and the growth of the petrochemical industry were underpinned by Bourbonist corruption, which both limited and offered targets for political opposition. The rapid development of the oil, gas, and petrochemical-based economy beginning during World War I, but most particularly in the 1930s and during World War II, led to a crisis of consumption. These industries became highly rationalized, requiring Fordist production techniques and labor discipline.[9] In Louisiana, as in the nation as a

whole, consumption of productive output could not keep pace with rapid production during World War I and the 1920s. As capital had not found a solution
to this crisis by the 1930s Depression, it was up to the state to find a way. Huey
Long's brand of New Dealism created an important outlet for accumulated capital
from the oil and gas industry, investing it in social infrastructure such as roads,
schools, and hospitals.[10]

Huey Long came to power as a neopopulist who sought to "share the wealth"
with the broad working classes. Supplanting the Bourbons and modernization
elites, Long was instrumental in creating a social welfare state that helped
modernize Louisiana. The advent of Longism on the heels of Progressive urban
reformism signified the beginning of alternating periods of populist and reform
policy guiding the local state. Neo-populism, despite its rhetoric, and liberal
reformism enabled rapid capital expansion, particularly of the oil, gas, and petrochemical industries. While imposing an excise tax on oil and gas, Longism
instituted industrial property tax breaks beginning in 1936. These tax breaks
were considered "lagniappe," or icing on the cake, doing little to attract new
industry to the state, or stimulate job creation or economic development
(Louisiana Coalition for Tax Justice, 1992).[11] Long's most important contribution
was his introduction of a bifactional political system into a previously oligarchic
system (Carleton, Howard, and Parker, 1988). Longist social welfarism, in concert
with the national New Deal, generated a climate of democratic ideology that
created fertile political space for labor to challenge suppression by capital and
for African-Americans to resist white supremacy (Fairclough, 1995). The introduction of class-oriented social welfarism, however weak, signified the creation
of a Fordist state that would distribute the wealth from Fordist production
more equitably.

The petrochemical boom during World War II and the immediate post-war
years led to higher wages and increasing private consumption in a broad segment
of Louisiana's working class, and a resulting significant growth of the middle
class. Material conditions for the poor, however, particularly African-Americans,
barely changed until the 1960s. The rapid growth of Louisiana's welfare state and
post-war social programs was financed largely by industry excise taxes, rather
than by individual property and income taxes. With attainment of mature Fordism
after World War II, Louisiana's growing middle class came to tolerate government
corruption due to their extremely low tax burden.[12]

Throughout the Fordist period, Louisiana continued its role as resource colony,
dependent on outside capital, with huge wealth siphoned off to New York and
other financial centers. At the same time, environmental devastation became
increasingly evident, particularly due to the unregulated growth of the state's
petrochemical industry and the import of hazardous waste from other states.
The growth of industrial capital in Louisiana was accompanied by increasingly
powerful offensives by business to contain the power of labor through open
shop campaigns. Beginning in the 1920s, right-to-work campaigns mobilized in

response to labor militancy, and in particular against the prospect of increasing African-American power in unions.[13]

THE FORDIST CRISIS: A CRISIS FOR THE PETROCHEMICAL INDUSTRY, ENVIRONMENT, WORKERS, AND COMMUNITY

The petrochemical industry in Louisiana was relatively immobile, despite restructuring within the industry. At the same time, the industry was not mono-lithic, but vulnerable to outside pressures from government and civil society. The industry grew steadily from the 1930s to the 1970s, establishing itself mainly in two regions: the Mississippi River corridor from Baton Rouge to New Orleans, and around Lake Charles. Beginning with the Standard Oil (now Exxon) refinery in Baton Rouge, the industry grew to include nearly 100 facilities in the Baton Rouge/New Orleans corridor, while fifteen facilities operated around Lake Charles. By the 1970s, petrochemical industry accounted for 45 percent of the state's GDP. Facilities were often arranged in complexes of five to ten plants. Petrochemical companies were drawn to Louisiana for two important reasons: good transportation and abundant nearby critical natural resources. An added incentive was a very welcoming and porous state government, which enabled quick expansion of facilities and provided important infrastructure and services. As is the case in other places, the petrochemical industry in Louisiana was relatively immobile, being fixed in locations because of close proximity to vital mineral resources, such as salt brines, and oil and natural gas. During the Fordist period, hardly any efforts were made at environmental management; thus petro-chemical facilities were exceedingly polluting. Indeed, decades of production created dozens of uncontrolled hazardous waste sites, contaminated huge areas of groundwater and surface water, and created some of the most toxic air in the country. By the mid-1970s the Baton Rouge / New Orleans industrial corridor had earned the title, "Cancer Alley," and for good reason, since preliminary health surveys indicated cancer rates well above the national average.

OCAW's orchestrated campaign against BASF and coalition strategies came in the immediate context of the crisis of Fordist production in Louisiana and elsewhere, which had resulted in a crisis for workers, the environment, and economic development. In much of the country, by the early 1970s Fordism had become characterized by a profitability crisis for capital, while creating crises for labor and the environment. In Louisiana, the Fordist crisis had a delayed impact on the economy and state's political leadership because of the domestic oil boom resulting from the OPEC embargo of 1973. For much of the 1970s the oil and petrochemical industries expanded production. Increased revenues filled state treasury coffers and more funding flowed into state social services. Yet while the state's economy flourished, Louisiana unions were dealt a serious blow by the passage of right-to-work legislation in 1976, which was part of the overall weakening of labor around the country.[14]

By the early 1980s, Louisiana's economic growth had slowed markedly and unemployment rose quickly after oil prices plummeted. The base of industrial revenues for social welfare declined accordingly, as social programs were cut back. The 1980s oil bust and recession again exposed the economic ramifications of the "tooth-fairyism," to which Louisianans had been long accustomed; indeed the lack of revenue generated by private income and property taxes left social infrastructure and welfare programs directly vulnerable to the rise and fall of revenues from industrial exports. While petrochemical, oil, and gas development had soared during Fordism, Louisiana remained the least industrialized state in the South (Chapman, 1992). Louisiana could still be considered a resource colony, dependent on outside capital, suffering a lack of industrial diversification, and with unemployment consistently higher than the national average.

The petrochemical industry was seriously affected by the Fordist crisis. In the aftermath of the second oil price shock of 1979-80, and the recession of that period, the industry underwent a major period of restructuring in the 1980s, largely in response to intensified competition and takeover pressures. These pressures led to industry consolidation—through mergers and takeovers—overproduction, and replacement of workers through mechanization. Many companies were forced to increase their debt and slash their workforces in order to pay off interest.[15]

Pressures from real or potential corporate takeovers gave rise to worsening health and safety conditions in the petrochemical industry. Companies cut their permanent workforces, particularly shop floor operators, replacing them with remote operators in control rooms. Moreover, companies significantly reduced preventive maintenance by operating at full capacity while delaying major overhauls. They retired their experienced workers early, replacing them with less-experienced, often poorly trained, and increasingly contract workers.[16] The situation was not easily corrected, in that management customarily segregated contract workers from permanent workers, who were more often highly trained and unionized. OSHA had allowed the petrochemical industry to regulate its own health and safety conditions, despite efforts by the United Steelworkers to get the agency to implement tougher standards for the industry in the aftermath of the 1984 Bhopal tragedy. Thus, by the mid-1980s, conditions in the petrochemical industry were primed for accidents, given that the restructured industry was operating at overcapacity, and was undermaintained and hardly regulated.[17]

Investment in manufacturing in the Gulf Coast petrochemical regions was slowed by customarily high wages in the industry, a reputation for labor-management confrontation, and public perception of environmental contamination. Regardless of important pollution reduction made in the latter part of the 1980s, the concentration of these facilities in huge complexes exacerbated local environmental contamination. As Chapman (1992) argues, after thirty to forty years of development along the Gulf Coast, the petrochemical industry matched the characteristics of growth poles. Yet such poles lacked any notable diversification of the economy.[18]

The restructuring of the petrochemical industry, in Louisiana and nationally, was a way of ensuring continued capital accumulation in an increasingly competitive global economy. Restructuring involved the uncoupling of mass production from mass consumption. A stable and growing middle class was no longer necessary for industrial development. In Louisiana, protecting middle-class living standards was more of a factor in political stability than a precondition for industrial growth. When Governor Edwin Edwards raised private income taxes to stabilize a state treasury rocked by declining industrial inputs in the wake of the 1980s oil bust, he was voted out of office in large part by an angry middle class. While the petrochemical industry restructured to stabilize and increase profits, it did so without regard for a capital-labor accord and without accountability for the livelihood of working people. Louisiana's political leaders, on the other hand, had to weather the recession, the loss of corporate revenues, and the persistence of "tooth-fairyism" to retain power. State political leaders faced the dilemma of ensuring both the stability in the state's leading industries and the stability of the electorate, particularly the middle class, hit hard by recession and unemployment.

In geographic terms, the response to the Fordist crisis in Louisiana was a continuation and intensification of agglomeration economies and urbanization established under Fordist petrochemical development. Louisiana's industrial cities—New Orleans, Baton Rouge, and Lake Charles, in particular—retained their urban concentration while expanding. Indeed, the 1980s and 1990s brought an urbanization of rural areas around previously peri-urban industrial facilities, like the petrochemical corridor between Baton Rouge and New Orleans. With the encroachment of residential areas in proximity to growing petrochemical complexes at the urban periphery, the potential for conflict between residential and industrial land uses increased.

At the same time, the toxics crisis brewing during the Fordist period became more apparent, particularly with a well-publicized incident in 1978 in which the driver of a tractor-trailer dumping hazardous waste was asphyxiated by toxic vapors at Bayou Sorrel, near Baton Rouge. This incident made clear the degradation of work and living environments in a petrochemical economy. Conditions of environmental degradation and overdependence on a narrow petrochemical economy provided a point of departure for local collective action in the 1980s. The neo-populist/reform cycle in state administration continued through this period. In the aftermath of overt white supremacist control of the governor's office in the early 1960s, African-Americans gained electoral power and ultimately shaped the outcome of the 1971 election. Edwin Edwards won election in 1971 through an unprecedented black-white electoral coalition. He ensured greater funding for social welfare programs by raising oil and petrochemical severance taxes, while at the same time promoting continued capital expansion and endorsing policies detrimental to working people. Defying his promise to the AFL-CIO, Edwards signed Right-to-Work legislation into law in 1976. During his four administrations (1971-1979, 1984-1988, 1992-1996) he consistently opposed environmental protection and promoted industrial property tax breaks. Edwards fit the mold of colorful rogue neopopulist, in the Huey and Earl Long tradition, who taxed the corporations to fill state coffers and reward his friends. He chose to quit the 1987 gubernatorial race, after his campaign foundered due to previous business dealings, particularly a federal indictment and subsequent acquittal on racketeering for procuring hospital permits for campaign contributors.

Edwards' administrations were interrupted twice by moderate reformers; David Treen, a Republican (1980-1984), and Buddy Roemer (1988-1992), initially a Democrat who became a Republican. During the Treen administration, the Louisiana Department of Environmental Quality was formed, opening up a necessary arena for environmental discourse among citizens, industry and the state.[19] Buddy Roemer turned back Edwards' gubernatorial negligence by bolstering the DEQ and instituting an environmental scorecard at the Board of Commerce and Industry. The scorecard was designed to reward industry by giving property tax breaks on the basis of environmental performance.

The 1970s brought an era of multiracial electoral alliances, an expanded African-American electorate, and a rapidly growing number of black public officials. This injected a voice of racial moderation into Louisiana politics that helped check a highly resilient white supremacism. David Duke's 1990 and 1991 campaigns for U.S. senate and governor were turned back in no small part by high black electoral turnout. Edwin Edwards defeated Duke in 1991 largely due to a black-white electoral alliance which boasted an unprecedented 85 percent turnout among registered African-Americans. Once in office, Edwards appointed industry-oriented bureaucrats to run the DEQ and eliminated the environmental scorecard. Nevertheless, progress made under the two previous reform administrations—creating and strengthening DEQ, elevating the discussion over corporate environmental accountability—established an arena for citizen participation and public dialogue that could not simply be erased with the return of a pro-industry neopopulist.

In summary, the crisis of Fordism in Louisiana created a capital politics that exacerbated existing crises for labor and the environment. Business unionism had reached its own political limits, as demonstrated by the passage of right-to-work legislation. The environmental crisis, resulting from Fordist industrial development, had grown steadily, finally erupting into the public consciousness in the mid-1970s. The state responded to the environmental crisis initially with nominal environmental protection in the early 1980s. Restructuring by Louisiana's petrochemical industry put labor on the defensive, and put communities and workers at greater risk through gradual replacement of the permanent workforce with poorly trained contract labor. The state did little to check this alarming trend. Petrochemical capital politics was further defined by a relative local dependency on natural resources and transport links, which made the industry potentially vulnerable to innovative labor and environmental politics.

AN EXISTING ENVIRONMENTAL NETWORK
AND BRIDGE BUILDERS

OCAW's ability to link with environmental community was facilitated by a decades' old environmental devastation wrought by petrochemical and oil and gas industries, by an incipient environmental network that arose to combat this devastation, and by bridge builders within the environmental community who quickly understood the plight of the locked-out workers. The union's environmental link was also aided by reformist leaders in government who had taken steps to address the environmental crisis, most notably, the reformist attorney general, who in 1978 established a citizen access unit for environmental affairs.

Modern environmentalism had its beginnings with Progressive reformism and northern upland populism and agrarian radicalism. Progressive reformism, driven largely by urban elites, tended to be promodernization and focused on wetland preservation, oil, gas and timber preservation, and urban health and sanitation. Northern populism and agrarian radicalism, largely working-class driven, tended to be antimodernizationist and were oriented toward preservation of rural livelihoods against the wholesale landscape destruction by the timber companies and railroads. The emergence of these two streams of environmentalism was indeed connected to the onset of New South industrialism and its attendant environmental destruction of wetlands and northern forests.

Environmentalism during the Fordist period was limited largely to wetland and forest preservation. The toxics crisis had yet to break into the public light, although public awareness about pollution related to industrial development was growing. In fact, by the late 1960s the "selling of the South" approach among government leaders intent on attracting industry to Louisiana and other southern states in the post-war decades began to be tempered by the knowledge that industrial development had definite environmental costs (Cobb, 1982).

Environmentalism entered a new stage, as working-class whites and people of color mobilized to defend their communities against decades of toxic contamination. In the 1980s, African-Americans organizing against polluting industries could not help but connect their threatened health with institutionalized racial bias that failed to protect their communities. The greatest concentration of petrochemical development coincides with a high concentration of rural and urban African-American communities along the Mississippi River. Former plantations were bought up by the petrochemical industry, while African-American communities neighboring the old plantations remained. There is no mistaking the heaviest impact in the Mississippi River petrochemical corridor, both economically and in terms of public health, as being upon low- and middle-income African-Americans (Bullard, 1990; New Orleans Times-Picayune, 1991).

In the mid-1980s, petrochemical companies began dealing with the contamination of adjacent African-American residences by buying out and moving the communities. Over a ten-year period, four African-American communities in the Baton Rouge-New Orleans petrochemical corridor were bought out and moved, while another was in the buyout process.[20] Such buyouts and forced migration were the basis for the environmental justice activism of the Gulf Coast Tenants Organization (Janice Dickerson, interview, 1991).

Prior to the mid-1970s, environmentalism in Louisiana was restricted largely to preservation and conservation of natural environments, despite federal and state investigations of toxic mishaps. Incidents of toxic contamination, and subsequent citizen activism, remained highly localized.[21] Yet several activists based in New Orleans had begun making links to citizens in poisoned communities across the state. One activist well-networked with communities on the frontlines was William Fontenot, a volunteer with the Sierra Club. Fontenot was tapped by the state attorney general to run the Citizen Access Unit in 1977.[22]

While incidents of contamination occurred frequently in the 1970s, many giving rise to community collective action, the aforementioned toxic asphyxiation of a waste hauler at a toxic dump at Bayou Sorrel in 1978 significantly raised public awareness about industrial pollution statewide. The Bayou Sorrel incident helped catalyze the formation of numerous local antitoxics groups, which helped build the necessary pressure to bring about the creation of a state environmental protection agency. With regional organizing assistance, local communities targeted sites like the massive Petro Processors waste facility north of Baton Rouge, and International Technologies' proposed commercial hazardous waste incinerator in Ascension Parish. In 1982, Calcascieu League for Environmental Awareness Now (CLEAN), based in Lake Charles, was formed, and over the decade became one of the better organized antitoxics groups, with a large local base. In the mid-1980s, the Gulf Coast Tenants Organization began organizing numerous African-American communities to challenge polluters.

An informal network of grassroots activists, spearheaded by Fontenot of the attorney general's office and by the New Orleans Ecology Center, helped create the Department of Environmental Quality in 1980 during the Treen administration. Environmental awareness grew further in 1985 with the proposed dumping of radioactive gypsum sludge into the Mississippi River by Freeport McMoRan's fertilizer production facilities between Baton Rouge and New Orleans.[23] By 1986, there was sufficient critical mass to form a statewide clearinghouse for local antitoxics organizations, the Louisiana Environmental Action Network. In LEAN and the many local antitoxics groups, women were key leaders.

OCAW's ability to link to community was enhanced by community leaders steeped in civil rights activism, in particular civil rights activists with a union background. Civil rights activism in the workplace has a long tradition in Louisiana, which allowed for the possibility of union leaders with civil rights experience. The convergence of civil rights activism and union membership in southern Louisiana only elevated the possibility of bridge builders emerging who could help forge links between unions and community organizations. Indeed, OCAW would find strong solidarity from one particular African-American trade unionist, Amos Favorite of Geismar, who had a strong connection to community and extensive experience in confronting authority, at the workplace and as a civil rights activist.

RIGHT-TO-KNOW ACTIVISM
AND ENVIRONMENTAL SOLIDARITY

The union's ability to link with right-to-know activism was influenced by a national community and worker right-to-know movement hitting its peak in the mid-1980s. OCAW found significant support among national antitoxics organizations at an auspicious moment for the movement. OCAW had developed a particularly close link to the National Toxics Campaign, a national network of grassroots antitoxics groups that emerged in 1983, through NTC's founder, John O'Connor. O'Connor had organized briefly with OCAW in Massachusetts and had developed a connection to Tony Mazzocchi, a national leader of OCAW International and premier bridge builder to the public interest and environmental communities.

The backdrop for the lockout and OCAW's collaboration with environmentalists was the Fordist landscape of severe environmental contamination and ensuing rapid growth of the chemical right-to-know movement, which had developed on two flanks: worker health and safety, on the one hand, and grassroots and national environmental, on the other. Since the 1970s, union health and safety activists and Coalitions on Occupational Safety and Health (COSHes) had promoted worker right-to-know about potential workplace hazards, particularly chemical hazards. The national antitoxics movement, which had taken flight in the aftermath of Love Canal in the late 1970s, advocated not only for waste site cleanup but for community right-to-know legislation in the early 1980s. The Bhopal, India, catastrophic release of deadly methyl isocyanate at a Union Carbide pesticide plant in December, 1984, accelerated right-to-know activism, and led to much closer collaboration of worker and community right-to-know activism in many states and at the national level.

The National Toxics Campaign, for its part, emerged in 1983 as an effort to link local antitoxics groups around the country in campaigns for legislative and policy changes on toxic chemicals and hazardous waste. NTC was staffed by policy strategists and community organizers, involved community leaders in its strategy development, and lent assistance to local struggles. The other national antitoxics network, the Citizens' Clearinghouse for Hazardous Waste, founded by Lois Gibbs, similarly employed community organizers and policy strategists, while engaging local community leaders in its direction. It is not surprising that OCAW had strong links to both these important national networks. OCAW leaders in Niagara Falls had assisted Lois Gibbs in the late 1970s in her Love Canal organizing campaign against the Hooker Chemical Company, to win compensation for the affected families, and to get the contaminated areas in her community cleaned up.

The lockout, then, occurred at a propitious moment, when the antitoxics and right-to-know campaigns were reaching a national presence. Moreover, OCAW had already developed important links to right-to-know and antitoxics activists. The international union's experience in collaborating with environment activists—from the fight to pass the Occupational Safety and Health Act, to the OCAW strike at Shell Oil in 1973, to OCAW's assistance to Lois Gibbs' organizing at Love Canal—on the one hand, and the previous links by environmental and antitoxics networks with OCAW on the other, enabled the union to reach out for environmental allies when it needed them during the BASF lockout.

BASF's POLITICS OF UNION ELIMINATION: THE LOCKOUT OF OCAW 4-620

The BASF Corporation, a German chemical producer, is the largest chemical company in the world, with 130,000 employees worldwide and 20,000 in the United States. It began as a producer of synthetic dyes in 1861, and expanded into the production of fertilizers in the late 1800s. As a member of a German dye producers cartel, BASF helped control the dye market in the early 1900s, while producing mustard gas and explosives during the First World War. From the 1920s through the end of World War II, BASF was the principal member of the infamous IG Farben cartel, together with its modern competitors Bayer and Hoechst. IG Farben financed Hitler's military effort while producing, with slave labor from Auschwitz, Zyclon-B, the lethal gas used to exterminate inmates in the Nazi death camps. After the war, IG Farben executives were convicted of Nazi war crimes and the cartel was dismantled into several independent companies, including BASF, Bayer and Hoechst, three of the biggest chemical companies in the world. Germany outlawed most of the antiunion practices—such as lockouts—eventually used by BASF at its U.S. facilities. BASF grew rapidly in the 1950s and 1960s to become a world leader in the production of plastics, paints, and fertilizers. Motivated by the presence of abundant oil, gas, and mineral resources, as well as lower labor costs, BASF expanded significantly into the United States beginning in the late 1960s. It purchased Wyandotte Chemicals in 1969, with its Geismar, Louisiana, works. The company increased its investments in the United States during the 1980s by buying up synthetic fiber, dye, and other chemical operations. After its five-and-one-half year confrontation (1984-1989) with the Oil, Chemical and Atomic Workers International Union at its Geismar, Louisiana, facility, BASF shifted the focus of its expansion to Eastern Europe (Mattera, 1992).

BASF had relatively harmonious relations with its German unions since its reincarnation in the 1950s. The company was highly confrontational, however, with the unions of the companies it purchased in the United States. Beginning in 1979, under the leadership of Edwin Stenzel, the new president of BASF Chemicals USA, the company undertook a campaign to eliminate unions at its facilities in the United States. The company took advantage of the relative weakness of American unions and the lack of social democratic political power to back up unions. Between 1979 and 1985, BASF forced the elimination of unions at its plants in Wyandotte and Holland, Michigan, and Jamesburg and Belvidere, New Jersey. In 1980 the National Labor Relations Board found the company guilty of coercing workers in a union organizing drive in Anderson, South Carolina. At plants in Rensselaer, New York, and Huntington, West Virginia, the company forced the unions into accepting major contract concessions, including taking away union provisions allowing them to effectively regulate the contract. The concessions at Huntington in 1981 were forced by an eight-month lockout, after which the company allowed only 200 out of 350 OCAW members to return to work. The directive for the U.S. union-busting campaign originated at BASF AG's headquarters in Germany, an NLRB investigation ascertained. OCAW Local 4-620 in Geismar was ripe for a challenge from BASF, in that it was one of the last of the union locals to be confronted by the company and represented 100 percent of the permanent workers at the Geismar facility, unusual in a right-to-work state. Moreover the Geismar facility was the largest of BASF's 80 plants in the United States, accounting for half the company's profits in the United States. Thus it was a major trophy to be won (Leonard and Nauth, 1990; Oil, Chemical and Atomic Workers, 1988).

The company's lockout of 370 OCAW workers at its Geismar facility on June 15, 1984 was thus part of a concerted campaign to remove unions to boost profits in a highly competitive, restructuring petrochemical industry. Lowering labor costs by replacing high-skilled, high-paid union workers with nonunion, often contract, labor was a prevalent, lucrative practice for boosting profitability in the petrochemical industry by the mid-1980s. While BASF was busy trying to bust unions, it had gradually phased in the practice of contracting-out work customarily carried out by permanent—union and non-union—plant operators and maintenance workers. Indeed BASF's 1984 lockout of OCAW was the eighth lockout by industry against OCAW within ten years.[24]

BASF set numerous conditions for settlement of the contract with OCAW Local 4-620 during the 1984 contract negotiations, to which the union would not agree: reduction of wages and health benefits; replacement of all 110 union maintenance workers with contract workers; end of seniority; and power to the company to replace any union worker with a contract worker. Regarding the company's contract demands, BASF Geismar plant manager Les Story commented, "When you work for BASF, you leave your constitutional rights at the gate" (Oil, Chemical and Atomic Workers, 1988). After sixty negotiating sessions, the union was unwilling to accept these terms, but at the same time was not prepared to strike, given the high unemployment rate in Louisiana and the lack of available jobs for OCAW members. The result was a company lockout, which began when the company escorted union officials and negotiators out of the plant on June 15, 1984 (Leonard and Nauth, 1990).

While it appeared that BASF was prepared to outlast the union in a lockout, the company was vulnerable. Its vulnerability was the huge investment in its Geismar operation, which was bound to Louisiana's important natural resources and to the locally extensive petrochemical agglomeration. It was highly unlikely that BASF had any plans to leave the state. Unlike other industries, which responded to the Fordist crisis by threatening to move operations, or actually doing so, BASF could not credibly do so in Louisiana. By locking out the union, then, the company opened itself potentially to a local political struggle.

OCAW's ANTI-LOCKOUT CAMPAIGN

At first OCAW did not believe the lockout would last long. Six months into the lockout, however, with no end in sight, they called in two representatives from the international union to organize a campaign against the company. National resources were vital to fighting a multinational corporation. OCAW corporate campaign organizers began looking for allies and tactics to be employed to damage the company enough to force an end to the lockout. They developed several strategies: building community support against the immorality of locking out workers; corporate environmental pollution; contract labor and workplace health and safety; and BASF's fascist past and ties to apartheid regimes. OCAW's project organizers from the international union, particularly Richard Miller, made the strategic move to foster solidarity from environmentalists and the local community (Fontenot, interview, March 13, 1991).

The company counted on rapid surrender by the union, given the dire economic situation in the state and the lack of alternative job opportunities for the locked-out workers. When surrender did not come, BASF began employing divisive tactics on three fronts: pitting maintenance workers against operators, black union members against white members, and union members' wives against their locked-out husbands.

The union employed an elaborate set of legal strategies, persistent research, grassroots organizing, and innovative public relations. OCAW boycotted BASF's consumer products, such as antifreeze and audiotapes. Together with national allies they conducted a "lock-in" of company executives at BASF headquarters in New Jersey. Using legal means, they discovered numerous company documents, which they used to disrupt BASF's business wherever possible. For instance, using company documents, the union obtained information regarding BASF's future plans. The union disclosed some of its findings in its regular newsletter, revealing information such as personal items about company executives, and company marketing and future expansion plans. The union produced a video on the lockout, linking BASF to its fascist past. Moreover, OCAW conducted countless demonstrations and rallies, wrote numerous newspaper articles, erected several billboards in Ascension Parish, and directly lobbied executives and stockholders in Germany. Yet union members and strategists recognized that the campaign against the company could work only if it was grounded in building solidarity with the community, which became the most important component of the campaign (Leonard and Nauth, 1990).

Bridge Building to the Local Community

The union consciously employed geographic strategies against the company. It soon recognized that its central strategy in the campaign against the company had to be local, building an effective local politics. Before the lockout, OCAW's connection to the community was distant and their relationship to environmental groups nonexistent. As Leslie Vann, an OCAW leader from local 4-620, notes,

> Before the lockout, we weren't very receptive to the environmental groups. We assumed that the company was giving us all the information that we needed, that if there was anything out there harmful they would tell us about it. We were naive, we believed it. They're not going to allow us to breath anything that would hurt us. They're not going to allow us to take anything home on our clothing that would affect our families. So we really figured that environmental groups were just a bunch of kooks wanting to shut all the chemical plants down and put a lot of people out of work. (Vann, interview, 1991)

This statement indicates union members' lack of class consciousness and environmental awareness before the lockout. Workers trusted the company to inform them of workplace exposure, on the one hand, and had little understanding of pollution at the workplace or in the community.

During the first year of the lockout the union gradually recognized the importance of building solidarity within local communities, as a way of keeping the 370 idle members busy, and tactically as a way of preventing the public from putting blame for the lockout on the union workers. Then-OCAW International Representative, Ernie Rousselle, made the observation:

> If people sit idly by doing nothing, there's a tendency to assess blame against the union, rather than the cause of the problem. The involvement of the community gave our people an opportunity to express their feelings relative to who they thought was to blame for the situation. There was a sense of acceptance of the reasons. It became a fight between not just the labor union and the company. It was a people-fight rather than an organizational fight. (Rousselle, interview, 1991)

Involvement in the community was thus made to ensure that the lockout was seen as a fight for individual freedom and not for building support for the union. Outreach also helped union members clarify their class relation to BASF. The company was portrayed as "doing away with liberties and economic freedom of people, more so than taking on the union" (Rousselle, interview, 1991). With the community's assistance, the union characterized its struggle as one involving the community and the union over the economic freedom of the individual workers. This characterization counteracted frequent chemical industry portrayals in the media of the union "reaching out to environmental kooks," according to Rousselle. The union thereby took a significant step in defining the lockout as a moral issue by expanding the population of those affected beyond the union workers to include the community. As such, the union involved community in its strategy against the company.

To union leaders, outreach into the community seemed imperative, not just an optional strategy. As Esnard Gremillion, OCAW chair at BASF during the lockout, said, "All of that helped us build a foundation, to get past the selfish agenda, which was getting back our jobs." OCAW members talked to business people in towns around the Geismar complex. Reaction of the business community to the workers being locked out was understanding, but not supportive. As Gremillion reported,

> Most of them told me, "Look, I'm sorry you lost your job. It wasn't right for BASF to do that. But I really want to get involved in the environmental issues that are coming up. I'm worried about the polluted air and groundwater and how that will affect me and my children and grandchildren." (Gremillion, interview, 1991)

This reaction from the business community helped the union members realize that they had to begin organizing on environmental issues in order to gather broader support from area residents. The union, then, chose to reach out to the existing Louisiana environmental community in order to broaden the message about the immorality of the lockout and its impact on the economic lives of the workers. OCAW members recognized that people were hearing the message and it had a "tremendous impact on keeping the morale of people together" (Rousselle, interview, 1991).

Taking the strategy of building solid ties to the community came at the advice of both labor and the environmental community. OCAW's Rousselle asserted that his experience with lockouts—having been through a forty-four-month lockout in the 1970s at American Cyanamid in New Orleans—taught him that it was vital to build support for the economic plight of the workers within the local community. Rousselle's leadership, as informed by this community experience, helped shape the union's community outreach strategy.

A key factor in developing links to the community was the support role played by the female spouses of locked-out BASF workers. During the first year of the lockout, a group of female spouses, in close cooperation with the union leadership, formed a women's support group. This support group was a vital presence at open union meetings, rallies, and press conferences. More importantly, they helped union families deal with financial and personal stress and channeled the International Union's Adopt-a-Family financial support to the most needy families. As in most strikes and lockouts, family solidarity is an essential element in building a larger community of solidarity. In the BASF lockout, the women's support group helped in important ways to communicate the immorality of the lockout to a family's network of friends and community contacts, particularly through various church congregations. The message carried by the women's support group had a palpable effect within the largely rural and urban-fringe Ascension Parish, where over half of the 365 locked-out workers resided. Moreover, the efforts of the workers' spouses and families—particularly in the African-American community of Geismar—paved the way for union-community collaboration on environmental health concerns. Family solidarity, led largely by the women's support group, served as a vital bridge in the union's inclusion of community in its politics (Leonard and Nauth, 1990; Vann, interview, 1991).

The union's community of solidarity expanded to include the Catholic Church. In a tradition of assistance and solidarity to labor and working people, the Catholic Church lent support to the locked-out workers. Church leaders drew the link to *Rerum Novarum,* the papal encyclical of 1891, which gave church leaders a codified basis for promoting social justice among working people. Father George Bundy of Loyola University condemned the lockout as an immoral act. Sisters from the Baton Rouge Catholic Diocese spoke against the prolonged deprivation of the locked-out workers. Later during the lockout, Loyola University's Institute for Human Relations co-sponsored, with OCAW, LAWATCH (Louisiana Workers Against Toxic Chemical Hazards), a watchdog organization on worker exposure to toxic chemicals.

OCAW's attempt to win the backing of local political officials, however, was not successful because of the petrochemical industry's strong influence. The union asked the Ascension Parish police jury (county commissioners) to not issue a parish bond to BASF to construct a hazardous waste incinerator until the lockout was over. Although such solidarity was forthcoming by the Jefferson Parish police jury during the American Cyanamid lockout of OCAW in the 1970s, the Ascension Parish officials failed to lend that support in this case. The police jury voted 9-0 (with two abstentions) against OCAW's request, in spite of the fact that three members of the eleven person jury were from organized labor, including the jury president who was an OCAW member. Several of the police jury members, however, were petrochemical plant managers or supervisors. Because of the explicit class confrontation between OCAW and BASF and the close ties of leading officials with petrochemical management, it was difficult to convince the police jury that the union's struggle was at once a larger community struggle that they should support. There is little doubt that industry pressure forced the police jury members to reject the union's request. As such, political opportunities at the parish government level were limited as long as local officials perceived the conflict as largely a labor-management matter (Rousselle, interview, 1991; R. Miller, personal communication, February 17, 1992).

Environmental Bridge Builders and Strategies

By developing local environmental strategies, however, the union was able to move beyond the limitations of parish government politics and take advantage of other political opportunities. The 370 locked-out OCAW members were replaced largely by nonunion contract workers, poorly trained in operations and maintenance. The union used this issue as the basis for debating the link between worker health and safety and the environment. Contact with current and former contract workers, and access to internal company documents, provided the union with information about the increased number of workplace accidents since the lockout began, involving contract workers, and often involving worker exposure to toxic chemicals. The union believed that the substantial increase in use of contract labor posed a significantly higher threat to worker and community health and safety. The union documented the increased accidents and hazards, filing complaints with OSHA. Local 4-620's efforts ultimately came to the attention of Rep. John Conyers (D-Michigan), who launched a congressional investigation. As a result, OSHA commissioned the John Gray Institute of Lamar University to investigate contract labor and chemical industry accidents. The groundbreaking John Gray study found a strong positive correlation between the increased use of contract labor and an increasing accident rate. (Leonard and Nauth, 1990; Moberg, 1990).

Environmental leadership helped set the stage for the union's use of environmental strategies. Union leaders and strategists met with a leading progressive voice in Louisiana's environmental movement, William Fontenot, director of the Citizen Access Unit of the state Attorney General's Office.[25] Fontenot urged the union to build environmental campaigns in the Geismar area and beyond. He recommended that the union take on the other plants in the area on environmental grounds to bring pressure to bear on BASF. As Fontenot said,

> Taking on just BASF, it's the union versus the plant. But if you take on all the other plants and show how bad they all are, they're going to all of a sudden scream at BASF, "Hey look, get these goddamn union guys off our back. Why don't you guys just settle up with these guys? Can't you keep your problems on your plant boundaries? Why do you have to bring the plague upon us?" So that's exactly what OCAW did. [OCAW campaign organizer] Richard Miller played the game to the hilt. And it worked. (Fontenot, interview, March 13, 1991)

Fontenot, then, introduced an important geographical tactic to the union's campaign; moving beyond BASF to include other industrial polluters offered the union potentially greater political leverage against the company. The union's ultimate success was certainly attributable in part to class-conscious leadership from the community, in this case from an important environmental leader.

Once the union decided to pursue this strategy, locked-out union members began cataloging chemical releases and spills and sites of buried chemicals at the

BASF facility. The very exercise of monitoring BASF's waste stream helped raise environmental awareness within the union. Active environmental practice by union members, fostered by union leadership and the example set by grassroots community activism, made union members environmentally conscious. The union tracked and made public the environmental practices of numerous Louisiana chemical plants, from New Orleans to Lake Charles. Campaign strategists pointed out environmental problems at these facilities, challenged their permits, and forced environmental regulations to be adopted. As a result, BASF received intense pressure from other member companies of industry associations. OCAW organizers, in particular lead strategist Richard Miller, organized numerous citizens in their respective communities to address the corporate environmental problems the union had made public (Fontenot, interview, March 13, 1991).

OCAW put much effort into building an effective environmental alliance with community residents of Geismar as an important vehicle for effecting state regulatory pressure on BASF and the rest of the Geismar industrial complex. Community residents and OCAW workers who lived in the vicinity of the Geismar complex knew that the ten area chemical plants emitted dangerous chemicals into the environment. Many families in Geismar had lost members to cancer, and many attributed the cancer to polluted air and water. At William Fontenot's suggestion, the union approached a seasoned civil rights activist and retired union steelworker named Amos Favorite about assembling a community group that could fight pollution from the plants. Favorite then approached other Geismar residents and found them reluctant at first, believing that OCAW was seeking to build alliances purely to get the union members' jobs back and to not to help the community. But residents supported the idea after the union demonstrated that it was willing to help them fight pollution, and promptly founded the Ascension Parish Residents Against Toxic Pollution (or "APRATP") (Fontenot, interview, March 13, 1991; Favorite, interview, 1992; Gremillion, interview, 1991). It is notable that, as a primary bridge builder from the neighboring community, Favorite brought union and civil rights experience to bear on building community solidarity for OCAW.

APRATP served as a vehicle for OCAW-community investigation of environmental violations by BASF and other area plants beginning in 1986. Relying on research performed by the union or by hired technical experts, aided by the legal talents of the faculty and student attorneys of the Tulane Environmental Law Clinic, APRATP won two lawsuits against BASF, other chemical companies and the state.[26] The lawsuits set several state precedents. First, in assessing pollution penalties, a court called on state agencies to factor in economic benefits that companies enjoyed by not taking appropriate pollution reduction measures. The court threw out a $66,700 fine against BASF for five environmental violations as too small, arguing that the company had benefitted financially by not installing proper pollution controls. Second, they forced the Louisiana DEQ to meet a legislative deadline to write new rules restricting underground injection of hazardous waste. The new rules (Act 803) surpassed current federal regulations by banning underground injection unless monitoring, proof of no migration, and no alternatives are demonstrated. Third, the state denied BASF construction permits for a $50 million production unit due to groundwater contamination at the site, thereby establishing a new policy of prohibiting such construction.[27]

In another important Geismar environmental issue, OCAW discovered in 1987 that BASF had continued to receive a ten-year industrial tax exemption on the closed Basagran unit at its Geismar works. The union filed suit against the company, forcing BASF to pay $225,000 in back taxes. Taking cues from Oliver Houck's important 1986 Tulane Law School study on corporate tax giveaways, the union developed a tax justice component to the campaign, helping to launch the Louisiana Coalition for Tax Justice in 1989.

The union's close collaboration with Geismar community activists and a legal clinic made an important impact on state environmental policy and enforcement. It worked because of the union's central leadership role. When the union was a secondary player in an environmental struggle against the petrochemical industry, however, the results were mixed, as illustrated by the union's peripheral involvement in an environmental struggle in St. Gabriel, several miles away from Geismar. Working with the Sierra Club's Delta Chapter in 1986, OCAW produced a study on air quality in the Geismar-St. Gabriel industrial complex. Researched before the federal right-to-know law was passed, the study documented that 196 million pounds of toxic chemicals had been emitted into the air by eighteen Geismar-St. Gabriel area petrochemical plants over a one-year period. Soon after, the union and the Sierra Club produced a study documenting the discharge of 76 million pounds of toxic chemicals in one year into the Mississippi River by fifteen area plants. In both these studies, OCAW did most of the research and writing, while the Sierra Club lent its credibility to the study. In the air pollution study, the union and the Sierra Club sought to relate the pollution levels to a high incidence of miscarriages in the St. Gabriel area, brought to light by St. Gabriel environmental activists (Malek-Wiley, interview, 1991).

A controversy ensued over the possible link between pollution and elevated miscarriage rates. The St. Gabriel activists were isolated and forced to close their local pharmacy by an effective campaign waged by industry, much of the local nonunion industrial workforce, the local Catholic Church and the state.[28] Job blackmail successfully isolated the local activists because their local group was small and unable to make necessary links to local workers, virtually all nonunion, and because the nearly all-male workforce targeted a woman activist as the enemy. While the OCAW/Sierra Club study helped spark public awareness over the link between pollution and public health, inasmuch as the union did not play a central role, it was unable to help relieve the pressure put on the St. Gabriel activists by the chemical industry, the state, and others. Without effective backing by a well-organized mediating institution, such as a union or a church, St. Gabriel's local activists were overwhelmed by the isolating tactics of local industry. The

Geismar environmental activists never faced this type of pressure because they had a solid base in several local African-American churches and had the full support of OCAW's leadership and resources. The St. Gabriel activists' struggle against Ciba-Geigy and the Louisiana Chemical Association, however, was not in vain. Despite the isolation the activists suffered, their efforts would become a key force in subsequent struggles over tax justice and environmental justice in St. Gabriel in the 1990s.

The OCAW corporate accountability campaign challenged environmental violations well beyond the Geismar-St. Gabriel industrial complex. OCAW made links with community organizations in other communities in which BASF had facilities in order to publicize the company's negligent environmental practices. OCAW worked with civic and union groups in Terre Haute, Indiana, to stop the siting of a huge hazardous waste incinerator and waste dump complex at a BASF facility. It helped union workers at Schuykill Metals and Reynolds Aluminum in North Baton Rouge, where workers were being exposed to toxic vapors given off by the adjacent Petro-Processors Superfund site. Workers from this struggle helped form Louisiana Workers Against Toxic Chemical Hazards (LAWATCH). For several years LAWATCH advocated for better enforcement of OSHA standards at industrial facilities. LAWATCH was ultimately taken under the wing of Loyola University's Institute for Human Relations (now called the Louis Twomey Center for Peace through Justice), and helped create the Injured Workers Union in 1990. OCAW was instrumental in building Louisiana's environmental movement, worked to raise $207,000 from progressive foundations for various grassroots efforts in Louisiana, and helped create several grassroots advocacy organizations. The union worked closely with the Tulane Environmental Law Clinic in 1989, helping it gain funding for a community outreach organizer to support third-year law students in their environmental legal work assisting contaminated communities challenge corporations and the state. OCAW's strategic engagement, thus, went well beyond the union's struggle with BASF. Its politics were not merely about gaining a union victory but about broader movement building. The union was transformed by its struggle with BASF to reach a new level of involvement in Louisiana environmental politics and beyond, a transformation explained by the specific relation between the union's intellectual leadership and community and environmental intellectual leadership.

National and International Solidarity

As the lockout dragged on, OCAW took the campaign to a national and international level, seeking new allies and developing international pressure against the company. Union strategists made a conscious effort to craft a campaign to mirror the company's global reach as a way of exploiting BASF's numerous potentially vulnerable points. Owing to the company's global and local politics, union strategists recognized that the union's politics had to be simultaneously global and local as well.

By the mid-1980s, concern about environmental degradation had become widespread. In the aftermath of the 1984 Bhopal disaster and through the grassroots community right-to-know campaign, national antitoxics organizations such as Greenpeace and the fledgling National Toxics Campaign (NTC) had much greater credibility among the general public and within the OCAW membership. The union won support from Greenpeace and NTC. NTC joined OCAW in the union's sit-in at BASF's national headquarters in New Jersey in 1987. OCAW built international ties to German workers and Green Party members. A delegation of OCAW members and community allies joined demonstrations against BASF's pollution on the Rhine, while West German counterparts participated in demonstrations against the company's pollution of the Mississippi. The union lobbied BASF stockholders in Germany, the International Labor Organization in Geneva, and the European Organization for Economic Cooperation and Development. In one of the most costly tactics for BASF, OCAW revealed BASF's trade of computer equipment to South Africa, leading to a cessation of shipments, costing the company $47 million in lost business. Finally, BASF workers in France, Belgium, and Brazil lent financial and moral support to the locked-out OCAW members (Leonard and Nauth, 1990).

Overcoming Obstacles to Solidarity

The OCAW's five-year-long effort to end the lockout and win back the jobs of its locked-out workers confronted numerous obstacles that undermined or threatened to undermine the union's ability to broaden its base of solidarity and build political and regulatory pressure against BASF. Many of these obstacles directly constrained the discourse of collective action, that is, they sought to limit the union's ability to expand and shape discussion about the lockout, environmental contamination, and underdevelopment.

OCAW's politics of collaboration with community were confronted by potential divisions during the lockout. Such division did occur, sometimes for complex reasons, other times fostered intentionally by BASF. Once the union's corporate accountability campaign commenced, the company sought to portray the union as driven by elements from outside the community. In flyers and in the press the company portrayed the International's two campaign strategists as carpetbaggers, living out of an office in a motel room. Depicting union organizers as outside agitators and carpetbaggers is a rich tradition by companies and government, particularly in the South. While this tactic may have resonated with some community residents, it was by itself insufficient to turn the community against the union.

More effective in preventing community support of the union during the lockout was the entrenched antiunion bias found in many American communities, including Ascension Parish. Decades of antiunion propaganda, reenforced by the Cold War, in concert with a general lack of union involvement in the community, helped create an ongoing distrust of unions as community-based institutions. Many Ascension Parish residents did not come to support the union until it demonstrated its commitment and expertise in addressing environmental issues. Union members were perceived as out to get back their high-paying jobs with good benefits, thereby begging the question, "Why should I be worried about the OCAW?" as William Fontenot posed it. Indeed, the union's activism and organizing ability around environmental health issues were vital, first steps toward challenging the persistent perception of the selfishness of unions and establishing the credibility of the OCAW in Ascension Parish. Without such community engagement, corporations can successfully portray unions as self-centered, selfish people. As William Fontenot notes, "The more management can foster that view, the weaker you become. When you get to the bargaining table, you've got nothing to work with." Corporations are able to do this through their own engagement in the community, often as a way of countering local environmental activism. In Geismar, petrochemical companies "adopted" the elementary school and donated an old fire engine to the local fire department.[29] As Fontenot notes, "The unions have to play that game, but not at the same level. They can't give a fire truck to the local fire station. But they can be the volunteer firemen. They can go down and repair the problems at the local school." Thus for their own survival, unions need to become community institutions, committed to issues that transcend their own jobs and working conditions (Fontenot, interview, March 13, 1991; Favorite, interview, 1992; Gremillion, interview, 1991).

Other actions also fueled antiunion sentiment. BASF took out full-page newspaper advertisements, claiming they were a good neighbor paying huge taxes and creating many jobs for area people. Moreover, the company, and subsequently the media, persisted in calling the lockout a "strike." This perception succeeded in casting the union as the bad guys and the company as the good guys. "I think it's going to stay that way until the union has control over who does and who does not get jobs with local industry," said Esnard Gremillion. "That's the only thing that they have the upper hand on us; they've got the money and the jobs" (Gremillion, interview, 1991).

OCAW's attempts to build support within the community often met with reluctance on the part of workers at other petrochemical facilities to support the union. For nonunion plant workers, this reluctance was grounded in their fear of losing their jobs. How well-founded these fears were, whether they were backed up by subtle or overt job blackmail on the part of employers, is not well-known. It is certain, however, that many workers were afraid to express open and active sympathy for the locked-out OCAW members. Former OCAW chair Esnard Gremillion commented,

> The thing we couldn't accomplish was to really get the community behind us, because, in part, there was a close knit community with kinfolk working at BASF and the plants. And they don't want to say anything bad, afraid their kinfolk are going to get blackballed. Job blackmail ended up blocking a coalition with the community at large. (Gremillion, interview, 1991)

While fear of job loss hampered the building of community solidarity, job fear was partially offset by the organizing success of the women's support group and the union's community environmental initiatives. The women's support group communicated through networks of friends and through churches the union's commitment not only to getting the locked-out workers' jobs back but to the community environment as well (Gremillion, interview, 1991; Vann, interview, 1991; Women's Support Group, interview, 1991).

The union did not expect to win the support of all segments of the grass-roots environmental community, given class and racial tensions, both subtle and obvious. One predominantly white local environmental group, Save Our Selves (SOS), refused to support the union, despite the union's high level of environmental activism. The union contended the SOS leader was beholden to BASF due to business connections. SOS's principal spokesperson claimed that she could not support the union because its attempts at blocking construction of a hazardous waste incinerator at BASF would force those wastes to be burned in her community.[30]

The class tensions that hindered the union in gaining support of certain local organizations were to a certain extent grounded in remnants of the plantation political structure. While the union won the solidarity of some citizens within Ascension Parish, it failed to gain the backing of local government, namely the police jury (county commissioners). The police jury's refusal to support the union was symptomatic of the tight relationship between local officials and petrochemical management and was a direct extension of political relationships during the plantation era.

The politics of the river parishes between New Orleans and Baton Rouge were, and continue to be, heavily influenced by white power structures, manifested in white families of planter heritage, tied to the old plantation economy. The growth of oil, gas, and petrochemical development in the river parishes since the 1930s simply overlaid new business interests on residual planter-merchant power structures. As the previous hegemonic relations were partially driven by patronage, so too did patronage politics prevail in most of the river parishes.

During the lockout and afterward, several Ascension Parish police jurors were employed in plant management as managers or supervisors. As previously mentioned, the policy jury's 9-0 vote against the union's request to delay BASF's bond for a hazardous waste facility construction until after the lockout was ostensibly heavily influenced by the plant management presence on the police jury, even swaying the vote of the jury president, a locked-out OCAW member.

Industry dominance of the parish government indeed inhibited the union from employing local ordinances to pressure BASF to end the lockout. With the local level political arena impeded by the vestiges of the plantation system, the union's search for political opportunities continued, with far greater success, at the state level.

Union Resistance to Divisive Tactics

BASF attempted, without success, to foment racial and gender divisions within the union during the lockout. The company's efforts to divide workers along racial lines were based on tried and true corporate practices against unions in the South, particularly in Louisiana. As the union refused to surrender to BASF's conditions to ending the lockout, the company attempted to split the African-American union members from the predominantly white union leadership. BASF mailed out letters to the African-American union members, telling them that it was the selfishness of the maintenance workers—comprised of the union's leadership, which was at that time nearly all white—which was sustaining the lockout. The company called on the black workers—who were almost exclusively operators—to break from the maintenance workers' demands to get their jobs back. While this ploy was, on the surface, an attempt to turn operators, who were the majority of the membership (260 out of 370), against the maintenance workers, it was at a deeper level an effort to turn black workers against white. The union quickly recognized the company's tactic in part because the union leaders had relied upon the leadership of an African-American to maintain close lines of communication between black and white members. (Vann, interview, 1991)

Similarly, the company attempted to turn female spouses against male union members. They did this by mailing a letter to spouses encouraging them to get their partners to give up the fight because of the devastating financial consequences it was having on the union members' families. The atmosphere of open communication provided by the women's support group, in concert with the union's elevated solidarity and ongoing open communication at weekly meetings, was able to defuse the company's divisive effort (Vann, interview, November 21, 1991).

More generally, the local's democratic structure—with open discussion of, and membership vote on, all union business—provided the context for building a durable solidarity within the local and establishing clear channels of communication between black and white members, and between female spouses and male union members. This democratic tradition originated in part in the OCAW's industrial unionist past and its association with the CIO in that organization's militant years. Thus, a tradition of open discourse within Local 4-620 and the OCAWIU helped minimize the effect of BASF's divisive tactics.

State Political Opportunities

While the parish government failed to provide the union political opportunities to build pressure against BASF, the state political structure offered various openings, primarily in environmental regulation. During the first years of the lockout, under the Edwards Administration, the union and its environmental allies used the courts to penalize BASF and other polluters, which lent important force to the union's corporate campaign. The shift in political opportunity structures from the Edwards administration to the reformist Roemer regime in 1988 created greater opportunities for the union coalition to influence policy.

Although the DEQ had been in existence since 1983, it's leadership during Edwin Edwards' 1984-1988 term was not responsive to federal right-to-know statutes or to citizen involvement in environmental issues. Prior to Roemer, the DEQ was largely an ineffectual regulatory agency known for rubber stamping industrial operating and construction permits. Laws created during previous administrations, such as Act 803 (the land-ban decision), had not been implemented. During the three administrations before Roemer, impetus for environmental reform came from grassroots mobilizing efforts led by the state attorney general's Citizen Access Unit. This mobilization effort helped pave the way for Roemer's revamping of the DEQ to be more responsive to grassroots environmentalism.

Buddy Roemer, in his 1987 gubernatorial campaign, perceived Louisiana's sorry environmental state to be a crisis situation that needed to be faced squarely. The Roemer administration of 1988-1992 responded to the crisis, the changes brought on by the community right-to-know legislation, and the demands being made by the state's growing antitoxics movement. By appointing Paul Templet, a Louisiana State University environmental scientist, as DEQ secretary, Roemer opened the doors for encouragement of citizen participation in environmental decisions on a formal level. Templet created offices of local programs and citizen participation, and policy and planning, regarding them as the brains of the new DEQ. He nearly tripled DEQ's staffing, and for the first time DEQ drew some of its funding from the state treasury. Under Templet, DEQ was no longer beholden to industry as it had been in the past. Prior to Templet, permits to industry were denied only through a forceful outside show of opposition from citizen groups. During Templet's term, DEQ's open door policy in some divisions came to encourage, expect, and rely upon inside pressure from the environmental grassroots to influence the outcome of facility permitting, litigation, and penalty assessment. Templet raised the hazardous waste tax to nation-leading levels. Further, by commencing a "corporate challenge" publishing lists of the top 12 polluters, DEQ set a precedent of bringing about significant reductions in the release of toxic chemicals to the environment, as well as established itself as a serious watchdog of industry that would frequently deny permits (Templet, lecture, 1992).

Despite the reforms initiated by Templet, DEQ continued to be plagued by several important problems: the "revolving door" of employment for scientists and engineers between the agency and industry; the shared culture of industry and DEQ experts; and inadequate pressure from citizens to match industry pressure on the agency.

Within the context of shifting political opportunities at the Louisiana DEQ, the OCAW corporate campaign helped provide an important thrust to maintaining and enlarging the political opportunities for grassroots environmentalism in Louisiana. Not only did the campaign give rise to several environmental policy precedents; more importantly, its work led to the creation of new institutions that continue to promote enforcement of environmental laws and regulations and to broaden environmental policy itself. These new institutions are discussed in the next chapter.

The Last Straw

With pressure mounting against the company, particularly from the chemical industry itself, several events pushed BASF to break the lockout and hire back the remaining 110 maintenance workers. Leonard and Nauth (1990) argue that the settlement was reached due to three actions. First, the OCAW's campaign against the company stopped the construction of a $50 million glyoxal unit at BASF's Geismar facility. Second, working in tandem with Indiana environmentalists, the union successfully blocked the construction of a hazardous waste incinerator in Indiana. Finally, the campaign threatened to block BASF's acquisition of New Jersey state forest land, at a cut-rate price, for a new company headquarters.

While each event added substantially to the already formidable pressure exerted against the company to settle, it was the compromise reached in the permitting of BASF's glyoxal unit that finally brought the company to lift the lockout, as OCAW campaign organizer Richard Miller argues ®. Miller, personal communication, October 10, 1991). By 1989, BASF had already lost well over $75 million in profits as a result of the corporate accountability campaign waged against the company by OCAW and its allies. The potential profit loss if operation of the glyoxal unit continued to be held up amounted to tens of millions of dollars.

Thus the campaign's blocking of the Geismar expansion warrants closer examination. The company's Geismar facility experienced major groundwater contamination at a site where the herbicide Basagran was produced from 1979 to 1987. Basagran and several other organic chemicals had leached 75 to 100 feet vertically into the ground at the production facility. BASF had applied for a permit to operate a glyoxal production facility on top of the old Basagran site. OCAW and the Ascension Parish Residents Against Toxic Pollution were opposed to the new facility on the grounds that the old site had not been cleaned up and that granting a permit to operate a new facility on top of it would prevent the company from doing an effective remediation of groundwater and soil contamination.

OCAW campaign organizer Richard Miller had developed a vital line of communication to the Louisiana DEQ assistant secretary for water pollution control,

Maureen O'Neill. O'Neill had come under much pressure from BASF to grant the operating permit on the glyoxal plant. BASF was losing millions of dollars because the unit was not up and running. A high-ranking official from BASF's U.S. headquarters in New Jersey had visited Louisiana in late 1989 to plead for a settlement. The union did not want to back down on blocking the glyoxal plant, but it wanted to end the lockout, and saw this as a way out. O'Neill's effectiveness in administering other groundwater cleanups was being challenged by her resistance to the permit in the BASF case.

O'Neill, an activist environmental official since her tenure with the New Orleans municipal water department,[31] had come to expect sufficient pressure from OCAW and the citizenry to counteract the severe pressure she would receive from industry. O'Neill commented that if she would withhold issuing permits, she expected industry representatives to camp on the couch in the waiting room to her office. If citizen and union pressure, in the form of visits and phone calls from a variety of groups and individuals, was not sufficient enough, she stated she would have no recourse but to cave in to industry pressure. If she issued the permit to industry, while there was some opposition from citizens, she would put the blame on the citizens for not being vocal enough. The "Basagran case" had put her into an unusually difficult predicament. Citizen and union pressure was more than sufficient to keep her from issuing BASF a permit. However, by withholding a permit, she jeopardized other cleanups that needed to go forward.

The dilemma was resolved by the action of DEQ Secretary Paul Templet. In close communication with the OCAW and Governor Buddy Roemer, Templet interceded by issuing an operating variance, rather than a permit, on the grounds that a permit could not be issued until a corrective action order on the Basagran contamination had been approved. BASF had not yet proved an effective course of corrective action on the contamination. This compromise was instrumental in settling the Basagran issue sufficiently to facilitate settlement of the lockout.

In addition to support from the two DEQ officials to help move BASF into the position of compromise, OCAW made arrangements for Governor Buddy Roemer to apply additional pressure. Roemer met with a BASF official from the company's global headquarters in Ludwigshafen, Germany, and OCAW. The governor confronted the company on the injustice of the prolonged lockout and how the whole affair was bad for Louisiana's business and bad for the workers. Roemer's pressure on the company to settle quickly allowed DEQ's Templet to propose the compromise in which BASF would call off the lockout if the DEQ would grant the company an operating variance for the glyoxal unit ®. Miller, personal communication, October 10, 1991).

The lockout, in effect, was brought to an end by an environmental issue, or more accurately, by the relationships the union had developed over five years with the environmental community and the state environmental agency. The reformist Roemer administration provided significant opportunities for the union to influence environmental permitting and, more importantly, to shape environmental policy in Louisiana. The union had taken advantage of the shift in political opportunity structures from the last Edwards administration by building close communication with DEQ Secretary Templet. Indeed, the union had worked with Templet even before his appointment as DEQ secretary, while Templet was part of Roemer's citizen environmental advisory committee. The untiring presence of OCAW's Richard Miller in DEQ's offices and in the permitting process built up substantial credibility for the union as an environmental watchdog. The union and its influence in the environmental community made the jobs of activist-oriented DEQ officials such as Templet and O'Neill easier, by providing the necessary citizen pressure for more effective environmental cleanups.

CONCLUSION

A historical analysis of labor-community collaboration in Louisiana reveals instances of community solidarity with labor but no pronounced pattern for such politics. The pre-Fordist and Fordist periods demonstrated an abundance of militant industrial unionism, some multiracial unionism, and some informal support from the community. The Catholic Church provided recurring community institutional solidarity with labor from the 1880s to the 1950s, but its support was always short-term tactical, never strategic. The only instance for any possible, although not demonstrated, long-term labor-community collaboration was in the African-American community, primarily the churches. Removed from the electoral process by a virulent segregationism over a fifty-year period (1890-1940), African-Americans focused their militancy on the workplace. Blacks were important leaders in building a racially diverse unionism in New Orleans. Industrial unionism, if left to run its course, might have developed long-term institutional relations with community organizations during Fordism and pre-Fordism. It was, however, consistently abandoned and attacked by a narrow craft unionism; attacked by capital's racially and skills-based divisive tactics; and divided by a pervasive state-sanctioned segregationism. Anticommunism and a fifty-year-long open shop (right-to-work) movement made matters worse. When right-to-work legislation finally passed in 1976, business unionism was bereft of effective political strategies. Thus Louisiana's infrequent experiments with multi-racial, multi-class labor-community collaboration had been systematically undermined by corporate politics and the exclusionary, economically-focused practices of business unionism. New political-economic conditions demanding new labor and community intellectual leadership would be needed to break this trend.

The crisis of Fordism and the destructive impact of the petrochemical industry helped set the conditions for the emergence of a new labor-community collaboration. OCAW's five-and-one-half year struggle (1984-89) against BASF was an unprecedented campaign in Louisiana. No union had waged such a long battle with a company before, and much less won. What set OCAW's struggle apart was the union's leadership, environmental and coalition-building experience, and the local dependence of the petrochemical industry. The union sought out vulnerable points in the company, one of which was its environmental record. This led the union into a collaborative relationship with the local community and key environmental leaders over pollution issues. The sense of shared place among union members and community residents, particularly from African-American river communities, enabled OCAW and community leaders to forge links. Bridge builders emerging from the environmental community and local African-American community, maintaining an affinity for union and working class issues, were critical to launching collaboration with OCAW. The union members developed an environmental consciousness through their interaction with local, primarily African-American, community activists. The union's spatial strategy went beyond the immediate confrontation with the company's Geismar, Louisiana, facility; OCAW incited pressure among other petrochemical companies against BASF, and waged an international public relations campaign targeting other BASF facilities and practices. The union, then, matched the company with a local and a global political strategy. The lockout ultimately ended because of an environmental issue and the union's exploitation of state political opportunities. Effective relationship building by the union with key state environmental officials pressured the company to end the lockout in exchange for a temporary operating permit on a chemical processing unit.

OCAW Local 4-620 likely never would have collaborated with community and the environmental movement were it not for the national union's extensive experience in coalitions with environmentalists. More specifically, OCAW International had worked with community leaders on environmental issues in a number of other places, including Love Canal and the Shell Oil strike of 1973. Significantly, several environmental groups had developed an openness to collaboration with OCAW even before the BASF lockout, particularly the very recently formed National Toxics Campaign. Thus, when the lockout began, OCAW was already well-positioned to garner national solidarity from progressive environmental organizations. The union effectively drew on that experience to develop its alliances during the campaign to break the lockout. From a Gramscian perspective, the union's intellectual leadership, at the national and local levels, in tandem with the astute guidance of key environmental leaders helped devise the strategies and mobilize the necessary resources to break a lockout imposed by a petrochemical giant. The intellectual leadership and class capacity of OCAW and community leaders established a new standard of labor-community collaboration in Louisiana.

ENDNOTES

1. Research for Chapters 4 and 5 was conducted on the Labor-Neighbor Project from January 1991 until April 1992 in the form of participant observation, interviewing, and archival research. Subsequent visits to interview activists and collect archival material

were made from 1992 to 1998, while further telephone interviews and archival research were conducted from 1998 until 2005.

2. Craft unionism, it must be said, enjoyed a moderate degree of success in challenging capital and shaping state policy. Where industrial unions failed, craft unions often succeeded in overcoming employers' strikebreaking attempts because of the leverage of skilled workers' unions. The craft-union hegemony promoted some progressive causes in the legislative and political arenas, notably on issues of gender equality, child labor, workplace health and safety, public schooling, workers' compensation, and labor law reform (Cook and Watson, 1984).

3. Support by leftist CIO unions helped the growth of the Southern Negro Youth Congress, the Louisiana Association for the Progress of Negro Citizens, and the Louisiana Farmer's Union (Fairclough, 1995).

4. The labor movement assumed a purely defensive mode, as the CIO abandoned its militant left-wing unions. The post-World War II labor-management accord brought the CIO into line with AFL accommodationism and its industrial partnership mentality.

5. The Federation opted to sacrifice agricultural workers to open-shop laws, in return for a delay by the state in 1954 on the promulgation of right-to-work provisions across all economic sectors. Owing to an antidemocratic, top-down structure, the state AFL (and subsequently the CIO) was unable to mobilize a political force among the rank-and-file to oppose right-to-work. Moreover, the leadership's craft and racial exclusionary philosophy became pervasive among the membership. Hence top-down political lobbying—against right-to-work or segregation—met with little success because it ran counter to grassroots educational campaigns.

6. Bussie, a racial liberal along the lines of Earl Long, was unable to bring the AFL-CIO to actively push for integration. Indeed, the lack of grassroots mobilization against segregation and against the open shop severely hampered the movement in building effective political power (Cook and Watson, 1984).

7. The Bourbon oligarchy derived centralized power from the Spanish and French tradition of authoritarian centralism, including wide-ranging powers for the governor, and supported by attendant Catholic and European attitudes of submission to authority. These early attitudes fostered a political culture—persisting into the modern era—which tolerated undemocratic, elitist, and corrupt state political leadership (Carleton, Howard, and Parker, 1988; Maginnis, 1984).

8. The Bourbons were severely weakened by black disfranchisement—which they and the progressive reformists actively promoted—as well as huge public resentment with their antidemocratic methods. Drawing on national-level tendencies in urban reform of that period, the urban progressives—dominated by business boosters and upper-class professionals—sought to upgrade urban infrastructure, diversify industry, and, in the wake of widespread labor union and populist militancy, restore social order. Like the Bourbons, they resorted to antidemocratic tactics to carry out their agenda, notably restricting African-American suffrage as well as restricting direct election of public officials (Grantham, 1983; Jeansomme, 1990).

9. Fordism incorporated a bureaucratically regulated social contract between organized labor, capital and the state built on negotiated compromises. The state, for its part, assumed a Keynesian role and created new powerful institutions. Corporate capital committed itself to a steady increase in investments to elevate productivity and living standards as a basis for securing profitability. Organized labor agreed to collaborate

with capital and the state in supporting corporate production techniques and strategies for increasing productivity—in effect, disciplining workers to a Fordist system—in exchange for increased power in collective bargaining, performance in production processes and labor markets, and social policy. The political ground for this balance of power was set through years of struggle and the ultimate defeat of militant working-class movements of the immediate post-war period.

10. Although the Progressives were the ones to introduce the severance tax on oil and gas exports to fund modernization projects, it was Long who made it the centerpiece of his share-the-wealth populism to improve the livelihood of the poor and working class (Grantham, 1983; Jeansomme, 1990).

11. The tax burden on industry was not huge, contrary to the reputation Louisiana had gained during the 1940s as a high-tax state for industry. Indeed, the Louisiana 1936 Constitutional Convention established significant industrial property tax exemptions as an attraction to businesses to come and stay in the state. The ten-year industrial exemption was instituted at that time. This exemption consists of a five-year exemption from property taxes, and renewable for another five years, for the purpose of promoting job creation and investment in new construction or maintenance at industrial facilities, and to make the state competitive with other states. In its early years the ten-year exemption was applied discriminately by the Board of Commerce and Industry, as almost one-half of the requests were denied. But with the growth of the petrochemical industry through the 1950s and 1960s, the Commerce Board approved an ever greater number of requests by industry for the 10-year exemption. After the 1973 constitutional convention, Commerce Board approval of requests became a sure bet, despite the reservations of many convention delegates that the exemptions were being abused and costing the local governments millions of dollars. The industrial property tax exemption continues to the present day, yet it has never been able to stimulate substantial industrial diversification (Cobb, 1982; Louisiana Coalition for Tax Justice, 1992).

12. The white middle class was not given to social unrest during times of prosperity, as long as state programs were largely financed by industry, a situation regarded as "tooth-fairyism" (Carleton et al., 1988).

13. While the 1920s campaign stalled, right-to-work forces returned with a vengeance in 1944 and 1946, each time more successful. Right-to-work legislation finally passed in 1956, with the cooperation of the AFL-CIO, which allowed the open shop in agricultural enterprises with the agreement that nonagricultural enterprises would be exempt (Cook and Watson, 1984).

14. The weakness of the labor movement in the aftermath of right-to-work passage facilitated a prolonged wave of antiunion attacks, in the form of corporate lockouts, union decertification campaigns, and replacement of permanent union employees with contract labor.

15. Overall employment in oil refining and petrochemicals declined over a ten-year period, reaching its low point in 1987. Unlike other industries that abandoned or mothballed plants during the 1980s, the petrochemical industry instead reduced capacity by focusing production on the most efficient units, often consolidated into highly integrated complexes (Chapman, 1992; Moberg, 1990).

16. The petrochemical industry began using contract labor in the 1960s, mainly in large-scale construction. But due to significant cost savings—contract workers earn

two-thirds the pay of permanent employees and with no benefits—and flexibility, companies increasingly used contract labor for routine maintenance. By 1989 contract workers accounted for 26 percent of all petrochemical workers. Yet, with turnover rates averaging 50 percent per year, contract workers never learned well the finer points of plant maintenance, leading to a higher rate of plant accidents. A study of contract workers conducted for OSHA by the John Gray Institute of Lamar University in 1989 documents the correlation between increasing use of contract workers and rising accident rates. The Gray study asserts that 46 percent of petrochemical industry accidents involved workers with no safety training, meaning contract labor (Moberg, 1990).

17. Indeed, injury rates at petrochemical facilities increased by 30 percent in petroleum and coal products sections and by 100 percent in industrial organic chemicals sections, from 1985 to 1988. This is not a complete figure, given that contract workers' accidents are not included and, overall, many accidents are not documented (Moberg, 1990).

18. Petrochemicals actually hindered the development of other industry to the extent that public perception of a polluted environment dissuades investment in a diversified economic base away from oil and petrochemicals and promising long-term sustainable growth (Chapman, 1992).

19. Prior to the formation of the Louisiana DEQ in 1980, environmental regulatory functions were carried out largely by the Department of Natural Resources, which had little capacity or expertise to handle issues of toxic chemical waste in water, air, or land. DNR's previous expertise lay in regulating oil field contamination (Latour, 1985).

20. Good Hope was bought out by a Shell refinery in St. Charles Parish. Reveilletown was bought out by Georgia Gulf near Plaquemine (Iberville Parish). Morrisonville was bought out by Dow Chemical, also near Plaquemine. Sunrise was bought out by Placid Oil in Port Allen (West Baton Rouge Parish). Currently, Exxon was in the process of buying out the largely African-American Garden City neighborhood in North Baton Rouge (Times-Picayune, 1991).

21. For instance, the Food and Drug Administration in 1972 investigated contamination of cattle in Ascension Parish by hexachlorobenzene transported by waste haulers from a nearby chemical plant. The FDA quarantined all the cattle contaminated with hexachlorobenzene in East Ascension Parish in 1973. Subsequently the EPA found extensive hexachlorobenzene contamination in the parish, which persisted in the 1990s (Fontenot, interview, March 13, 1991).

22. In addition to the Attorney General's Citizen Access Unit, also working to help local groups organize was the Ecology Center of New Orleans, an extra-local organization formed in the late 1970s.

23. The Freeport gypsum dumping proposal sparked a debate over health versus economic necessity. CEO Jim Bob Moffett pushed for dumping into the Mississippi as an economic necessity. The Sierra Club, behind the organizing leadership of the head of the New Orleans Water and Sewer Board, Maureen O'Neill, rallied the popular opposition, including that of some businesses such as Colonial Sugar, to the proposed dumping. The opposition argued that the dumping would seriously contaminate New Orleans' drinking water supply.

24. OCAW was locked out by National Gypsum (1974), Johns Manville (1974-75), American Cyanamid (1975-79), National Gypsum (1977), Chevron Chemical (1977), Bunge Grain Elevator (1977), BASF (1980), and BASF (1984-1989) (OCAW, 1988).

25. Fontenot had been working in that capacity since 1978, helping citizens across the state to organize local environmental campaigns—more than 150 groups from 1978 to the early 1990s. Appointed by Attorney General William Guste, who had a strong appreciation for environmental protection, Fontenot was given abundant freedom to organize citizen participation in the environmental policymaking process.

26. By 1993, Ascension Parish Residents Against Toxic Pollution had won five of six lawsuits intending to force stricter state regulation of polluters (Evans, interview, December 1, 1993).

27. While the state denied BASF the construction permit for one unit, it granted the company a variance—that is, a temporary operating permit—on another unit at the same site. The granting of this temporary permit was a compromise in settling the lockout in 1989. In 1992, the company received a formal operating permit for the unit.

28. In 1986, Kay Gaudet, a St. Gabriel pharmacist, began documenting a high rate of miscarriages among her customers. Gaudet, her husband Chris, and several other local residents started East Iberville AWARE to address these concerns. The Sierra Club and OCAW included these findings in their pollution study. The results were explosive. Governor Edwards declared a state of emergency in St. Gabriel. The state and the Louisiana Chemical Association commissioned Tulane University to do an epidemiological study. Highly criticized for its methodology, which relied on telephone interviews of women, the study concluded that St. Gabriel's miscarriage rate was no higher than the national average. Ciba-Geigy, the largest company in St. Gabriel turned against Kay Gaudet, as did the Louisiana Chemical Association, the local Catholic church, the local political boss, and even Governor Edwards. Gaudet was vilified by the nearly all-male workforce and industry leaders as a harbinger of economic ill to the community. Ciba-Geigy encouraged its workers to boycott Gaudet's pharmacy, eventually forcing it to close. While the African-American community was supportive of the Gaudets in their health campaign, they were not sufficiently organized to challenge the local plants and the local boss. Further, the Gaudets did not enlist the full support of OCAW in challenging Ciba-Geigy; rather, they preferred not to be closely linked to the union in order to establish their own identity as an environmental group separate from OCAW's corporate accountability campaign. At the same time, the miscarriage issue prompted the local chemical industry to conduct expensive public relations actions. Local industry put on a local fair, began giving away more local scholarships, and donated $100,000 to the Catholic church to replace the church's roof. (Gaudet, interview, 1991)

29. Local environmental activism stimulated a strong corporate public relations campaign in nearby St. Gabriel during the lockout. In response to the OCAW/Sierra Club air pollution study and St. Gabriel miscarriage documentation, Ciba-Geigy and other local companies began a series of well-publicized charitable donations to local schools and churches. Ciba-Geigy, ICI, and Stauffer paid for the $100,000 worth of renovations to the local Catholic church. The public relations campaign culminated in 1990 with local chemical plants proclaiming, through huge billboards in the community, that they were "turning over a new leaf" with their new "responsible care" principles (Gaudet, interview, 1991).

30. SOS had established itself in a struggle in the early 1980s to block construction of a commercial hazardous waste incinerator by the IT Corporation in Burnside, Ascension Parish. The community prevailed, and the "IT decision" became precedent, requiring

polluters to seek alternatives to incineration and introducing cost-benefit analysis. SOS's lead spokesperson refused to lend support to the locked-out OCAW members. OCAW members argued that this lack of support was due to the SOS leader being beholden to BASF, as well as several other area chemical plants, given that her husband owned a fuel oil business which supplied the BASF Geismar facility. While the union supported the environmental efforts of SOS, demonstrating with them at the state capital, SOS did not extend its formal, open support for the union during the lockout (Gremillion, interview, 1991; Robert, interview, 1991).

31. O'Neill was instrumental in 1985 in swaying the New Orleans water board to block Freeport McMoRan's request to dump radioactive gypsum into the Mississippi from its several facilities between New Orleans and Baton Rouge.

CHAPTER 5

The Flow and Ebb of the
Louisiana Labor-Neighbor Project

After the lifting of the BASF lockout, the work of OCAW's corporate account-ability campaign against the company did not come to an end, as is often the case after victorious union-led corporate campaigns. The union and the National Toxics Campaign (NTC) wanted to continue. OCAW members wanted to create a project which could give something back to the communities that had stood by the union during the lockout. NTC sought to invest in a cutting edge collaboration that could advance the environmental organization's grassroots organizing agenda.

By the lockout's end in December, 1989, the corporate accountability campaign had already spun off creative projects on corporate taxes and economic development, environmental legal assistance to local grassroots organizations, and redressing workplace injury and illness for primarily nonunion workers. The campaign's work fostered the creation of the statewide Louisiana Coalition for Tax Justice in 1989, ensured foundation funding for a community outreach liaison at the Tulane Environmental Law Clinic beginning in 1989, and inspired the formation of the Injured Workers Union, an outgrowth of LAWATCH (Louisiana Workers Against Toxic Chemical Hazards) housed at Loyola University's Institute for Human Relations.

Yet the centerpiece of the union's investment in continued labor-community collective action, the Louisiana Labor-Neighbor Project, would carry on the environmental coalition work in Ascension Parish and nearby parishes. The Labor-Neighbor Project grew from a coalition based largely in one parish and one community in 1990 to a four-parish coalition representing more than twenty organizations in eight communities in 2000. The Labor-Neighbor Project developed and succeeded through the 1990s for the following reasons: a systematic consolidation and then expansion of leadership; a broadening of its agenda, beyond pollution issues, to take on many issues at once; a turn to mass-based organizing, while expanding the base spatially; continued political openings in the state, particularly the local state; and continued organizational resources (skills and funding). After a decade of expansion and success, however, the Labor-Neighbor Project suffered organizational and financial setbacks in 2001 and 2002. These setbacks were due to the following: problems in recruiting a new skilled project coordinator and organizing supervisor; problems in deepening union leadership in the coalition; insufficient capacity building among both union and community leaders; difficulty in mobilizing workers when workplace crisis is not present; and, taking on too many issues at once.

In early 1990, members of OCAW Local 4-620 voted to invest $5 per member per month to fund an organizer and operating budget. The union's $25,000 per year investment was matched by the National Toxics Campaign, a national environmental grassroots network doing organizing and policy work that promoted pollution prevention. NTC had been an ally of the locked-out OCAW members, particularly since the corporate campaign's 1987 "lock-in" of BASF employees at the company's U.S. headquarters in Parsipanny, N.J.

OCAW International was committed to supporting the further development of Local 4-620's community projects. The international provided the services of corporate campaign strategist Richard Miller to oversee the development of an ongoing labor-community organizing structure in Louisiana. The international's support was ensured and strengthened with the election of Robert Wages as president in August, 1991.[1]

With the lockout over, OCAW Local 4-620 was committed to sustaining a political project incorporating community issues along with its own. Union members, however, had not yet developed any long-term strategy for their coalition with the community. During the lockout, the union's relationship to the community was primarily tactical, framed by the short-term objective of breaking the lockout; now it was faced with thinking in fundamental ways about its political role in the region. Further, the union faced a relatively unknown relationship with a new coalition partner, the National Toxics Campaign. Despite these uncertainties, OCAW members were excited about the new projects.

POLITICAL OPPORTUNITIES AND THE REGULATORY STATE

The larger political backdrop for the beginning of the union's new coalition politics was Governor Roemer's environmental and fiscal reforms and the industrial challenges to them. Roemer's first fiscal reform proposal was defeated in the legislature in 1988. It had called for an increase in income taxes, a reduction in the homestead property tax exemption, a reduction in sales taxes, new business incentives, and elimination of the 10-year industrial tax exemption. Industry pressure forced the removal of provisions benefitting working and poor people even before the plan was defeated. Roemer returned in 1989 with a more modest proposal that excluded the ten-year industrial tax exemption. This plan, however, was so diluted—lessening sale tax cuts, restoring income tax loopholes, and increasing business tax exemptions—that a public referendum rejected it soundly, as people saw it benefitting only big business (Louisiana Coalition for Tax Justice, 1992).

Roemer's efforts to restrict the issuance of industrial tax exemptions dovetailed with growing citizen concern about corporate tax breaks and lack of accountability for pollution and for local hiring. The December 1989 Petition for Rulemaking filed by the newly created Tulane Environmental Law Clinic with the Board of Commerce and Industry, on behalf of twelve citizen groups, including OCAW, attempted to achieve what Roemer could not do in the legislature. The petition's intent was to force implementation of new rules that would link tax exemptions to environmental performance.[2]

At the same time, labor leaders from Lake Charles began attending Board of Commerce and Industry's meetings, and presented evidence that Lake Charles-area industries were hiring out-of-state labor, which violated the board's rule calling for preference in hiring of local labor, contractors, and suppliers. The labor leaders had documentation of significant use of out-of-state labor. Further, the state AFL-CIO, at its March, 1990, convention, passed a resolution calling for corporate tax exemption reform, on the basis of environmental degradation, excessive out-of-state hiring, and declining revenues for schools and public services. Public support for tax-exemption reform and for the institution of an environmental score card was running very strong.

Public support for the regulatory efforts at the Louisiana Department of Environmental Quality under Paul Templet was also very strong. The environmental community regarded Templet's leadership as vital to building citizen participation and better environmental enforcement.

The price of these reform efforts in tax exemptions, economic development, and environmental protection was intense corporate pressure on the governor, his staff, and the DEQ to not institute reforms which, it was argued, would damage Louisiana's business climate. Predictably, the avenues for citizen input into economic and environmental policy making opened up under Roemer—through the efforts of various citizens groups—were quickly and consistently challenged by the Louisiana Chemical Association and other business groups.

THE LOUISIANA COALITION FOR TAX JUSTICE

At roughly the same time OCAW Local 4-620 initiated the Labor-Neighbor Project in 1990, it helped launch the Louisiana Coalition for Tax Justice (LCTJ). LCTJ grew most directly out of OCAW's experience during the lockout that citizen research on economic and environmental issues can potentially shape policy and force companies to change their environmental and community practices. The union had used the issue of BASF's continued tax exemption on a dismantled production facility at its Geismar plant. Insofar as LCTJ was brought into existence largely by OCAW, its efforts should be seen as an extension of OCAW's labor-community collaboration beyond Ascension Parish and across the state. Although conceived during OCAW's tactical campaign to end the BASF lockout, LCTJ quickly developed more along strategic lines, with the goal of organizing citizens to force industry to share more of its wealth with low- and middle-income communities.

LCTJ's formation was initially inspired by a 1986 critical study and proposal for reform of industrial property tax exemptions by Oliver Houck of Tulane University's School of Law. While part of a growing public resentment over the 10-year industrial exemption since the 1973 Louisiana Constitutional Convention, Houck's study initiated a concerted effort to restrict the use of exemptions.[3] Houck, weighing the costs and benefits of the program, concluded that they were not effective and were literally billion dollar windfalls for companies that were destroying the environment. He argued that granting exemptions be contingent upon a given company's compliance with environmental laws; the greater the environmental violations the less the amount of the exemption (Houck 1986). OCAW's corporate accountability campaign organizers took notice of this study and began supporting Houck's proposal.

Patterned after the highly successful Kentuckians for the Commonwealth, LCTJ became a statewide grassroots voice against the 10-year industrial property tax exemption and other tax giveaways to industry at the expense of progressive economic development. Sharing office space with OCAW Local 4-620 and the Labor Neighbor Project, LCTJ had a grassroots board made up of leaders from Lake Charles, New Orleans, Baton Rouge, and several rural communities. By 1993, with an organizing staff of three, it had helped organize community groups in six communities to challenge tax breaks given to local polluters or to challenge permitting of hazardous waste facilities.

LCTJ's primary strength was its research and education. It investigated the four kinds of current industrial exemptions in Louisiana: the 10-year industrial property tax exemption; the enterprise zone program; industrial area designation; and municipal revenue and pollution-prevention bonds. Yet its main focus for public education was on the 10-year industrial tax exemption, the biggest tax exemption for industry.[4] The tax coalition compiled extensive information, parish by parish and company by company, on corporate tax exemptions, jobs provided, and pollution levels, for the period 1980 to 1989. For Ascension Parish alone, on average annually from 1980 to 1989, at least $16.7 million of $31 million total annual revenues, or 54 percent of potential tax revenues, were lost through the various tax breaks (LCTJ, 1992). By the mid-1990s LCTJ had gone into decline; it continued to operate through the end of the decade, although primarily with no staff.

THE LOUISIANA LABOR-NEIGHBOR PROJECT

Formation as a Long-Term Strategy

In 1990, OCAW Local 4-620 and the National Toxics Campaign hired a full-time organizer to build an ongoing union-community coalition in the Mississippi River parishes and to continue the union's monitoring of environmental and health and safety conditions at the Geismar area petrochemical facilities, particularly BASF and Vulcan Chemicals, the two bargaining units of Local 4-620. The project's principal goal was to build a longer-term strategic relationship between the union, community organizations, and public health advocates. Union and community strategists recognized the severe limitations of the tactical relationships developed during the lockout. The union/community collaboration was mainly oriented toward pressuring BASF to end the lockout, not toward building labor-community power for a multiplicity of ends. As OCAW strategist Richard Miller said, "It's easy to build tactical relationships when the boss is the enemy. The key is to build strategic relationships based on longer-term interests, not short-term alliances" (cited in Schafer, 1993, p. 45).

Yet the coalition-building process during the lockout forced the union to re-invent itself as a community institution, oriented toward bettering the environmental and economic conditions of working people in Ascension and nearby parishes. This redefinition by the union meant that not only did they owe something to the broader community for its support during the lockout, but the union had also developed a new commitment as a self-recognized community institution.

Commitment by the union and the National Toxics Campaign to the project was insufficient to prevent a near-disastrous staffing decision in the early months of the new project. Indeed, the union's new strategic sense as community institution was lost on the first coordinator of the labor-community coalition, hired in August, 1990.[5] The first coordinator aligned himself against the union leadership and with several militant rank-and-file members, and underestimated badly the union's commitment to building local power through community and coalition organizing. The most important lesson to emerge from this inappropriate choice of personnel was that, given adequate funding, a project's success is based largely on the skills of, and oversight over, its coordinator. A skilled organizer will nurture communication with union leaders and rank-and-file workers, constantly eliciting their input, listening well to what they want, and agitate when necessary. Inasmuch as the union was embarking on a new, uncertain coalition relationship with the community and a national environmental organization, it needed a coordinator who was an intellectual motivator and agitator.

By March, 1991, although the union was prepared to withdraw support for the project, union leaders chose to continue investing in the project, but with the recommendation that per capita commitment be reduced from $5 to $2.50 per person per month. The consensus was that the project was too important to drop, but it was now on probation. OCAW and NTC project supervisors recommended to the union that the author be employed as interim project organizer during the initial four-month probationary period, to which the union agreed.

Regardless of the project's early mishaps, it did begin an important community organizing process in Ascension Parish. The first coordinator organized a meeting of residents of Geismar and environmental activists in February, 1991, to discuss ways of dealing with the area's pollution problems. While the meeting was well-attended, drawing about seventy people, including several area plant managers and local politicians, it was poorly conceived and conducted. It neither helped develop local organization nor effectively established community demands on a specified target, such as the plant managers. Yet the meeting did serve as a basis for subsequent, more-rigorous, organizing in the community.

First Step at Base Consolidation:
Geismar/Dutchtown Residents for Clean Water and Air

Union and NTC strategists began formulating a plan to build systematically a broad community base in Ascension Parish. The larger purpose of this plan was to better challenge corporate pollution, build a greater degree of local popular control over the tax base as a way to influence economic development, and establish a popular base for the union for future solidarity in struggles with employers. The process of building a broad community base would involve developing one community group after another. The union's only current allied community group in the parish, the Ascension Parish Residents Against Toxic Pollution, lacked a sufficiently large core of leaders and broad base. Rather than expand that group, the union chose to build an entirely new community organization with a larger stable of leaders. A strategy designed in April, 1991, focused on organizing a community group in Geismar to demand that the petrochemical companies pay for a municipal water and sewer system. This plan was patterned after a neighborhood organizing model employed by NTC's organizing director. A water quality survey was sent out to 1000 residences, querying residents on their perceptions of local water quality, whom they considered responsible for bad water quality, and whether they supported the idea of the area petrochemical facilities financing a municipal water and sewer system for the community. The survey was designed purely as an organizing tool; thus, it intentionally had leading questions. As an organizing tool, the survey was invaluable. With a 25 percent response rate, it identified three to four good leaders. One-on-one meetings with respondents and other interested residents led to five house meetings, after which a steering committee was formed.

Three members of the steering committee, including one OCAW rank-and-file member who lived in Geismar, met with DEQ officials in the air quality division to ask DEQ to provide a 24-hour-operating air monitor for the community. DEQ officials showed interest in setting up such a station in Geismar, given the high concentration of petrochemical plants and the fact that no outside community monitor was present in the area.

The steering committee then organized and ran a community meeting at the local school that drew 175 people. In contrast to the meeting held six months earlier, this meeting, run by residents, made several clear demands of the specific target, the petrochemical plant managers. The meeting was used to inaugurate the Geismar/Dutchtown Residents for Clean Water and Air (or GDR). It helped galvanize the multiracial steering committee, composed of six African-Americans and six whites, three women and nine men. The meeting also ratified the next actions and gave a reason for a second meeting. One action, approved by those in attendance, was a letter sent to all area petrochemical plant managers, requesting that the companies finance a municipal water and sewer system and a system of air monitors in the community. The letter also requested a meeting between the steering committee and the plant managers. A second meeting was held one month later, at which the steering committee reported back to the community the response of the plant managers to the request for petrochemical financing of a municipal water and sewer system. The community residents in attendance ratified the committee's upcoming meeting with the plant managers.

In preparation for the meeting with the plant managers, an OCAW leader coached steering committee members on how to negotiate with plant management. This action was one way in which union members contributed their knowledge to help the community organization. Another union member, who worked at BASF, was a consistent member of the steering committee and often volunteered his insight on worker exposure to air toxins and the frequency of chemical spills at the facility. Thus, the union's presence on the steering committee and in support of it helped lend the group greater legitimacy and provide it with useful information and skills.

Good Neighbor Negotiations

Seven members of the multiracial steering committee of GDR, organized by the Labor-Neighbor Project, met on October 15, 1991, with plant managers from eight of the twelve petrochemical plants in the Geismar industrial complex. The community group called the meeting to request that the companies finance a municipal water and sewer system for the communities of Geismar and Dutchtown, with a combined population of 2,500. The discussion went as follows.

The GDR members told the plant managers that their community was suffering from bad water, bad air, and high cancer rates, which the residents attributed to the growing presence of the petrochemical plants in the area beginning in the late 1950s. One GDR member, Donna Carrier, stated that the local petrochemical facilities cheated the community by "getting huge tax breaks and not putting much back into the community." GDR's preliminary request was that the companies finance an engineering feasibility study on the creation of a municipal water/sewer system for the community. Members argued that the plants owed the community for endangering the health of the community's residents. GDR leader Izeal Morris said, "What you're doing and putting into the air, individually and collectively, it is harming the people. Both my mother and father died of cancer. All we are asking is that you give something to the community."

The lead plant manager, Bill Moran, not coincidentally the BASF facility chief, acknowledged the community's concerns as genuine, but focused on the need for a third-party risk assessment of water contamination to allay the residents' fears that the industrial facilities were endangering the residents' health. Another plant manager, Wayne Leonard of Borden Chemical, insisted that the plants were not polluting the residents' water: "Our best people will say that there is no risk. Remediation gets most of the contamination early on."

GDR members responded to this by stating that the companies needed to do something to alleviate the problem immediately, rather than just commission third-party risk assessments. They argued that a third-party risk study would do nothing to address the problem and people's fears. As Donna Carrier of GDR noted,

> A lot of studies won't ease people's minds. People are very reluctant to take third-party views. We know that the water issue is a see-saw. What goes up comes down. Air pollution goes into water. We don't agree with testing. It won't satisfy the people here. Patting us on the head with an analysis is not enough.

Moreover, GDR members argued, the contamination extending out from the chemical plants is so extensive that it would eventually contaminate the community. GDR leader Hubert Armond said: "The water table breathes back and forth. Nothing you say can stop us from believing our drinking water will get contaminated."

Indeed, residents argued that what local residents knew from their own personal experience—their local knowledge—was for them far more believable than the results from any third-party risk assessment commissioned by the plants. GDR member Sheila Blair stated, "As long as people smell it and taste it and see it, people won't believe what you're saying."

As regards the issue of funding of a water/sewer system, the plant managers stated that they would not pay for a system because that was the government's job. As BASF plant manager Bill Moran said, "The chemical companies here pay half of the property taxes in the parish [. . .] It's a government responsibility to pay for a system and find a way."

GDR members contended that the federal and state governments did not have the money to fund such a system, because funding had been severely reduced. Moreover, the residents argued that government was not responsible for the pollution. Izeal Morris of GDR stated,

People in Geismar don't feel like the government has polluted their water. People here think that they have to drink polluted water and breath polluted air the rest of our lives. So we go to you, our neighbors, to ask you to assist us to get done what needs to be done, to ease our discomfort. [. . .] We can argue all night over studies. The problem is in the people's minds. [. . .] The burdens on the people's minds won't go away. As corporations of responsibility, we're asking you to help us improve the situation. [. . .] My question is, are you willing to assist our people by giving us peace of mind, by satisfying our request.

The companies' position remained negative on corporate funding of the water/ sewer system and the feasibility study. While the company made no concessions during the meeting, the most important results were that a second meeting was agreed upon and that the GDR members gained valuable experience in dealing directly with industrial leaders.

The lines of discussion of the GDR members and the plant managers could not be more strikingly contrasting. GDR members spoke of local experience that made them find the petrochemical companies to be responsible for significant degradation of the local environment. Such "structures of feeling" (Williams, 1977), or local understandings of political economic relations, informed the community leaders that the chemical plants were responsible for degraded public health. Given this degradation of health in tandem with the massive tax breaks industry received for operating in the area, the community leaders felt that the industry owed it to the community to finance research into and install a municipal water/sewer system. Community members firmly believed that what industry had extracted from the community in terms of wealth and public health was owed back to the residents in the form of better services to preserve public health. Industry, rather than government, was responsible for the damage and therefore responsible for rectifying it.

The plant managers, on the other hand, spoke in terms of unfounded fears among residents, fears informed by a lack of sound scientific information. The managers played down the importance of local experience, arguing that it was not a good basis for finding solutions. For industry, the only problem was local perception, not actual everyday experience or alternative scientific information that pointed to massive groundwater contamination under the plants with the potential for long-term migration into the community's primary aquifer. The industry representatives were prepared to accept responsibility only for providing their scientific assessments to the community.

Thus, it was a clash of two lines of knowledge: industrial science and local knowledge (informed by competent science). For the industry representatives, the answer was technical; for the residents, one of equity. Industry attempted to sidestep the requests for equity by proposing a low-cost technical solution.

In follow-up public relations work, the BASF general manager characterized the GDR members as poorly informed, unable to provide specific cases of air and water pollution problems, and unwilling to accept industry's assistance with a third-party study on water quality. The companies, in effect, misrepresented the residents' experience with pollution and disease, not regarding it as relevant to the search for technical solutions.

Three months later, GDR steering committee members again met with the plant managers to request once more that the companies fund a feasibility study on a water/sewer system, fund the system itself, and fund a community air-monitoring network. The dialogue at the January 15, 1992, meeting was similar to that of the previous meeting. In addition, company representatives—this time only three, from the lead companies, BASF, Borden, and Vulcan—enthusiastically proposed testing residents' wells for chemical pollutants. GDR members stated that residents would not believe the results if they came up negative and thus were not interested in a well-testing project. The managers argued that a third-party study was needed to "understand the difference between fact and the [community residents'] perception of fact."

GDR leader Donna Carrier responded to the companies' proposal for a third-party study by saying,

> We know about lots of sickness and cancer. People still have questions. They know that the chemicals [in the groundwater] are still there. You can't deny it. No magic wand will make it go away.

Throughout the meeting, GDR members remained wedded to their requests that the companies fund a water system. The managers, however, were adamant about the companies' not being responsible for financing a municipal water system. Wayne Leonard, the Borden Chemical plant manager, said, "If we didn't contaminate the water, we shouldn't have to put in a system." As the meeting progressed, the BASF plant manager agreed that the companies would discuss what they could do about funding a feasibility study.

When asked again about funding an air-monitoring network, the managers told GDR members to go instead to the Louisiana DEQ for support, which GDR members said they had already done. A GDR member pointed out to the managers that the *Responsible Care* principles of the Chemical Manufacturers Association state that association members shall assist communities in establishing air-monitoring networks. This appeared to catch the managers off guard. They promised to review the principles in order to respond to the GDR members' request, but stated that for now the companies would not fund an air-monitoring network.

GDR member Ben Clark related the local experience that a large number of children were contracting cancer, relating it to air pollution coming from the plants. "If you kill the kids off, there's nothing left," he said. To this, Borden Chemical plant manager Wayne Leonard responded in a condescending manner that the GDR member's belief was not based in fact, because the manager, who lived in Dutchtown, had a different experience. Leonard said, "I lived in

Dutchtown for 15 years and would have moved if I didn't like it. I don't think what you feel is happening."

GDR members challenged the managers' assertion that the chemical companies paid 55 percent of the parish's property taxes, arguing that they paid only 26 percent. To this, the managers replied that the income of one-third of the 2,600 permanent employees at petrochemical facilities in the parish—amounting to over $8 million—goes back into the parish via local spending. The managers also argued that companies need the tax breaks as an incentive to come to the state because it is more expensive for them to operate in Louisiana than in northern states. The managers stated that the companies would not help finance a water/sewer system not only because they had not polluted the residents' water, but because the companies were already paying more than their fair share to parish residents through corporate taxes.

While GDR members gained the managers' promise to look into funding a feasibility study, to provide groundwater contamination maps, and to review the companies' policy on funding community air monitors, the managers granted no concessions. Yet clearly, GDR had further established itself as an important voice in the community. The plant managers recognized they were talking to community leaders. The meetings served not simply to advance discussion and requests, but provided a chance for plant managers and GDR members alike to assess strengths and weaknesses of the other side. For GDR members, both meetings demonstrated that the plant managers held slightly different positions on some issues—such as the willingness of the plants to fund the feasibility study. It also became apparent which plant managers were the area leaders in addressing community mobilization against their environmental and economic practices. For the plant managers, the meetings helped them to identify GDR's leaders, and the strengths and weaknesses of the group's arguments.

GDR came away from the meetings with greater credibility in the community and a heightened sense of purpose and self-empowerment, despite the minimal concessions by the plant managers. The meetings, and more generally GDR's "good neighbor" strategy, helped define community, who is a part of it and who is not. The good neighbor strategy was a spatial strategy to include the petrochemical companies as part of community to get them to act responsibly. The process of inclusion had one obvious goal of getting the companies to finance municipal public works projects (a water/sewer system and air-monitoring network) and reduce pollution.

The politics of GDR members and chemical industry representatives, as demonstrated at the two good neighbor meetings, had a spatial component. GDR members defined their political allegiance with the local community of Geismar/Dutchtown. Their identity was therefore primarily locally informed, although they drew on outside organizing resources—from (Boston-based) NTC, OCAW, and the broader Louisiana environmental community.

The chemical industry representatives had a more complex identity politics. The plant managers defined themselves as part of, and apart from, the Geismar/ Dutchtown community. This, too, was an important spatial strategy. On the one hand, the managers asserted that the companies were being good neighbors by contributing their fair share to the community and the broader parish, by paying half the parish's property taxes and by providing jobs that infused millions of dollars of personal income into the local economy. On the other hand, the managers defined the plants as separate from the community on the issue of negative externalities such as pollution. They defined the plants as falling under DEQ's or EPA's jurisdiction—both outside bodies—rather than being obligated to local requests based on local knowledge, in part supported by scientific evidence. One plant manager conveniently defined himself as a resident of Dutchtown in order to contradict the GDR members' local experiences with pollution and illness, while at the same time situating himself within industry, apart from the local community and not obligated to it. Moreover, the managers indicated their membership in a global industrial community by arguing that industrial operating costs are higher in Louisiana than in northern states, thereby justifying Louisiana's generous industrial property tax exemptions to attract them to and keep them in the state.

Establishing Identity: Formation of the Louisiana Labor-Neighbor Project

The creation of the Geismar/Dutchtown Residents served to build a rudimentary community base for the labor-community project sponsored by OCAW and the National Toxics Campaign. The project could not simply be OCAW's vehicle, but rather had to transcend the union to take on challenges of importance to community residents. The campaign for a water/sewer system and community-based air monitoring identified and developed local community leaders. Two of those leaders, one a veteran of the Ascension Parish Residents Against Toxic Pollution, the other a new leader emerging from GDR's creation, were selected to serve on the board of the Louisiana Labor-Neighbor Fund, incorporated in early 1992. They joined two leaders from OCAW's BASF group, two from the union's Vulcan group, one representative from the National Toxics Campaign, one from OCAW International, and one from the larger Louisiana environmental health community. Meeting twice annually, the fund's board was empowered to define the organization's mission and organizing strategy, and to direct the organizing efforts of one paid staff member, the project coordinator. What was previously a project directed by several supervisors and the project coordinator with approval by the union, was now a formalized organization with a democratic structure involving legitimate community leaders. The Labor-Neighbor Project's incorporation signaled the development of a coalition consciousness on the part of union and community leaders. Community and union leaders viewed each other's organizations as necessary, long-term strategic partners. More so than during the lockout, community leaders increasingly regarded the union as a legitimate community institution.

Building Local Control: A Community Water District

Following the second meeting with the plant managers, it was apparent to community residents that the local petrochemical plants were not prepared to finance a municipal water system or an air-monitoring network. The project and GDR, therefore, examined possible ways to force the companies to pay for such a system. One idea was to create a water/sewer district that included the plants. Following this concept, GDR members, working with the project, defined the boundaries of a proposed water and sewer district. The proposed district included the Geismar petrochemical complex and the communities of Geismar and Dutchtown. By including the industrial facilities within the district, these would be subject to municipal governance, including the levying of taxes for local economic development. The community could, therefore, more effectively challenge industrial tax breaks. Following the state legal requirements for establishing water and sewer districts, GDR members drafted a petition calling for the creation of water and sewer districts. The group presented the petition and signatures to the Ascension Parish police jury, which agreed to the creation of a Geismar/Dutchtown water district and an attendant water board, comprised of five community members proposed by GDR. While four of the five water board members had been active in GDR, GDR and the board understood that the board members were to act as a technical/administrative body, distinct from the community organizing function of GDR. Indeed, the creation of the water board served to bolster GDR's legitimacy as a local political agent, while allowing GDR the freedom to continue organizing.

The police jury then assigned a parish consultant to help the newly formed water board and GDR to pursue federal funding for the water system. A preliminary task was to come up with funding for a feasibility study on establishing a water system. The source of the municipal water supply was foreseeably the Baton Rouge system, which would run a five-mile extension line to the community. At the same time, the Labor-Neighbor Project, with the assistance of the Louisiana Coalition for Tax Justice, began exploring the possibilities for challenging the Geismar petrochemical companies' industrial tax exemptions. The project sought to change the tax exemption policy to provide additional sources of funding for the municipal water system.

Ongoing Environmental Advocacy

The Labor-Neighbor Project continued the environmental advocacy support for OCAW undertaken during the lockout. The focus of such a servicing role was production-related environmental violations. True to its name, the project was committed to finding resolutions to problems of worker and community exposure to toxic chemicals. In one case, the project attempted to force BASF to follow the most effective remediation of groundwater contamination under the old Basagran facility at the company's Geismar works. In another case, the Labor-Neighbor Project pursued the investigation of massive groundwater contamination at Vulcan Materials, where OCAW represented 135 workers. The project and OCAW leadership at Vulcan met with Vulcan management several times in 1991 and 1992 to discuss the company's remediation plans, which followed a 200-year schedule of pumping and treating the extensive contamination.[6]

In the Basagran and Vulcan groundwater cases, the Labor-Neighbor organizer fulfilled his responsibility to the union to continue pushing for worker and community protection. The union members sensed an immediate value in having an environmental advocate who could facilitate efforts to make management more accountable to worker and community protection. Whereas the community organizing on environmental and public-service issues was more long-term and its results less palpable, plant-site environmental advocacy was more visible to union members. It more readily justified the January, 1992, increase in their investment from $2.50 to $4.00 per member per month. However desirable it was for union workers to have an in-house professional environmental advocate, a dual focus on community organizing and environmental regulatory advocacy required a huge effort.

Two Small Victories:
Air and Hazardous Waste

On the heels of its success in establishing a local water district and water board, Geismar/Dutchtown Residents for Clean Water and Air in 1992 succeeded in getting the Department of Environmental Quality to install, maintain, and finance a twenty-four-hour air monitor in a Geismar residential area. While GDR had requested the chemical companies to finance a network of monitors, the group won DEQ's support for the proposal to set up a monitor in the community. The relationship-building with DEQ's air quality division paid off when the agency chose to site one of its new stationary monitors in Geismar. Only upon installation of the monitor did the area chemical facilities express their support, though not in financial ways.

During the same year, GDR successfully pressured the Ascension Parish police jury to ban the transport of hazardous chemicals on two roads leading through the heart of residential Geismar and Dutchtown. Tractor-trailer transport of hazardous chemicals had long been a concern of community residents, particularly since one such truck had overturned in front of the Dutchtown elementary school, although no chemicals had been released. Road signs marking "no hazardous chemicals" were installed along the two roads. Chemical trucks were required to use roads outside of the primary residential areas.

With these two small victories, GDR continued to establish itself in small, yet incremental ways as a local citizen force. Nevertheless, its influence was limited to issues mainly concerning the Geismar community, not the parish at large.

Reaching Beyond Geismar: The Airport Coalition

The Labor-Neighbor Project's opportunity to expand its base occurred in early 1993 with Ascension Parish's plans to serve as the site of a new international airport. Officials at New Orleans International Airport were looking for a site between New Orleans and Baton Rouge that could accommodate air cargo traffic and ultimately be the principal passenger airport in the state. The eastern part of Ascension Parish, including part of the Geismar area, was proposed as a potential site for the airport. The Labor-Neighbor Project and GDR quickly called a series of meetings, culminating with a community meeting attended by more than over 200 residents. The Labor-Neighbor organizer met with residents of other Ascension Parish communities, including Darrow, and the St. Landry section of Gonzales, and formed local committees to address the airport issue. The community groups in Gonzales, Darrow and Geismar/Dutchtown, largely African-American, together with a predominantly white middle-class environmental organization in Burnside, as well as church leaders from the proposed impacted area, and citizen groups from other parts of the parish, formed a loose tactical alliance, called Neighbors for a Quality Life, to bring pressure to bear on the Ascension Parish Police Jury. Leaders of most churches in the proposed impacted area in the parish took a stand against the airport. Cumulative citizen opposition ultimately prompted the police jury to reject the airport proposal for the parish. The alliance experienced racial tensions when white activists sought to hold private planning meetings without including the alliance's African-American leadership. Although the tensions threatened to dissolve the coalition, discussion facilitated by the Labor-Neighbor coordinator helped to resolve the immediate difficulties (Nicolai, interview, May 10, 1993).

The airport controversy presented the Labor-Neighbor Project with an opportunity to organize community groups in other Ascension Parish communities. Two of the groups emerging from airport fight, from Gonzales and Darrow, held together to take on other issues such as emergency response, toxic releases, and local hiring.

The citizens' group, Concerned Citizens of Gonzales, represented the largely African-American rural St. Landry residential neighborhood, located less than a mile from Rubicon, a chemical company. Rubicon had been cited several times over the previous few years for releasing nitrobenzene fumes into the air from open waste pits at its Geismar facility. OCAW Local 4-620 filed a complaint because its workers at the adjacent BASF facility had complained of respiratory problems and eye irritation resulting from nitrobenzene from the Rubicon facility. The nearby residents complained of the same symptoms. Several "good neighbor" meetings between community members, OCAW members, Rubicon plant management, and DEQ officials produced no progress in minimizing the contamination problem. The Labor-Neighbor Project then sought to prevent the Board of Commerce and Industry from granting Rubicon a $2 million industrial property tax exemption. To improve its chances of blocking the exemption, the project tried to enlist the support of the building trades unions. A meeting between OCAW and several building trades leaders was fruitless, in that the building trades leaders said they could not help because they were expecting to win construction jobs from Rubicon, which they claimed Rubicon had promised them. Ultimately Rubicon received its tax exemption and gave all the construction jobs to nonunion contractors, largely from outside the parish (Nicolai, interview, November 30, 1993).

Rubicon's lack of emergency response to toxic releases and its flagrant use of poorly trained non-union contractors—who historically had posed a greater threat to local health and safety—helped to mobilize local citizens and workers to push for local government intervention. The Labor-Neighbor Project gained the support of a pipefitters' union local in a campaign to promote local hiring and emergency response by companies in the parish. The pipefitters joined the project, the Concerned Citizens of Gonzales, and the Darrow/Hillaryville community group, to lobby the parish council[7] to pass an ordinance requiring companies and their contractors to report their hiring when applying for municipal bonds. Such an ordinance, the citizens groups contended, would help promote local hiring and a more transparent process of company emergency preparedness. Working together with the steering committee from Darrow, an African-American community located close to a Texaco refinery and a grain elevator, the project won the support of a longshoremen's union local in the campaign to promote local hiring and transparent emergency preparedness. The Darrow committee and the longshoremen sought to stop a local grain loading company from leaving the community. A meeting was held in Darrow with the parish council president and the parish sheriff to push the ordinance on mandatory reporting of hiring and to discuss emergency response. Meetings with the council president were held in other communities as well. The effort in Darrow, in concert with the involvement of the pipefitters, the Gonzales community group, and various church lay leaders, who attended the meetings with the parish council president, ensured the passage of the ordinance on company reporting (Nicolai, interview, January 26, 1995).

The Labor-Neighbor Project's expansion in Ascension Parish demonstrated how its politics addressed interrelated production and reproduction issues. Before the Labor-Neighbor Project, no previous citizen organization in the parish had organized on issues such as local hiring, and worker and community exposure—that is, community *and* labor issues—in an integrated way. By blending production and reproduction issues, the project's politics developed a more solid basis for confronting vexing pollution and employment problems.

Losing a Coalition Partner:
The Dissolution of the National Toxics Campaign

The Labor-Neighbor Project lost its principal environmental partner when the National Toxics Campaign voted to dissolve itself in April, 1993. The reasons for NTC's dissolution were later discussed among organizers, journalists, and scholars.[8] My analysis of the dissolution comes from these sources as well as my participation in meetings of the NTC staff and board before and after the breakup. In short, NTC's demise can be attributed to two general factors. First, NTC could not accommodate its own rapid growth from a small group run largely by white men into a large multiracial, gender-balanced network, with attendant tensions over organizational mission and management. Second, the organization's over-dependence on liberal philanthropic funding put it at odds with foundation agendas gravitating away from NTC's consistent focus on grassroots organizing for pollution prevention. Both factors were highly interrelated. Tensions over the organization's direction and management style were exacerbated and partially fostered by the liberal capitalist agendas of the funders. NTC's dissolution illustrates the volatility and fragility of national environmental partners in contrast to the greater stability of union partners. NTC sometimes brought complications to the partnership with OCAW. It never succeeded in appointing an OCAW leader to its board of directors because of the animosity of one board member, a local environmental leader from Kansas, toward any union member employed at Vulcan Materials; the proposed board member from OCAW was a Vulcan worker. Despite NTC's dissolution, its organizing director continued to provide training and supervision to the Labor-Neighbor coordinator until 2000. In general, the supervision and training provided by NTC was instrumental to the success of the Labor-Neighbor Project from 1990 onward.

Shifting Political Opportunities After 1992

Edwin Edwards' final term as governor signified a return of the rogue neo-populist and power broker in the Long tradition. As before, Edwards helped his friends in the business world who helped him in politics and in his private business affairs (Maginnis, 1992). Although Edwards was the choice of African-American and liberal voters seeking a state government active in diversifying economic development, protecting the environment, and boosting economic opportunity for working people, he was tied closely to powerful development forces. The petrochemical, oil, and gas industries readily backed him because they saw him as someone who would work to stop environmental reform policy created under Buddy Roemer. Gambling developers supported him, and in return he pushed hard to bring legalized gambling to the state, including floating Mississippi River casinos and a huge river bank casino in New Orleans. He rewarded allies in the state AFL-CIO and the construction industry by appointing state AFL-CIO chief

Victor Bussie to chair the Louisiana Public Facilities Authority, an autonomous agency that issues municipal bonds for various construction projects.[9]

Edwards' fourth term as governor immediately established a new approach to environmental protection. He eliminated the "environmental scorecard" that Buddy Roemer had put into place for one year in December, 1990, justifying this move by stating that environmental protection and economic development should not be linked because the results could be detrimental to economic health. He appointed industry-friendly people to the top positions at the Department of Environmental Quality, replacing the progressive reform-minded environmental scientist Paul Templet with Kai Midboe, previously a lobbyist for the Mid-Continental Oil and Gas Association. The former heads of the water resources and air quality divisions during Edwards' previous term returned to their old positions in the new administration.

Edwards' appointment of Kai Midboe as DEQ secretary came as no surprise, given Edwards' own strong ties to the oil, gas, and petrochemical industries, despite his own reputation as a populist. Edwards' 1991 election campaign was heavily underwritten by these industries. Midboe's record stood in stark contrast to the enforcement agenda set by Paul Templet. In two years in office Midboe lowered the tax on importation of hazardous waste into Louisiana, nearly granted a permit for a hazardous waste recycling plant in a low-income black community near St. Gabriel, and gave the go-ahead for lead-contaminated soil from Dallas to be dumped in Monroe, Louisiana. Moreover he challenged the Tulane Environmental Law Clinic, which represented citizen groups' lawsuits, urging the governor to put the clinic under tight control. Midboe resigned in January, 1994, after intense animosity from many environmentalists over his laxness toward industry, particularly his liberal issuance of environmental permits for contested industrial facilities.

His replacement, William Kucharsky, deputy secretary at DEQ, was far less confrontational with the environmental community yet was as friendly to industry as Midboe. Kucharsky had previously worked as an engineer for Woodward-Clyde, an engineering consulting firm holding numerous large contracts with petrochemical companies. Although he did not promise to be any friendlier to environmental health than Midboe, his behavior in his earliest actions as DEQ chief indicated conciliation with environmental groups. He denied an operating permit to Supplemental Fuels, Inc., for a hazardous waste recycling plant near St. Gabriel, a permit that Midboe had all but granted. Further, he planned to reintroduce the hazardous waste tax at its Roemer-era level. Kucharsky was more politically pragmatic than his predecessor, with a better understanding of public opposition to shoddy environmental practices. Two years into Edwards' fourth administration, the general public had perceived that the governor had gone too far in trying to roll back environmental gains made during the Roemer years. Support even within the business community for a restoration of the environmental scorecard and the hazardous waste tax appeared to be strong and growing.

It is likely that many business leaders viewed strong environmental standards as important for building Louisiana's reputation as a good place for business. Despite the promising situation, the environmental scorecard did not return on Kucharsky's watch.

Under Midboe and Kucharsky, DEQ was no longer an active agent in expanding opportunities for citizen participation and in designing a clear environmental vision for the state, as it had been during Paul Templet's tenure. The citizen-oriented assistant secretaries and policy analysts were largely gone; abolished were the divisions of local programs (oriented toward setting up DEQ advisor positions for each of the state's parishes) and policy and planning, the department's "brains" division. During 1994 and 1995, Secretary Kucharsky did not actively promote any environmental legislation.

With the shift toward antienvironmental decision making by state government, one would expect the grassroots environmental community to respond with a rise in concerted activism and lobbying at the state level. This was generally not the case. Whereas the environmental community applied intense pressure on the legislature during the second half of the 1980s—fueled in part by the formation of the Louisiana Environmental Action Network and by OCAW's intense corporate accountability campaign—this lobbying presence tapered off consistently during the mid-1990s. The Louisiana Environmental Action Network was indeed successful at reacting against and stopping some proindustry bills, but these efforts had been piecemeal, reactive, and not part of an alternative strategy such as pollution prevention and right-to-know. LEAN promoted the formation of a Louisiana environmental PAC, in close collaboration with Clean Water Action's efforts to form eco-PACs in a number of states. Eco-PACs have the professed goal of backing the election of pro-environmental legislators and other public officials. The Louisiana eco-PAC was formed in 1995 but was unable to secure national foundation financing (Nicolai, interview, July 28, 1995). It struggled since that time.

On labor issues, true to his past record, such as his signing of the right-to-work bill in 1976, Edwin Edwards had a poor record on worker protection during his fourth term. His overtures to labor during the 1991 campaign about reinstituting the closed shop turned out empty. Yet he did little to further undermine worker protection. He maintained a friendly relationship with the state AFL-CIO by rewarding state construction contracts to building trades unions and appointing AFL-CIO chief Bussie to chair the Louisiana Public Facilities Authority.

The election of Mike Foster as governor in November, 1995, signaled a worsening of conditions for labor in Louisiana. While Foster was expected to follow Edwards' hostile stand toward environmental protection, his record on labor as a state senator was far worse than that of Edwards. Foster was expected to push for conservative reform on issues such as workers' compensation and was not expected to have a warm relationship with business unionism (King, interview, December 19, 1995; Nicolai, interview, November 30, 1995).

Tax Breaks and Toxics in Iberville Parish:
Victory for the Tax Coalition

DEQ Secretary William Kucharsky's 1994 denial of an operating permit to Supplemental Fuels, Inc., for a hazardous waste processing plant in Carville, near St. Gabriel in Iberville Parish, proved to be a big victory for the Louisiana Coalition for Tax Justice. The tax coalition had helped organize the local opposition to the facility by forming a local group called Neighbors Assisting Neighbors. Supplemental Fuels wanted to locate the waste processing plant adjacent to an African-American neighborhood. The facility would blend industrial hazardous waste into a fuel to be burned out-of-state in cement kilns (*Baton Rouge Advocate*, July 2, 1993). The campaign to stop the recycling plant successfully won the support of the Louisiana House of Representatives, the Iberville Parish and Ascension Parish police juries, and the Gonzales Board of Aldermen, all of which passed resolutions against the siting of the facility (*Baton Rouge Advocate*, July 2, July 27, 1993). Broad popular support for the campaign came about because the proposed facility, with its attendant transport of hazardous waste, would pose a serious threat to public health and local water resources. The proposed siting of the facility in Carville was thought by many, including some Iberville Parish Police Jury members, to be a clear case of environmental racism. Despite a strong, vocal campaign, then-DEQ secretary Kai Midboe granted SFI the operating permit in late 1993. After Midboe resigned, however, the new DEQ Secretary revoked the permit.

LCTJ's organizing in St. Gabriel, and the active engagement of its president, Chris Gaudet, a St. Gabriel resident, set in motion a local initiative that led the Louisiana Supreme Court to declare tax-exempt "industrial areas" unconstitutional. The court decision was rendered after the Iberville Water District filed suit against Ciba-Geigy, located in St. Gabriel. Community activists in St. Gabriel urged the Iberville Water District to sue Ciba-Geigy because the company was not paying to support the local water system, by virtue of its large property tax exemptions, while being a major polluter in the area. In a 1992 district court decision, the judge ruled unconstitutional the state law creating industrial tax exemptions. The judge also ordered that Ciba-Geigy give $500,000, which the company paid under protest from 1985-1992, to the water district. The Louisiana Supreme Court decision in January, 1994, flowed directly from the Iberville case. This victory for LCTJ was thought to be significant for municipalities that lose out on potential revenue from petrochemical plants that are geographically within a municipal service area, but for their special industrial area status exempt themselves from it. LCTJ's involvement in the parish also led local activists to win a police jury ordinance making the issuance of tax exemptions contingent upon a company's provision of jobs to parish residents. St. Gabriel's incorporation in 1995, which included the industrial facilities in the area in the new municipality, constituted a major victory for local activists pushing for tax justice and corporate accountability to local communities (*Baton Rouge Advocate*, June 23, 1993; Nicolai, interview, January 28, 1994; Orr, interview, December 20, 1995).

A Shift to Mass-Based Organizing

While the Labor-Neighbor Project continued its activist-based organizing on environmental and public service issues in Ascension Parish, beginning in 1994, the project began a new effort to build a broader community-labor coalition by developing relationships with churches and other labor unions. The new model added to the project's organizing repertoire was congregation-based organizing. It emerged after the dissolution of the National Toxics Campaign, which had prompted a rethinking among the remaining organizers about political strategy. Congregation-based organizing entailed a close attention to selecting issues. Leaders and member organizations advanced their issues in discussions at house meetings and larger leadership meetings. The upshot was a broadening of Labor-Neighbor's agenda, beyond traditional ideas of environmental health to include various issues of concern to member organizations. Yet, the more common unifying issues continued to be environmental or economic development.

The congregation-based model of the Industrial Areas Foundation is oriented around developing "sponsoring committees," comprised of church leaders who are prepared to help fund a congregation-based organizing project and to ensure turnout of a set number of members for various actions, such as meetings with public officials. The Labor-Neighbor Project coordinator began one-on-one interviews with church ministers and labor leaders from Ascension Parish, to build appropriate relationships and assemble a sponsoring committee in the parish.

Meeting at least three times one-on-one with pastors from various churches, by mid-1995 the Labor-Neighbor coordinator was able to win the support of eight to ten churches, including Baptist, Methodist, Lutheran, and Pentecostal churches, but not the Catholics. Lack of Catholic support threatened to be a significant obstacle to building an effective committee. The project arranged for some of the supporting pastors to attend a five-day training course in New Orleans conducted by PICO (Pacific Institute for Community Organizations), an IAF-style congregation-based network operating mainly in the West Coast, Gulf Coast, and mid-Atlantic regions. Developing a link to PICO was considered important for the incipient sponsoring committee, as PICO could lend ongoing support in training and building relationships to a broader range of churches. The issues of concern expressed by the pastors were job opportunities for youth, youth activities, water/sewer service, and growth issues, including related flooding. Concerns about pollution and the environment were not high on the pastors' agenda. In late 1995, the Labor-Neighbor Project sought to formalize its relationship with ten churches in Ascension Parish, through the incorporation of a sponsoring committee consisting of autonomous chapters. All of the churches were Protestant, eight of ten African-American, and two predominantly white.

The Labor-Neighbor Project agreed to support the sponsoring committee with research on economic development, employment, and provision of public services in the parish. PICO was not interested in entering any formalized relationship with Labor-Neighbor regarding the Ascension Parish project (Nicolai, interviews, Jan. 26, July 28, and Nov. 30, 1995).

That the Labor-Neighbor Project's efforts to establish a formalized relationship with PICO in Ascension Parish were fraught with tension was not surprising. PICO in Louisiana was wary of working with unions, as were other PICO organizations and the Industrial Areas Foundation. This wariness stemmed in part from the close ties that church leaders often had to company management and the business community, which were customarily distrustful of unions. One of the basic principles of IAF and PICO is "no permanent allies, no permanent enemies" (Industrial Areas Foundation, 1978; Jonathan Mayer, interview, October 15, 1994). This translated to an openness to work with anybody, including big business, given the proper conditions. In 1995, PICO held two community meetings in St. James Parish cosponsored by two banks. Freeport McMoRan, the fertilizer giant, sponsored PICO's New Orleans affiliate, ACT (All Congregations Together), an organization with sixty member-churches. PICO's record of working with industry, alternatively, made unions affiliated with the Labor-Neighbor Project nervous about entering a relationship with the church-based network (Nicolai, interview, July 28, 1995).

Organizing the pastors faced a potentially formidable obstacle in the concurrent organizing efforts by the Christian Coalition. Already strong in Ascension Parish, the coalition organized on school prayer and censorship of gangsta rap music, and had gained the support of many church pastors. While the Christian right had not yet taken control of the school board in Ascension Parish, they swept the 1994 Baton Rouge school board elections, united with the Chamber of Commerce and using an antiunion agenda focused on downsizing the number of public-school employees (Nicolai, interview, January 26, 1995).

The Labor-Neighbor Project had to reconcile its new church-based organizing model with its previous "Alinsky-style" direct action organizing. The two paths were difficult for one organizer to coordinate, but the project nevertheless sought to follow them simultaneously. Organizing for big public meetings, such as those about the airport or emergency response issues, took time away from building an institutional sponsoring committee. Further, the project's history in fighting industrial pollution created for tension concerning the organization's direction. One project board member wanted Labor-Neighbor to turn people out to environmental hearings. The project's new organizing direction, however, could not accommodate this request. The shortage of grassroots environmental leadership at the state level had prompted the project board member to try to enlist Labor-Neighbor to mobilize on environmental issues. Yet the Labor-Neighbor Project had determined it was not its task to do the job of the Louisiana

Environmental Action Network in mobilizing grassroots environmental forces (Nicolai, interview, July 28, 1995).

Due to its new focus on congregation-based organizing, the Labor-Neighbor Project was unable to maintain its organizing investment in three community groups it had helped create in Abend, Gonzales, and Darrow. The coordinator hoped to draw the active leaders of those groups into the larger congregation-oriented organizing committee. Civic leaders involved in the project's previous efforts on employment and environmental issues, as well as lay leaders from local churches, were skeptical of the ministers' capacity to actively lead on issues such as local hiring and emergency response. The conventional belief was that the ministers were too heavily influenced by company management to take a leading role in local citizen initiatives facilitated by the union-sponsored Labor-Neighbor Project. Plant management, for its part, consistently regarded negatively OCAW's involvement in citizen initiatives in Ascension Parish. The importance of recruiting ministers to play a central role in such a labor-community organization was such that their involvement brought a church endorsement to the initiatives of already-involved community and lay activists (Nicolai, interview, November 20, 1994).

Moreover, once the organizing committee was fully operating, OCAW had to rethink its role in the congregation-based project. OCAW members' involvement in the early church-based organizing was somewhat limited. While the union was very supportive of the direction of the project in building and solidifying a community institutional base by including religious institutions, only a handful of members were active in congregational organizing. The issue drawing union members' interest most was the question of local hiring by industry. OCAW members had not been interested in issues of youth employment and after-school activity to the degree that churches had been. Union leaders, however, expected greater union engagement on youth issues once the church base solidified. An explicit agreement by participating congregations in such a project was to deliver people. Until then, OCAW had delivered only a handful of activists to the community-based initiatives. There was, however, rich potential in such parish-wide organizing with OCAW's active involvement of its membership (King, interview, December 19, 1995; Nicolai, interview, November 20, 1994).

The project's new orientation toward church-based organizing was in part financially supported by several foundations. Through such financing, the Labor-Neighbor Project hired on an additional organizer in 1995, a Mexican-American from Texas. However, another previous funder of the project reoriented its support from antitoxics organizing to antiracism organizing in communities of color. Visiting Louisiana nonprofit organizations in 1994, that foundation's program officer expressed interest in funding "consciousness raising" and "confronting racism." The foundation was purportedly disenchanted with Gulf Coast Tenants Organization, the preeminent African-American environmental justice organization in the state. The view of the Labor-Neighbor coordinator and other environmental organizers, however, was that communities of color in the river parishes did not simply want a discussion on racism, but rather wanted jobs and economic development (Evans, interview, October 28, 1994; Nicolai, interview, October 26, 1994).

Following this logic, the concern of activists in communities of color in the Louisiana river parishes seemed to be over economic development and employment opportunities, not overtly over identity politics. This position was supported by the author's observations while working with the Labor-Neighbor Project in Ascension Parish. While recognizing the persistence of racism, the mobilizing issue for African-American activists was the need for economic development, employment opportunities and a healthy environment (Favorite, interview, January 14, 1992; Morris, interview, March 13, 1992). Yet, one cannot deny the importance of confronting racism. The goals of the foundation are not misplaced; rather, the priorities of local communities are such that economic survival often precedes discussions explicitly about race.

The shift to mass-based organizing resounded well with some of the Labor-Neighbor Project's leaders who had previously been active on environmental issues. Irma Rixner, a community leader from Gonzales in Ascension Parish, was a leader of United Methodist Women in the campaign against Rubicon's release of nitrobenzene into the local environment. After the Rubicon campaign, as a leader in the new Concerned Citizens of Ascension Parish, most of whose members were churchgoers at a Methodist church, she guided a core of activists to take up broader community issues. As Ms. Rixner stated,

> We got into other issues, such as youth. We organized self-esteem classes for kids and put together a health fair for kids. Then we started tutoring sixty kids. We met with the school board, which provides resources for tutorial programs. [. . .] Recreation is important for all kids. We asked the parish council president for a building for recreation. We organized Arts for Kids and got volunteers to help. We had the parish put lights in the parks. (Irma Rixner, interview, November 17, 1997)

Winning a Local Water System and Shaping Parish Politics

The project continued its organizing to get a water system for Geismar/ Dutchtown. While the Baton Rouge water department had offered a service-and-supply contract to the Geismar/Dutchtown water board, the process of deciding on a system and securing funding was slowed considerably by the newly created Ascension Parish Council and by hesitancy on the part of the water board. The new Ascension Parish Council, replacing the police jury system, was governed firmly by a strong president. The president was capable of limiting the influence of the Geismar/Dutchtown council members who, if they had more power, could have advanced the process more quickly. Moreover, the

Geismar/Dutchtown water board quickly became resistant to confrontation and had not pushed strongly enough for the completion of a water system feasibility study. Not seasoned in institutionalized decision making, the board members allowed themselves to be lulled by promises from parish consultants, which resulted in the water system's feasibility study not being completed. Pressure from Labor-Neighbor's coordinator by itself was not enough to get the board to be more forceful. Such complacency by institutionalized bodies whose creation results from collective action has historically plagued many reform-designed organizations emerging out of social movements (cf. Piven and Cloward, 1977). The project coordinator had pushed the board to challenge the petrochemical companies' industrial areas status. Overturning the industrial areas status would have enabled the town to tax the companies. The water board, however, refused to take on the challenge, after being misinformed by the parish counsel, who erroneously claimed that industry was tax exempt. The parish council president had helped undercut any confrontational tendencies on the part of the water board by promising to work with the board to get a parishwide water system (Nicolai, interview, October 26, 1994).

In late 1995 the Geismar/Dutchtown water board arranged with the Baton Rouge water department that Baton Rouge would supply the community if it could get 350 residents signed up. Water provision would then amount to $15 per month per unit. The major obstacle to this arrangement was the intention by the parish council president to establish a parishwide water system, financed by a parishwide tax. With a parishwide system, politically weaker, poorer communities such as Geismar ostensibly would be the last to receive service. But given its years-long mobilization for municipal water service, the Geismar/Dutchtown community was in a far better position to push for its own arrangements for water service. In 1997, Geismar/Dutchtown successfully obtained water service from Baton Rouge. This signified a major victory for the Labor-Neighbor Project, in that winning a system for Geismar/Dutchtown was a first step in developing a water system for Ascension Parish. The project's role in bringing about a parish system was central. As Duke King, OCAW chair at Vulcan Materials, commented, "The Labor-Neighbor Project will be a driving force in getting a parishwide system" (King, December 19, 1995; Nicolai, interview, November 30, 1995). Not surprisingly, once Geismar/Dutchtown won the installation of a water line from Baton Rouge, industry approached the water board to obtain some of the water.

Helping to galvanize Geismar/Dutchtown against the parish council president's plans was a local campaign in Geismar, led by the "17 Members Committee," to incorporate the community. Formed in 1995, the 17 Members Committee petitioned the board of elections to include the Geismar area petrochemical facilities in the incorporated area. It had been heretofore legal for new municipalities to include industrial areas in their incorporated areas. The neighboring community of St. Gabriel had successfully incorporated in 1993 and had included industrial areas in their municipality. They had succeeded by keeping the campaign quiet until all the pieces were in place. In contrast, the Geismar/ Dutchtown incorporation campaign was very public from the start, and thus drew a quick challenge from the petrochemical plants to the Geismar committee. The plants' obtained a court injunction on the inclusion of industrial areas within municipalities. In November, 1995, the 21st Circuit Court ruled against the Geismar committee, declaring that new municipalities cannot include industrial facilities. The court ruling was enabled by passage of a bill in the 1995 Louisiana legislative session. The bill, blocked as a separate measure but passed as a rider on an unrelated bill, outlawed incorporation of industrial areas in new municipalities. The Labor-Neighbor Project and the 17 Members Committee had lobbied intensively to stop the bill and the rider, but pressure from the Louisiana Chemical Association ensured the measure's passage (Fontenot, November 17, 1997; Nicolai, interview, November 30, 1995).

Stopping Shintech

Perhaps one of the Labor-Neighbor Project's most significant and high-profile campaigns was its participation in a broad-based effort to stop the siting of a polyvinyl chloride (PVC) production facility owned by the Japanese conglomerate Shintech in a low-income, largely African-American community of Convent. Located on the Mississippi River in St. James Parish, Convent was already home to eight other petrochemical facilities. Labor-Neighbor was integral to the creation of St. James Citizens for Jobs and the Environment, working together with the Tulane Environmental Law Clinic to help organize the group in 1996. The local group was the first to come out against Shintech, and quickly several of its leaders become prominent spokespeople in the struggle. The struggle became known nationally as an environmental justice litmus test for application of civil rights protections in the siting of a polluting facility in a low-income community of color. Greenpeace joined the struggle and helped raise its profile nationally. Labor-Neighbor brought to the campaign a mass-based solidarity of its coalition partners throughout Ascension Parish and neighboring parishes. The presence of this base of leaders and activists proved invaluable in public meetings.

While OCAW leaders were firmly supportive of the Labor-Neighbor's involvement in the Shintech struggle, some of the members were nervous about the union taking an active role against Shintech. A BASF plant manager strongly urged an OCAW leader to make the union back off in the Shintech case. The OCAW leader responded to the BASF manager:

> My answer to the company was, "You know, y'all caught us off guard. It's like in the 1980s our building burned down on us and we didn't have any insurance. So we've spent 10 years to rebuild it, and now that we've got it, we're sure not going to get rid of the insurance on it." For the union part of it, that's how I look at it. Labor-Neighbor poses a threat to the company and

they don't know in reality what we can do against them. (Robinson, interview, March 4, 1998)

The plant manager then replied that the Shintech battle was disrupting DEQ's permitting process, thereby slowing down BASF from getting expansion permits. The union stood firm behind the Labor-Neighbor Project's involvement in the Shintech campaign.

The Tulane Environmental Law Clinic's involvement in the anti-Shintech campaign, lending legal support to citizens of Convent, in part by invoking civil rights statutes that protect individuals and communities from harmful economic activity, drew the wrath of Governor Mike Foster, who was a strong supporter of the Shintech PVC facility. The governor waged a public relations campaign to take away TELC's funding, characterizing TELC and the anti-Shintech activists as extremists and outsiders. The governor's forces argued that TELC should not receive state funding to organize communities against industrial development. Gov. Foster successfully challenged TELC's ability to wage local fights by going to the state level to restrict its funding. TELC, meanwhile, applied its best energies, including the full attention of its director Robert Kuehn, to stopping the facility. TELC and LEAN enlisted an LSU engineer to examine the Department of Environment Quality's air permit to Shintech and found the permit seriously flawed. This prompted the U.S. EPA to audit DEQ and the permit process. In September, 1998, Shintech abandoned its efforts to site the PVC facility in Convent, shifting its sights 20 miles up the Mississippi River to Port Hudson, and ultimately Donaldsonville, across the river from Baton Rouge.

Louisiana Communities United

The Labor-Neighbor Project expanded its congregation-based organizing into four parishes in 1996 and 1997. In November, 1997, the project held the founding convention of Louisiana Communities United, a regional umbrella organization representing twenty-five churches, community associations, and unions primarily in four adjacent parishes—Ascension, Iberville, St. James, and St. John the Baptist. Nearly all the groups were church-based or community organizations focused on several issues. The only union involvement was from OCAW 4-620 and the longshoremen's union. The longshoremen, however, representing barge and tanker workers and loading dock personnel on the Mississippi River, were only marginally involved because "it may not be in their self-interest" (Holt, personal communication, November 21, 1998). LCU pledged solidarity for all its member organizations in their various struggles, including stopping the discharge of sewage into wetland areas and promoting municipal funding for youth after-school programs.

LCU annual conventions drew around 200 people each year and were an important step in defining the organization and its mission. At the 1998 convention union participation was small (only six OCAW participants), yet OCAW's participation was critical. Retired OCAW International regional representative Ernie Rousselle provided appropriate discipline in moderating the convention and improving the delegate-voting procedure at a steering committee meeting the evening before. His involvement demonstrated how union leaders can bring democratic discipline to such a coalition meeting, particularly to the running of the meeting and the process of making motions and voting. The 1998 convention also reflected an even racial balance among the speakers, those presenting issues, and within the steering committee. The meeting was grounded in local religious culture, as gospel music and prayer helped guide the meeting. An inspiring keynote address by state representative Kip Holden of Baton Rouge had a strong religious cadence with a message of environmental justice, unity, and hard work, while serving to validate the accomplishments of LCU's coalition organizing:

> Louisiana Communities United is not a one-dimensional organization. This organization is on the cutting edge of making the quality of life better for all people throughout our state. To place this in perspective, we must understand what we are up against. When we look at our young people, one in two lives in poverty, one in two grows up without a father, one in two teens is out of work. We come at a time that a large number of children are dying from abuse and neglect. We come at a time that many of the children in our state have no health insurance. We come at a time when many babies are dying before their first birthday. We come at a time when pollution is still an enemy. Industry continues its push to locate in poor minority communities. Big corporations are allowed to name their price for locating in our communities. Public officials and organizations are willing to deal themselves in and keep the citizens out. We come at a critical time, a time when our children need health care, a time when our school systems are overpacked, a time when poverty is at an all-time high. We come with a national backdrop of corporate welfare in our state, a state that continues to give away billions of dollars to corporations that don't provide any jobs for our citizens. (Holden, November 21, 1998)

Holden's comments argue for the promise of a mass-based organization like LCU to mount a progressive campaign for social justice, in part by directly demanding corporate and government accountability.

Coalition leaders had numerous supportive comments about the creation of LCU. Addressing the LCU convention in 1997, Russ Bourgeois, one of OCAW's primary leaders in LCU, and a union leader at Vulcan Materials whose father had been a union activist at BASF during the lockout, stated, "This is a great day. We at OCAW realized we had neglected the community. Our involvement in the Labor-Neighbor Project and Louisiana Communities United is our gift to the community" (Bourgeois, address at LCU convention, November 15, 1997).

William Fontenot, a Labor-Neighbor Project board member, commented after the convention:

The Geismar, Louisiana, petrochemical complex.
Photograph by Thomas Estabrook.

Coco Road in Geismar, Louisiana, less than one-half mile from the
Geismar petrochemical complex. Photograph by Thomas Estabrook.

Press conference of Geismar/Dutchtown Residents for Clean Water and Air, 1992. Photograph by Thomas Estabrook.

Meeting of Geismar/Dutchtown Residents for Clean Water and Air, at Geismar, Louisiana, Volunteer Fire Department, 1992. Photograph by Thomas Estabrook.

Press conference to inaugurate a 24-hour air monitoring state in Geismar, Louisiana, 1993. Leaders of Geismar/Dutchtown Residents for Clean Water and Air and representatives from the Louisiana Department of Environmental Quality are present. Photograph by Jenny Bauer used with her permission.

> Louisiana Communities United is an incredible extension of [the Louisiana Environmental Action Network], but in a different way. For the first time, the racial and economic barriers in the citizens community are dropping. The Labor-Neighbor Project, because of where it originated, is one of the most exciting projects in the country. LCU, together with other networks such as LEAN and the Mississippi River Basin Alliance, mean that there is more and more mutual support, with member groups attending each other's hearings. This means there is a larger citizens community, with less isolation. (Fontenot, interview, November 18, 1998)

Albertha Hasten, a leader in LCU from Ascension Parish, commented on the importance of unions and community leaders working together in LCU:

> In our community we've got really bad problems: drugs, alcohol, lack of good housing. And there is no union local to protect people in the plants. At LCU we've got to take on these issues. Zoning is the most difficult, long-term issue. Union people have the money and the organizing experience to take on these problems. Grassroots community people don't have the money or the organizing experience, but we want action. Together this adds up to razzmatazz, which is what LCU is all about. (Hasten, interview, November 16, 1997)

Amos Favorite, veteran environmental activist from Geismar, speaking out against the siting of a Supplemental Fuels Inc. hazardous waste processing facility in nearby St. Gabriel, 1994. Neighbors Assisting Neighbors, with the organizing assistance of the Louisiana Coalition for Tax Justice and the Labor-Neighbor Project, halted construction of the facility. Photograph by Dan Nicolai used with permission.

Irma Rixner, a community leader from Gonzales in Ascension Parish and Labor-Neighbor Project board member, weighed in similarly on the important skills that OCAW and community bring to LCU:

> Louisiana Communities United is about unions and community. The union is organized and gives the grassroots a base. It's a good partnership. They want to see the people of the community come together. They're serious, by giving up their money and know-how and giving us direction. This helps the community come together in numbers. We need to develop solidarity like unions. When public officials and companies see that we stand together, there's no more divide and conquer. (Rixner, interview, November 17, 1997)

Welma Jackson, a minister from Donaldsonville in Ascension Parish and an LCU leader, commented on what motivated him to work with Labor-Neighbor in building LCU.

> I've been in this community about 38 years when Dan [Nicolai, Labor-Neighbor director] met with me. I'd seen a lot of people come in and say they

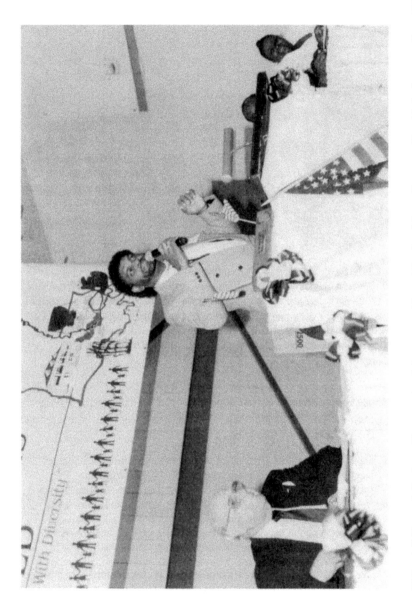

Reverend Wendell Normal, Sr. from Reserve, Louisiana, speaking at the Louisiana Communities United convention, 1997, Gonzales, Louisiana. Photograph by Jenny Bauer used with her permission.

Master-of-Ceremonies Ernie Rouselle, of OCAW, bestowing an award on Reverend Wilbur Green at the LCU Convention, 1997, Gonzales, Louisiana. Photograph by Jenny Bauer used with her permission.

Pat Melançon, a leader of St. James Parish Citizens for Jobs and the Environment, addressing the LCU Convention, 1997. Melançon helped lead the successful fight to stop the siting of a Shintech plastics production facility in Convent, Louisiana.
Photograph by Jenny Bauer used with her permission.

wanted to help and they had their own personal goals. I told Dan that was one of the things he would have to really overcome, because so many people came in, and once they got what they wanted, they were gone. And the people remember that. That's one of the things that started changing things. The other reason I became interested in working with Labor-Neighbor is because Dan didn't just come in and start dealing with the same old group of people who had benefited off of people for years. There are a lot of people who use the race issue just for them to live off of others. They're really not interested in helping anybody. There are a lot of people who use the problems of illiteracy and poverty just for their own benefits. They scream and holler about certain things, but they're really not interested in people. Dan and myself and everyone else, if we planned to do anything in this community, we had to overcome those things. (Jackson, interview, November 17, 1997)

Rev. Jackson's comments point to the importance of Labor-Neighbor's organizing skill in seeking out and developing a new pool of leaders who emerged out of a long process of one-on-one conversations with ministers, lay leaders, and community activists. Labor-Neighbor's organizers, beginning with its director, Dan Nicolai, worked with respected congregation leaders like Rev. Jackson to find a way to build a mass-based coalition that represented a diversity of interests, yet with the capacity to find common interests on which to conduct community campaigns.

The Labor-Neighbor Project's expansion into the creation of LCU brought both benefits and responsibilities to OCAW and the project. The creation of LCU gave OCAW additional leverage in workplace demands at Vulcan Materials and BASF. At Vulcan Materials, for instance, the union's reputation as part of an expanding community coalition helped bolster its health and safety demands of management. Duke King, OCAW chair at Vulcan, stated, "We wrote a letter to Vulcan management to fix some hazardous situations. They did 50 percent of what we asked. We have the confidence of the community. This strengthens our hand at work on wages and working conditions" (King, interview, November 17, 1997).

Similarly, William Robinson, OCAW chair at BASF, stated,

> The project has made BASF make sure they report everything, because it all needs to get reported. It used to be nothing was reported when it happened. I credit the project for being a large part of the reporting and the record-keeping and keeping the company from rubber-stamping everything. They know they have to meet the rules. We pretty well keep a close eye on them from the inside, so they pretty well stay in line. Surprise inspections haven't caught them doing anything but minor stuff. (Robinson, interview, March 4, 1998)

At the same time, Labor-Neighbor assumed new leadership responsibilities with LCU, which translated to offering guidance, but from behind the scenes. As Duke King noted,

We don't want to be big brother to the community organizations. LCU has to pick out its own problems. The ministers have to find outside funding. Our role is to be an outside entity to keep them on track. We want the churches and the ministers to be in there leading on finding solutions. (King, interview, November 17, 1997)

An Expanded Role as Labor-Community Watchdog

Despite the many accomplishments of the Labor-Neighbor Project and its environmental allies during the 1990s, Louisiana consistently ranked among the worst in the country on economic and environmental indicators. At the same time, the petrochemical industry expanded its production while maintaining high overall toxic releases. While the petrochemical industry expanded its production capacity and physical plant in the Baton Rouge-New Orleans petrochemical corridor during the 1990s, the industry was not a steady source of new jobs. The Louisiana state government continued to lavish industry with roughly $300 million in industrial tax exemptions each year (Louisiana Environmental Action Network, 2002), while doing little to diversify economic development or slow pollution. The Labor-Neighbor Project, therefore, had abundant political opportunities for labor-community organizing throughout the 1990s.

BASF expanded its area at its Geismar facility by one-third (Schneider, interview, March 3, 1998). Vulcan materials continued its production of "tail-end" products, slated for phase-out, such as 1,1,1 trichloroethane and carbon tetra-chloride (King, interview, October 15, 2002). Indeed, chlorine-based production, primarily as feedstock for plastics continued to grow in Louisiana, despite continued environmental releases and mounting international pressures to shift toward nonchlorine-based production. Industry successfully resisted efforts by LEAN and allied groups, including People First, a group promoting sustainable production, to force the state to withdraw the $350 million annual industrial property tax breaks.

With the return of Edwin Edwards as governor in 1992, the state reassumed its role as pro-big business, after the reform-oriented administration of Buddy Roemer. The Louisiana Department of Environmental Quality took a more pro-business approach during the administrations of Edwin Edwards and Mike Foster. The agency's directors presided over an agency that was far less responsive to citizen grievances and far more supportive of issuing industry operating permits than the reform agency of Paul Templet under previous governor Roemer. DEQ's policy was "do whatever the governor tells you, and whatever industry directs through the governor. That's always been the policy, even a little bit when Paul Templet was here" (Fontenot, interview, October 12, 2002).

Yet, citizen mobilization brought significant pressure to bear on DEQ, slowing the agency's customary rubber-stamping of industrial permits. The Shintech battle of 1997-98 led to an intense auditing of DEQ by the U.S. EPA inspector general and the Louisiana legislative auditor's office. This shifted DEQ's attention largely to the Shintech matter, diverting resources from the permitting and enforcement process for other facilities. The EPA and Louisiana state audits helped to expose the agency's proindustry stance—DEQ chief Dale Givens was a vocal proponent of Shintech—and its failure to fulfill its role of protecting public and environmental health. Citizen mobilization and federal and state audits combined to pressure the agency to change, which it sought to do with a restructuring into two functional divisions, permitting and enforcement; it remained unclear, however, as to whether this was an improvement over the previous DEQ structure, based on media: air, water, and hazardous waste. In 2002, a coalition of eight Louisiana environmental organizations, frustrated by DEQ's slowness to change, called on the U.S. EPA to assume primary control over environmental permitting and enforcement in Louisiana (*Baton Rouge Advocate*, April 9, 2002). Thus the Shintech battle helped generate momentum for reform at the agency, just as citizen mobilization in the 1980s—of which OCAW, LEAN, and their allies were a part—brought about reform at DEQ.

That DEQ failed in its mission of environmental protection is not surprising in a state rife with corruption at many levels. The 1990s were no different. From the governor to the parish president to state agency directors, official corruption contributed to a tapestry of unaccountability of government. Former governor Edwards was convicted of extortion for assisting the gambling industry and sentenced to five years in prison. At another level, the St. James Parish council president had served two prison sentences for extortion of two chemical companies. In the Shintech case, state government blatantly supported construction of the plastics factory, without regard for public health and social impacts or for an assessment of economic alternatives. Governor Mike Foster, the DEQ chief and a host of other public officials promoted the facility. As to why there was not a significant public outcry about such cases, Willie Fontenot, the state attorney general's environmental liaison and Labor-Neighbor Project board member, commented, "People are too used to being beaten down by an impenetrable, corrupt system" (Fontenot, interview, March 3, 1998).

Hard Times for the Louisiana Labor-Neighbor Project

After a decade of impressive expansion, Labor-Neighbor stumbled in 2001. With the departure of its director of eight years, Dan Nicolai, the directorship changed hands twice within a year. At the same time, Stan Holt, the project's organizing advisor since 1990, based in Vermont, discontinued his contract with Labor-Neighbor and no replacement was found. The successor to Nicolai sought to maintain the Labor-Neighbor agenda, despite operating increasingly without supervision, but resigned from the position within a year, moving out of the state. The second new director, starting in 2001, brought no experience in community organizing or with unions. Soon after the second new director began, a rift developed between her and the Louisiana Communities United leadership. Communication deteriorated between the Labor-Neighbor staff and LCU. The rift quickly led to the decision by several major foundation funders of Labor-Neighbor not to renew funding for the project or LCU. Labor-Neighbor, in effect, had "become unraveled." (Fontenot, interview, October 12, 2002). By 2002, the Labor-Neighbor board had all but ceased to meet.

The reasons for the unraveling can be attributed to several factors, among them a poor staffing decision, the departure of the organizing advisor, a lack of capacity building, and overextending the project's organizing resources. Labor-Neighbor board president Duke King gave his assessment of the factors of the project's decline.

> I think it was a combination of things. First, we really made a bad decision on a director after we lost Lynette [successor to Dan Nicolai]. Second, there was a power struggle among some of the groups, which tore the structure down. The money got harder to get, and we didn't have the expertise writing the grants. Also, we have had such a big changeover in the union, especially in the group at BASF. We've got only 30 percent of the people out there now that were involved in the lockout. There are so many people retiring at that age. So while it's still not difficult getting the okay from the members for our monetary support, we're not getting a lot of people support out of our union. (King, interview, October 15, 2002)

Thus, an unfortunate string of events had occurred, beginning with the selection of the interim director. The successor had no organizing experience and was not properly mentored, because the long-time mentor, Stan Holt, had left the project in 2001 as well. Communication broke down between the staff, the Labor-Neighbor board and the Louisiana Communities United leadership. Moreover, the union's attention was diverted from rescuing Labor-Neighbor by its own contract negotiations for the 550 union members at BASF in Geismar. When communications broke down, "we didn't have the expertise to put out the fire" (King, interview, October 15, 2002).

From the perspective of community leaders in Louisiana Communities United, the poor choice of director was a terrible blow to their organizing. Albertha Hasten, LCU president, stated,

> When things were clicking, we were able to be on the board and click with the union people, sit side-by-side with them. We were communicating, and we had people there who were communicating with us, and showed respect and responsibility, and being resourceful and making us feel like we were out here putting something back into the community, and not just being used. A lot of it came down to Dan [the director]. He listened to people and communicated with people and then made you communicate with people. To him it wasn't no 8 to 5 job, it was more. It was showing concern and commitment, it was showing that your hearts had to be changed, no matter what color you were, no matter how rich you were. When hearts change, then people change. And

we got that flowing in there. And every day it was a challenge, and I was grateful for it. But when it got to be only 8 to 4 with the new director, then it changed. It was just a job; it wasn't showing concern or commitment. Hearts got hardened. (Hasten, interview, October 21, 2002)

Clearly, having the right organizing staff was critical to the project's success. Managing the project was, even with the most skilled organizer, a difficult endeavor. Former Labor-Neighbor director Dan Nicolai observed that the project had grown too fast and expanded too far for Nicolai to coordinate effectively. "I had too many balls in the air," said Nicolai (Nicolai, interview, October 28, 2002). While it was a difficult challenge for Nicolai, the coordinator of eight years, to manage, it was a daunting task for the subsequent directors to maintain the project's high level of success.

Moreover, the poor staffing decision interrupted the ongoing process of capacity building of coalition leadership. The organization's ability to face the communication and staffing problems was limited because it had not yet developed to a point at which it could work collectively to resolve such issues. Labor-Neighbor board president Duke King remarked,

You've got to have everybody working on solving the problem. Some of the board members just didn't want to work on solving the problem. Maybe we did expand out a little too far, grew a bit too fast. In losing two directors, we lost control of communications between all them groups in LCU. I guess we didn't provide the adequate amount of leadership to do that. We should have spent more time, and brought the leaders in and given them more training as a group. They all got some type of training individually in national group conferences, but they really hadn't had the training to be objective leaders of an organization that big and diversified. (King, interview, October 15, 2002)

One of the critical communication problems had to do with the project's budget. Much confusion resulted from the lack of clear instructions to LCU's member organizations as to what grant funding was supposed to be spent for. "There was a lot of confusion that was created by lack of attention to detail in the financial relationship between Labor-Neighbor and Louisiana Communities United" (Fontenot, interview, October 12, 2002). This was a problem that preexisted the change in directors but was worsened by the new director's lack of experience and the declining confidence in her abilities.

Lack of capacity building also extended to union members. Labor-Neighbor had suffered from a lack of abundant union member participation since its beginning in the early 1990s. Labor-Neighbor board members recognized this. Willie Fontenot, who was an early bridge builder on the Project, stated,

While the Labor-Neighbor Project was functioning, it did some incredibly wonderful things. It filled a little niche that hadn't existed anywhere else. But you have to do a lot of nurturing for projects like this. You've got to have real training and support for the staff, director, and board members. The board members from the union were not involved enough with the organization. They let the director do his or her own thing. They didn't push to build the capacity of the union board members of the project, for being involved in the project itself. When the annual LCU meeting took place, labor was hardly there, only a handful. There should have been thirty members from the local. So it never was truly the *Labor*-Neighbor Project. It was the *project*. But for different reasons it never quite came together that way. Maybe the union guys didn't see the need to do it; they didn't want to put the time into it; they wanted to do other things. They had lives. They had been through the struggle of the lockout. They didn't need any more struggle. (Fontenot, interview, October 12, 2002)

Developing union members' capacity to recognize the political importance of the project and to take an active leadership role in it was seen as, at best, a long-term goal toward which the project did not yet have resources to work. As PACE (formerly OCAW) Local 4-620 president and Labor-Neighbor board president Duke King stated,

One thing that we let fall by the wayside was cultivating more interest among union people and getting more activity from the union people. But if we got the right person to come in as director, and make that part of their priority, say spend 25 percent of their time doing it, I think with a little support, some of the union people would do it, especially some of these younger people. Because we had all these people that were involved in the lockout, and they were educated to the things we were doing, and they could see the good of having organizations like that functioning, while we were negotiating with these companies, but then we lost a lot of these people. (King, interview, October 15, 2002)

Former Project board member Willie Fontenot similarly stated, "What came out of the lockout, in terms of challenging industrial permits and industry's actions has sort of been lost on the new members" (Fontenot, interview, October 12, 2002).

Younger union members who were quite engaged in union leadership positions did not have the militancy born of a crisis situation, like the lockout. The lack of such militancy meant that it was difficult to motivate union members to get involved in Labor-Neighbor activities. Former project director Dan Nicolai, stated,

Union members are not going to get involved in coalition organizing unless there is a sense of urgency. Union members aren't going to show up to another meeting like church members would. Church members are used to going to various types of meetings. Union members are not. (Nicolai, interview, October 28, 2002)

Union members could be mobilized by union organizing campaigns, which could also inspire participation by community leaders if the local community were active in the coalition. Yet it is unreasonable to expect union rank and filers and leaders to turn out for various community campaigns without being mobilized by a sense of urgency. However, building a sense of urgency in union leaders about the political importance of the Labor-Neighbor Project faced a potentially resistant attitude of the project as an insurance policy for the union against any future aggression by corporations. "Union leaders have had the attitude of the Labor-Neighbor Project as an insurance policy. That was an inherent weakness in the structure of the project" (Fontenot, interview, October 12, 2002). Fontenot's concern speaks to a tendency by some union leaders to view the project as a defensive measure rather than as a proactive political project.

Several coalition leaders were still hopeful that the project could be revitalized by a skilled organizer who could meet the project's many challenges. Yet these challenges would be daunting. William Fontenot stated, "With a different person in there it could still be very vibrant, but it takes somebody to understand how to work with the union and how to work with the community. Good luck" (Fontenot, interview, October 12, 2002).

Political Achievements

Despite the Labor-Neighbor Project's recent trials, over a ten-year period the organization succeeded in building substantial popular power by mobilizing a base. Through this mobilization, they were able to win numerous concessions from industry and the state: a twenty-four-hour air monitor; a ban on hazardous chemicals traffic; a rural residential water supply system; stopping construction of a large airport; a parish ordinance on local hiring; a court ruling on unconstitutionality of industrial areas; stopping the discharge of sewage into wetland areas; helping to stop a hazardous waste recycling facility; helping to stop a PVC production facility. Moreover, the Labor-Neighbor Project brought tangible political benefits to OCAW. Labor-Neighbor served as an effective "insurance policy" against future aggression by the corporations against the union. The project also served to improve the union's position in challenging BASF and Vulcan to operate more safely, thereby leading to safer operations and maintenance at the two facilities. Thus, the Labor-Neighbor Project won tangible increased power for both labor and community. It raised the union's role in local politics, and consolidated community forces to win an unprecedented number of concessions from the authorities, as Table 1 illustrates. The success of these projects was due in no small way to the development of new levels of awareness on the part of the union and community.

Furthermore, the Labor-Neighbor Project outlived the organizing spirit of the National Toxics Campaign and its would-be successor, the Jobs and Environment Campaign. Labor-Neighbor was one of the most successful field projects ever sponsored by NTC. Because it had the untiring support of a labor union and had the unique grassroots labor-community relationship-building that foundations like to fund, it was destined to live on during a period of downsizing among grassroots environmental organizations.

Table 1. Power Created by Local Interest Associations
(Affiliated with Louisiana Labor-Neighbor Project and
Louisiana Coalition for Tax Justice)

Alinsky-Style organization	Maximum # of people mobilized	Largest concession from authorities
Ascension Parish Residents Against Toxic Pollution	100	Forced state to implement law restricting land disposal of some hazardous wastes.
Geismar/Dutchtown Residents for Clean Water and Air (GDR)	175	Formation of municipal water system and water board.
Neighbors for Quality Life	300	Stopped siting of international airport in Ascension Parish.
GDR; Concerned Citizens of Gonzales; Darrow/Hillaryville Concerned Citizens	100	Ascension Parish ordinance requiring company and subcontractor reporting on hiring, toxic hazards.
East Iberville AWARE	100	Iberville Parish ordinance on local hiring; Louisiana Supreme Court ruling of tax-exempt industrial areas as unconstitutional.
Neighbors Assisting Neighbors	400	Stopped siting of hazardous waste processing facility.
Louisiana Communities United	200	Stopped siting of a plastics (PVC) production facility.

OBSTACLES TO COALITION-BUILDING

Coalitions are complex organizations. In the course of its existence, the Louisiana Labor-Neighbor Project faced numerous obstacles to its ability to function and thrive as a coalition of community and labor organizations. The project confronted two main sets of obstacles: organizational and political-economic.

Organizational Obstacles

The project faced numerous problems in deploying its organizational resources. Despite all its successes in growing and expanding throughout the 1990s, the organization was ultimately up-ended by its inability to use its resources, such as skills and relationships, effectively. Perhaps its most serious challenge was that of capacity building. While the project had the structure for developing experienced leadership in its board and the steering committee of Louisiana Communities United, it was unable to continuously train the leaders on the essentials of coalitions and nonprofit organizations. Community and union leaders needed to be trained on nonprofit financial responsibilities and board member leadership responsibilities. Such training was conducted in the early stages of Labor-Neighbor, but did not become a continuous process. Once the organization expanded and gave rise to the Louisiana Communities United, less and less training on leadership and financial responsibilities in a coalition was provided. Thus, the organization was not well-enough prepared to deal with grant monies designated for Louisiana Communities United, and LCU's relationship to its fiscal agent, the Labor-Neighbor Project. The board was unable to navigate the tensions arising over money.

Moreover, insufficient capacity building was done within PACE/OCAW Local 4-620 with regard to the political importance of the Labor-Neighbor Project. From the early 1990s onward, union participation in project campaigns was limited to a handful of leaders. Capacity building was difficult to do while simultaneously organizing new leaders in the community and taking on new campaigns. This points to the difficulty within the organization to "keep many balls in the air at once." Organizational resources were limited. Focusing on community issues, including developing community leadership, was a full-time job in itself for the project coordinator. Taking on the additional task of building union capacity within the coalition would require additional resources—a skilled organizer—that the organization did not have after 2000. Although building union capacity was recognized as an important issue, it was not a high priority.

Related to the lack of resources given to building union capacity within the project was the larger difficulty of building a sense of union urgency into the project's organizing agenda. During the first several years after the lockout, union leaders were clear about the importance of continuing the Labor-Neighbor Project. Having the project was regarded as a way of returning the favor of solidarity to the community, while providing the union with a level of protection against possible future corporate aggression as well as the expertise to promote improved environmental, health, and safety practices at Geismar area companies. What was missing, though, during much of the 1990s, was a sense among union members that the Labor-Neighbor Project was critical to the union's overall power and to promoting a progressive political agenda for working people in the region. Mobilizing union members for activities other than contract negotiations is exceedingly difficult. The union local's militancy from the lockout clearly waned throughout the 1990s, particularly as lockout veterans retired. While the old militancy would resurface at contract-negotiation time, as it did in 2002, this was directed largely at obtaining a good contract.

The project also proved itself unable to use its organizational capacity to deal with personnel changes. A change in directorship is clearly a vulnerable time for a nonprofit organization. The project was unable to tap its networking capacity to find a skilled replacement for a departing director in 2001. The seasoned advice and networking resources of the project's organizing advisor could have greatly assisted in this process, but the advisor was no longer in an effective mentoring position at that critical moment. Thus, it was up to the board to make the choice on its own, and it lacked the capacity to recruit for at least an interim coordinator replacement. With the departure of the organizing advisor, the project no longer had immediate access to outside networks and organizations with organizing experience. Labor-Neighbor, from its inception, had close links to outside organizations and networks, which lent critical skills and financial resources to the project. Once those links had withered through the departure of director Dan Nicolai and the organizing advisor, however, the board was deprived of vital resources in maintaining the project's organizing capacity. Labor-Neighbor was never just a local project, but rather was closely linked with national resources. Its ultimate survival might be found in resurrecting such national links.

The Labor Neighbor Project's trials after 2001 can be better understood when put in the context of national organizational changes. The project's staffing changes in 2000 and 2001 came at a moment when OCAW International was in flux. OCAW International's merger, in 1999, with the International Paper Workers Union (IPWU) to form PACE arguably may have temporarily weakened the international union's ability to provide critical resources—such as assistance in finding a competent staff director in 2000 and 2001—for a community project in need. More importantly, on the environmental side, the absence of a national environmental partner in the Labor-Neighbor Project, such as a National Toxics Campaign, meant that there was no organization with community organizing experience to assist Labor-Neighbor in finding a replacement for the director or the organizing supervisor. Thus, the shifting national landscapes for unions and environmental networks must be considered a factor in the Labor-Neighbor Project's staffing difficulties.

Political Economic Obstacles

The dominance of political elites, with its roots in Louisiana's Bourbon past, has made the creation of progressive coalitions difficult. Louisiana is plagued by severe injustices on which movement organizations have organized but made little headway: massive corporate welfare; huge disparities in wealth and economic development; and widespread lack of environmental enforcement. The Louisiana Coalition for Tax Justice, sister organization of the Labor-Neighbor Project, took on such issues, succeeded for several years, but ultimately faded, for lack of organizing skill and the ability to secure resources.

Louisiana culture, as dominated by political elites, has militated against the sense of "raising all boats" as being a good idea among the middle and upper classes. The Labor-Neighbor Project and the Louisiana Coalition for Tax Justice were largely working-class coalitions that could not tap into a base of support among the middle class, which could make such projects politically much stronger. Rather than being upset and motivated enough about blatant inequality, corporate welfare, and other injustices to do something about it, the tendency has been for the middle class to be demoralized by a corrupt political system. This makes multiclass progressive alliances such as living-wage campaigns and Justice for Janitors, which have succeeded in other states, less likely to happen in Louisiana. Moreover, the overall weakness of unions in Louisiana, owing to right-to-work legal conditions, has made their participation in progressive alliances also less likely.

Fear of Job Loss

Job blackmail is a powerful tool that can instill a strong enough fear in workers to prevent them from considering working in coalition with the community. Even union workers may give in to company threats that jobs will be lost if the company is forced to invest in environmental protection measures. Even for organized labor under contract, management may threaten job loss, overtly or subtly, due to the high cost of environmental compliance. In 1991, at Vulcan Materials in Geismar, management attempted to intimidate OCAW members with job loss by distributing a copy of the company budget which explained that the company could not invest in expanding production and jobs if it were forced to keep investing in rapid developments in environmental compliance. Duke King, OCAW Local 4-620 chair at Vulcan, said,

> The company says the bigger dollars they have to spend [on environmental protection], the more impact it has on the jobs and reinvesting. Whether it be directly related to people losing jobs, layoffs or the reduction in benefits and pay, it's equally threatening. (King, interview, November 20, 1991)

However, OCAW members at Vulcan, seasoned by the BASF lockout and the emergent labor-environmental coalition, responded generally in a pro-environment way to the company's allusions to the elimination of jobs. According to Duke King,

> Union members are pretty educated. They see that unless the company complies with environmental regulations, the company will be shut down. Therefore, workers believe they are really saving their jobs by pushing the company to comply. (King, interview, November 20, 1991)

This contrasts starkly with the union workers at American Cyanamid, in Westwego, near New Orleans, who did not have the benefit of the immediate BASF lockout experience to educate them on environmental issues. In 1990 at

American Cyanamid, OCAW members refused to work closely with the community and the Tulane Environmental Law Clinic to stop the company from being granted an exemption to operate its toxic waste injection wells. The company told OCAW that the company would have to shut down the plant if forced to continue testing its waste injection wells for contamination and to suspend deep-well injection. Cyanamid argued that following environmental orders was bad for their competitiveness and, moreover, that workers would have to sacrifice for the company to remain competitive. Ernie Rouselle, OCAW International representative said,

> The union membership buys that line 100 percent because there is still the "why would the company lie to us" attitude among our people. The members believe the company has the authority to do it and will do it, whether that's a fact or not. (Rousselle, interview, August 2, 1991)

The union leadership chose to support management's position, after management had successfully convinced the rank-and-file that jobs were in jeopardy. The Cyanamid workers did not act upon the experience of the locked-out OCAW members at BASF. "It's not in their experience," said Rousselle (Rousselle, interview, August 2, 1991; Evans, interview, March 7, 1991).

Even for the OCAW members at Vulcan, job loss was a real prospect, given the mandated phase-out in production of two of the company's principal products, both ozone-depleting chemicals. This put the Labor-Neighbor Project in the precarious position of supporting the phase-out in production, while at the same time trying to protect the union members' jobs at Vulcan. "The project is walking a tightrope," said Duke King. "How do you secure our jobs when the phase-out of production of our chemicals is imminent or possible?" (King, interview, November 20, 1991). In response to OCAW International's concerns, King spoke at a meeting of the International Joint Commission—which supervises environmental policy in the Great Lakes region—in 1993 in support of the union's proposal that a "just transition" be implemented.

It is difficult to translate the success of the OCAW campaign against BASF to workers in other situations in which job fear is very strong. Workers are caught in a dilemma in which economic stress is often necessary to force workers to act, yet those same hardships can prompt a fear that prevents them from challenging company blackmail. OCAW International Representative Rousselle said,

> Unless you put an economic burden on our people, they don't rationalize the issue. And that's the same economic burden that the company is holding over their head with the environmental issue. The company exploits this to the maximum. (Rousselle, interview, August 2, 1991)

It is difficult to communicate the experience of the job fear dilemma to those not directly involved. The transformative effect of fighting a huge corporation and winning comes mainly to those who experienced it immediately, not to those who admired the union's survival from a distance. Short of replicating the economic hardships of a company lockout, building a local organization involving workers and community members can be one way of addressing the job fear and the isolation workers feel. Without an adequate organizing effort, real job fear can run unchecked. Most workers have been doing the same job all their working lives and justifiably fear that they could find no other comparable job. Their fears are confirmed by Louisiana's narrow economic base, which makes it difficult to find comparable work elsewhere (Rousselle, interview, August 2, 1991; Summers, interview, April 25, 1991).

Some community residents who were nonunion workers at other, largely non-union, petrochemical plants did get involved in Labor-Neighbor Project campaigns, but they did so as community residents, not as workers at industrial facilities. Two such workers even took active roles, though not as chief spokespeople. One worker at Borden Chemical in Geismar, who was also chief of the Geismar volunteer fire department, was an important asset to Geismar Dutchtown Residents for Clean Water and Air. Not only did he bring the full support of the fire department to GDR's campaign and provide a space for GDR's meetings at the fire station, he also served on the community's newly created water board. Yet his role in GDR was as community resident, and he expressed several times that he could not take a visible role in demanding anything from Borden Chemical. His position was a difficult one, for while he did have an occasional visible role in requesting that the chemical companies finance a municipal water system, he recognized the necessary limits to his involvement in the group. Another community resident who was a worker at Texaco in Burnside also took a leadership role and served on the water board. Yet, generally, the nonunion workers at petrochemical facilities who did get involved remained behind the scenes.

Job blackmail in nearby St. Gabriel, a predominantly non-union industrial area, took on new, shifting dimensions after the 1986 miscarriage study. OCAW's study of area air pollution, in tandem with local activists' documentation of a high rate of miscarriages, unleashed a ferocious barrage of job blackmail in the St. Gabriel community. Job blackmail effectively isolated local environmentalists and undermined their organizing efforts. A campaign in St. Gabriel in 1992, however, rendered job blackmail less effective. Competent community organizing by the Louisiana Coalition for Tax Justice around the proposed Supplemental Fuels (SFI) hazardous waste recycling facility for a low-income African-American neighborhood in nearby Carville built a strong, vocal multiracial opposition to the facility. The political climate for siting hazardous waste facilities in communities of color was far different in 1992 than in 1986. By 1992, when the SFI struggle began, the environmental justice movement, nationally, had reached such a high profile that state and federal governments were responding with new policies. Companies adjusted their environmental practices to protect their image as good corporate citizens. Moreover, the Louisiana Coalition for Tax Justice and the local organization that it helped found, Neighbors Assisting

Neighbors, used the concept of environmental racism in their organizing and media work. Greater national prominence of environmental racism made it very difficult for SFI, the Louisiana Chemical Association, and Governor Edwards to discredit the citizens' groups.

The struggle against SFI, however, was not a production-facility struggle. It was a waste-treatment struggle. The producers of the waste could readily shift their waste to someplace other than the Carville site. The citizens' struggle, therefore, did not call forth the full force of job blackmail among area plants, as it had after the 1986 miscarriage study. No existing area plants or their production profits were explicitly targeted by local citizens. On the other hand, the struggles by citizens of St. Gabriel and Carville were limited by the complete absence of an active petrochemical workers' union in alliance with the community. The union-community coalition in nearby Geismar demonstrates how the presence of a union working in concert with local citizens' groups can indeed help to buffer job blackmail and other divisive methods coming from nonunion plants, and counteract elite forces, including the chemical industry, leading state officials, and the local political boss.

Relationship-building between the Labor-Neighbor Project and the building trades unions was hindered at first by perceptions on the part of the building trades that joining the community in fighting polluters could threaten potential union construction jobs. Historically, many building trades locals often used environmental issues to try to get jobs for their members (cf. Kazis and Grossman, 1982). But if environmental protection did translate into jobs for them, they were generally reluctant to join any fight against industrial polluters. Such was the case involving the building trades and the Labor-Neighbor Project's fight against Rubicon in Geismar in 1993. The project sought to challenge Rubicon's ten-year industrial exemption because of the air contamination originating from several open waste pits at the company's Geismar facility. Building trades unions refused to support the project on this issue, arguing that they would not challenge the company because it had promised them construction jobs. Yet, once Rubicon denied the jobs to the building trades, one trade union, the pipefitters, became open to collaboration with the Labor-Neighbor Project. Subsequently, the pipefitters joined the project and community groups in demanding a parish ordinance on local hiring. The lesson here was that job fear can cloud workers' ability to identify common interests. Only after the building trades had had their hopes dashed about the promised construction jobs did one of their unions open up to exploring common ground with the Labor-Neighbor Project.

Union Credibility and Corporate Influence on Church Leaders

Ascension Parish industrial facilities never approved of the Labor-Neighbor Project, but were unable to stop it from broadening its base and winning concessions from authorities during the 1990s. Nor were the corporations able to stop OCAW's credibility from growing, as the project expanded across the parish. The growth of the project helped to establish the union as an important force in the parish political landscape. Gone are the days when public perception was of a union solely interested in getting its members' jobs back during the BASF lockout.

As the project built relationships with area churches, however, it had to face renewed skepticism on the part of church leaders, mainly over the OCAW's involvement. While some of this skepticism derived from general popular mistrust of unions, much of it was fostered by the close ties between area petrochemical corporations and some church leaders. For well over a decade, some church ministers in the river parishes had been financially rewarded for being loyal to company management. The St. Gabriel Catholic Church, for instance, was renovated with financing from Ciba-Geigy (Gaudet, interview, October 2, 1991). Area petrochemical facilities have been extremely adept at weakening local opposition by winning over church leaders. Corporate buyouts of African-American communities were greatly facilitated by the companies first winning the support of the ministers, then buying out the black church, thereby severely undermining local opposition to the buyout (Dickerson, interview, November 20, 1991; Kirkland, interview, October 24, 1991). As demonstrated by the case of the St. Gabriel activists and the miscarriage issue, companies have enlisted the support of the church ministers to help isolate community activists who are congregation members.

Despite the reluctance on the part of some church leaders to get involved in a union-sponsored project, enough ministers and lay leaders showed sufficient interest to enable to the creation of a church-based sponsoring committee in 1996. With the creation of Louisiana Communities United in 1997, with representation in four parishes, it became increasingly difficult for industry to weaken the project's organizing. Yet it is not difficult to imagine corporate financing of new community projects as a way to draw supporters away from a church/community/labor coalition.

CONCLUSION

The Louisiana Labor-Neighbor Project grew and thrived during the 1990s, overcoming numerous obstacles to enhance its level of organization, expand its orbit, and engage a broad range of community leaders. It left an important political mark on environmental politics in the river parishes during the decade by building a broad-based environmentalism, which helped to halt the siting of several noxious facilities. More than any other organization in the state, it brought religious organizations into coalition with labor to address environmental and local economic problems.

Labor-Neighbor's sister organization, the Louisiana Coalition for Tax Justice was, for a time, a statewide progressive network promoting reform of an entrenched system of corporate subsidies. Despite the decline of LCTJ, its mission of economic justice and progressive reform remained vital and pertinent.

After the millennium, the Labor-Neighbor Project itself went into rapid decline after an unfortunate staffing decision and insufficient assistance from national networks to help the organization right itself. The organization's hardships demonstrate the fragility of coalition leadership, particularly in a changing national landscape for unions and grassroots environmental networks.

The Labor-Neighbor Project's political achievements during the 1990s illustrate Gramsci's emphasis on intellectual leadership and class capacity in devising effective political strategy, mobilizing multi-scale resources to challenge uneven development, the destructive impacts of the petrochemical industry on environmental health and workers, and the failure of the regulatory state to protect the health and well-being of area residents. In its prime years of the 1990s, the Project's intellectual leadership understood changing political economic conditions and the need for a different set of strategies to build labor-community power and make a political impact in the region. The project's shift to mass-based organizing, with an expanded agenda, and bringing together new coalition partners, including numerous churches, demonstrates the leadership's commitment to building new relationships and new institutions. This commitment to a wide-ranging agenda and new partners culminated in the creation of Louisiana Communities United, a broad-based, multi-class, multi-racial organization that made an impact in four river parishes. Yet the Project's rapid decline after 2001 demonstrates the fragility of labor-community coalitions and the importance of maintaining a rigorous intellectual and moral leadership and class capacity. The next chapter examines the lessons from the Labor-Neighbor Project's history and their relevance for labor-community and labor-environmental coalition building elsewhere.

ENDNOTES

1. OCAWIU President Robert Wages bolstered the international's support for hazardous materials training of workers and community residents around the country, and strengthened its commitment to a Superfund for Workers. Moreover, under Wages' leadership, the international began developing a rigorous union organizing program and launched, under the directorship of former Secretary/Treasurer Tony Mazzocchi, a successful campaign to form a Labor Party, which was founded in 1996. Thus, OCAW's innovative leadership provided important national support and understanding for Local 4-620's union-community initiatives in the 1990s.

2. The petition was based on the 1984 "IT" decision (*Save Our Selves vs. the Louisiana Environmental Control Commission*), in which the Louisiana Supreme Court pronounced that the state constitution required all state agencies and officials to protect the environment. The Tulane Law Clinic contended that the board was ignoring the

environmental impact of its decisions, in that the board had awarded tax exemptions to companies with recurrent environmental violations (Louisiana Coalition for Tax Justice, 1992).

3. Significant opposition to the abuse of the ten-year industrial exemption voiced at the 1973 Constitutional Convention was unable to curb the Board of Commerce and Industry's granting of exemptions. Many convention delegates believed that exemptions were being abused and costing local governments millions of dollars, and, moreover, that even industries who would have located in Louisiana regardless were granted exemptions. Despite these reservations, after the convention the Commerce Board approved requests almost automatically and at an increasingly higher dollar value in the 1970s and 1980s (Louisiana Coalition for Tax Justice, 1992).

4. The ten-year industrial exemption consists of a five-year exemption from property taxes, and renewable for another five years, for the purpose of promoting job creation and investment in new construction or maintenance at industrial facilities, and to make the state competitive with other states.

5. As a project intern and participant observer, the author worked together with this organizer from January to April, 1991, and thus was present at most meetings pertaining to the direction of the project.

6. Vulcan's groundwater remediation problems were further complicated by the tenuous existence of Vulcan's Geismar facility in light of the Montreal Protocol, the international agreement calling on industrialized nations to "sunset" the production of chlorine and several ozone-depleting chemicals. The two primary products produced at the Geismar facility—methyl chloroform and carbon tetrachloride—were slated for phase-out by 2000 in accordance with the protocol. With the phase-out, Vulcan management was concerned that it might have to shut down its Geismar facility entirely. In such an event, any ongoing remediation of groundwater contamination would be put in serious jeopardy, and the Vulcan complex would have to be turned into a Superfund site.

7. In 1994, Ascension Parish shifted from a police jury to a parish council system of government.

8. The National Organizers Alliance held a workshop in 1994 on the subject of the lessons learned from the NTC dissolution. Burke reported on management conflict at NTC before the dissolution (Burke, 1992), and discussed the organization's breakup (Burke, 1993). Kallick commented on the group's breakup and its meaning for grassroots environmentalism and progressive politics in general (Kallick, 1993).

9. A *Baton Rouge Advocate* investigation of the LPTA reported that it had acted as a slush fund for Edwin Edwards (*Baton Rouge Advocate*, August 16, 1993).

CHAPTER 6

Building Winning
Labor-Community Politics

This book is about labor-environmental collective action, seen primarily in a single case study, the Louisiana Labor-Neighbor Project, but situated within a history of labor-environmental initiatives and within a recent social movement landscape of labor and environmentalism. I have traced the development of the Labor-Neighbor Project over its sixteen-year history, as a participant observer and as a student of social movements.

In this chapter I re-examine the case study and the historical assessment of labor and environmentalism and consider what happened to make the Louisiana Labor-Neighbor Project develop, endure, and, recently, decline. Thus, I consider the particular structure and agency at play in the case study as well as in labor-environmental initiatives generally. I seek to draw conclusions about labor-environmental coalition-building in a petrochemical industrial context, but with explicit relevance to other political-economic settings.

The impact of the merger of OCAW into PACE in 1999 upon the work of the Labor-Neighbor Project is beyond the scope of this study. We cannot predict whether the United Steel Workers (PACE merged with the United Steelworkers of America in 2005) will be able to maintain OCAW's work. It is too early to tell, although we are optimistic. Labor-environmental struggles, such as those in Louisiana, are rooted in communities and regions and have a dynamic relatively independent of the particular politics of a national union such as PACE and the United Steel Workers.

This chapter makes the following points. First, the practice of labor-environmental politics is structured by: the spatial character of capitalist politics, in particular the regional character of the petrochemical industry; the regional character of the state, in particular, its relative openness; and the class experience of labor and community. Second, labor-community collaboration is usually pre-cipitated by an economic crisis for labor, which intersects with an environmental crisis for the community. Third, the labor-community agenda moves from narrow (several issues) to broad (many issues) over time, and involves tradeoffs such as the avoidance of issues confrontational to corporations. Fourth, to thrive and endure, labor-community must ultimately build coalition capacity—leadership skills and skills to run a coalition—among its union and community leaders, which includes the capacity to identify new urgent issues to maintain and build the interests of union rank and file and community residents. Fifth, maximizing the use of the coalition's resources, in particular its national organizing resources, is critical to its health and can only be accomplished through experienced leadership. Sixth, local political culture matters and can enable or frustrate multiclass coalition-building. Seventh, creating a progressive, durable coalition depends on capacity to broaden the coalition to include working class and middle class leaders and organizations. Eighth, over the long term labor-environmental coalitions must broaden the definition of environment to include economic and quality-of-life issues, and must ultimately challenge capital and the state over questions of taxation, distribution of wealth, pollution, jobs, etc.

EXAMINING LABOR-ENVIRONMENT

I examined the case of a successful labor-community coalition, the Louisiana Labor-Neighbor Project, in its geographic and historical context. This analysis focused on the political-economic context and dynamics of labor-community politics. I also assessed the history of labor-community coalition-building around the country to the present (Chapter 3) to draw comparisons for the case study and to better understand general historical currents of collaboration. I examined how the specific historical and geographical conditions, particularly petrochemical industry politics and the role of the state, might structure labor-community politics in Louisiana. I looked at the dynamics of class experience and intellectual leadership, and considered the process among movement leaders to craft a common agenda. Thus, I considered not only class dynamics, but also factors of race, culture, and gender relations in developing a labor-community politics. This examination of structure and agency entailed a historical assessment of labor-community initiatives in Louisiana (Chapter 4), a history of OCAW in its political-economic contexts (Chapter 4), and an examination of the local and national environmental movements' capacity to forge coalitions with labor in the 1980s and 1990s (Chapters 4 and 5). Thus, I sought to explain why the Louisiana Labor-Neighbor Project emerged, endured, and declined over a seventeen-year period, considering issues such as capitalist politics, political opportunities and the state, and labor-community leadership and organization.

The declining power of unions and community organizations during the era of industrial restructuring beginning in the 1970s has brought an increasing number of efforts to build a counterhegemonic politics by forging the energies of labor and community. Labor-community initiatives are an important phenomenon in and of themselves as well as for the potential they hold to create a progressive counterweight to destructive business practices, corporate-dominated governmental regulatory policies, and conservative civil society organizations.

THE DEVELOPMENT OF THE LOUISIANA
LABOR-NEIGHBOR PROJECT

Four important points must be made about the development of the Louisiana Labor-Neighbor Project. First, capitalist crisis set the stage for the development of OCAW's labor-community politics. Second, union and community leadership and its coalition capacity responded to the crisis, took advantage of political openings, and brought about collaboration in its changing forms. Third, while crisis helped form OCAW's original labor-community political response, this political project was transformed as it developed, expanding and diversifying its agenda, but sometimes moderating its potentially social justice oriented politics. Fourth, the project ultimately faced a period of great organizational difficulty, in part because of its own rapid success and other issues plaguing many labor-community coalitions, as well as issues related to Louisiana's political economic landscape.

Crisis as Context for OCAW's
Labor-Community Politics

A crisis in petrochemical capitalism, part of a larger crisis for Fordist capitalism, provided the context for the emergence of labor-community politics in Louisiana. This crisis for capital was at the same time a crisis for labor, motivating it to forge new collaboration with community. The Fordist crisis was also a regulatory crisis for public health and the environment.

In the late 1970s and early 1980s, responding to intensified international competition, the petrochemical industry restructured through increased automation, corporate consolidation, replacement of permanent workers with temporary contract labor, and operation of plant at overcapacity. Unlike mobile forms of production capital, Louisiana's petrochemical industry was fairly fixed in place, dependent on abundant oil, gas, and mineral resources and efficient water transportation. In this context of local dependency, BASF's lockout of union workers was a local political strategy used to deal with global competitive pressures.

The Fordist crisis also represented a crisis for labor. As a cost-cutting measure, the petrochemical industry waged a campaign to eliminate unions wherever possible. OCAW, in particular, had been targeted in numerous locations. For much of this century on the defensive against antiunion, right-to-work forces, labor in Louisiana suffered a serious setback with the passage of the right-to-work act in 1976. The act weakened labor's statewide political power and provided an opportunity for petrochemical companies to attempt to break union locals. Petrochemical companies locked out OCAW locals in 1977 and 1980 before the

1984 BASF lockout in Geismar. Nationwide, OCAW suffered a serious reduction in membership under petrochemical restructuring, losing numerous union locals through company-led decertification campaigns. The BASF lockout, therefore, constituted a critical moment for OCAW.

Louisiana faced an environmental regulatory crisis as well, the result of decades of Fordist production with insufficient environmental regulation. A grassroots eco-populist movement began to emerge by the mid-1970s, in response to widespread toxic dumping, high cancer rates and other illnesses, and general environmental destruction. At the same time, petrochemical regions of Louisiana experienced high levels of poverty in an economy that rewarded industry with huge subsidies. By the mid-1980s a national community and worker right-to-know movement was at its peak, having mobilized in response to worker and community exposure to chemical hazards at industrial facilities and a series of chemical accidents, highlighted by the 1984 Bhopal, India, chemical plant disaster. A propitious moment in the history of right-to-know activism, aided by national organizations such as the National Toxics Campaign, which had close ties with OCAW national activists, helped OCAW forge links with national environmental organizations and in some localities around chemical right-to-know issues.

Within this context of crisis, OCAW and community and environmental activists forged a coalition to take on the economic depredations of a petro-chemical giant and a variety of economic and environmental problems in an industrialized, economically underdeveloped region. As civil society organizations, labor and community groups intervened in the social-political regulation process to address the failure of the regulatory state to protect environmental health and the economic well-being of workers and communities. Louisiana's state institutions were compromised by conflicting state projects (industrial development versus environmental protection), resulting in a state legitimation crisis. Political opportunities for labor-community coalitions to influence the regulation process were thus heightened by the state's image and legitimation problem. In concert, the environmental, labor, and state legitimation crises provided opportunities for labor and communities to mobilize and intervene.

Leadership and Coalition Capacity
Forge Collaboration

Union, environmental and community leadership, and its capacity to form coalitions, forged collaboration as a response to the labor and environmental crisis. The BASF lockout promoted a populist solidarity (and sometimes class) consciousness among OCAW members. While Louisiana's labor history is rich in working class militancy, the union's tactical incorporation of an environmental populist perspective into its workplace-oriented populist solidarity consciousness was new. For the first time, the union local became aware of the detrimental consequences of local industrial pollution, in part inspired by environmental leaders within the community. Such a broadening of environmentalism into workplace-based consciousness was part of a national growth in environmental consciousness across classes during the 1970s and 1980s. For their part, key community residents and grassroots environmentalists developed a populist solidarity and provided important community leadership in return for the union's commitment to help the community fight its environmental struggles. Within the African-American community of Geismar, a history of oppression and poverty, combined with local knowledge of the impact of petrochemical pollution on local health, helped prepare many community activists to enter into an alliance with the union. For some community leaders, the petrochemical industry represented a continuation of the plantation economy.

With the BASF lockout over, the union began to rethink its collaboration with community institutions, shifting from short-term tactical concerns toward long-term political strategy, a coalition strategy. The Labor-Neighbor Project's formation in 1990 signaled a shift in the community's relationship with the union from tactical populist solidarity, during the lockout, also to a coalition strategy. Community leaders began to regard collaboration with the union, on a variety of economic development and environmental issues, as an important, long-term strategy.

The union's transformed awareness and its new form of politics were facilitated by multiscale intellectual leadership and financial resources. The success of the OCAW's corporate accountability campaign and the creation of the Labor-Neighbor Project were directly attributable to these resources. OCAW International's leadership was vital, during the lockout and the first years of the Labor-Neighbor Project. This leadership and support derived from the union's tradition of militancy and internal democracy in the oil workers union locals of the western states; the emergence of union militancy and democracy was facilitated by the hazardous working conditions in the early oil, gas, and petrochemical industries. The International also had a twenty-five-year history of coalition-building and organizing on environmental and health and safety issues, and had gained experience in corporate lockouts prior to the BASF struggle. The OCAW International was a formidable union foe for a hazardous industry. Moreover, the union's strategic leadership, backed up by important financial support, effectively exploited numerous political opportunities. These opportunities were vital to the union's corporate accountability campaign and to later struggles over industrial pollution, corporate welfare and tax justice, local infrastructure development, local hiring, and municipal incorporation. In Gramscian terms, the union's moral and intellectual leadership in coalition-building and militancy against aggressive corporate practices provided the capacity to mobilize the union and community during the crisis. Likewise, community and environmental movement leaders also brought moral and intellectual leadership to the coalition process, as they recognized the need for a strategy of coalition-building to confront serious environmental problems and the failure of the regulatory state.

A Politics Transformed:
Broader, Diverse, but Mainstream

As the original OCAW-community project developed, it first consolidated its base, then diversified its agenda, expanded its geographical reach and the number of coalition organizational members, while tending to move its politics to the mainstream. The coalition expanded its mission from job retention and retrieval, plus environmental issues during the lockout, to a wider range of economic and environmental issues, in the process balancing diversity with cooperation (Brecher and Costello, 1990), and continuing to address both workplace and community issues. The process of building a mass-based organization, comprised increasingly of religious organizations and civic associations, along with grass-roots environmental groups, meant that the center of political gravity increasingly shifted away from corporate confrontation to exacting concessions from parish government. While there were exceptions to this, such as the project's participation in the campaign to stop Shintech, the focus of the organization tended to be increasingly on supporting member organizations' local struggles, more often than not directed at local government rather than corporations.

Yet this consolidation and expansion of a mass-based organization filled an important niche and achieved some valuable victories in building local citizen power in the region. The OCAW-community collaborative project overcame one of the longest corporate lockouts in American labor history. During and after the lockout the coalition had a political impact on environmental and economic policy and politics. It helped shape the statewide debate over the "environmental score card," linking the issuance of industrial tax exemptions with corporate environmental performance. It helped win a court decision declaring tax-exempt "industrial areas" as unconstitutional. It brought about, directly and indirectly, two parish ordinances promoting local hiring by companies. It set into motion the development of a public waterworks infrastructure in Ascension Parish. It stimulated municipal incorporation drives in two communities, with the goal of accessing industrial tax revenue by including petrochemical facilities in the new municipalities. It brought about a ban on hazardous chemical-truck traffic in residential areas, improved community emergency preparedness practices, and won the installation of a twenty-four-hour community air monitor. It helped block construction of a plastics production facility in an already environmentally burdened low-income community of color. It built a mass-based organization, Louisiana Communities United, comprised of twenty-plus member organizations in four parishes.

Perhaps its greatest achievement, however, was its success in establishing a *process* of labor-community collaboration. This process allowed the project to build a mass base, well beyond the tactical alliance developed during the lockout, which could transcend corporate opposition, which at times had slowed the coalition's political initiatives. The open and dynamic process of crafting a common agenda, guided by skilled organizers and committed union and community leaders, prevented the coalition from falling into parochial, exclusionary politics. This collaborative process allowed the project to develop a host of local leaders, and for a time set up a structure upon which progressive campaigns could be conducted.

Challenging Times and the Importance of Capacity-Building

After a period of rapid expansion in the late 1990s, the Labor-Neighbor Project encountered difficult times in 2001. The project changed directors twice and suffered subsequent internal problems. Its board of directors lost members and stopped meeting regularly. This rapid decline can be attributed to a number of interrelated factors. First, the project expanded quickly in the late 1990s and then lost the organizing capacity to effectively manage the project. In addition to two quick changes in the directorship, the organization lost its organizing supervisor of eleven years, a person who brought important strategic thinking and prowess to the project. Thus, the project lacked the important combination of a competent director working closely with an organizing advisor.

Second, the project was deprived of a strong connection to national networks and their various resources, in part as a result of the departure of the long-term coordinator and the organizing advisor. But equally important, the project outlasted two national progressive networks, the OCAW International and the National Toxics Campaign, which had originally conceived and supported the Labor-Neighbor Project. The decline in Labor-Neighbor's connection to national networks deprived it of multiscale leadership and resources. Similarly, the project suffered from a lack of an effective progressive network in Louisiana. When progressive projects falter, as with the Labor-Neighbor Project and the Louisiana Coalition for Tax Justice, networks can assist those projects find key personnel or rebuild the organization. The lack of an effective progressive network is due in part to a local political culture that has impeded the development of progressive politics in Louisiana.

Third, the project struggled to build the capacity of its leaders, particularly its union leaders. Despite its great success in organizing Louisiana Communities United, it still faced the task of deepening its leaders' training in the fundamental workings of nonprofit organizations and organizing strategies, as well as the critical task of recruiting new union leaders to the core of coalition leaders and educating them about the political importance of labor-community action. Capacity-building can ensure that leaders remain invested, even when staff and directors change.

Fourth, the Labor-Neighbor Project struggled to sustain a progressive social justice organizing program. Although the project's mass-based organizing strategy built a broad coalition in four parishes, building unity often meant subsuming a progressive agenda. Occasionally, the project engaged in confrontational politics with a progressive theme, such as the environmental justice battle against Shintech. But to live up to their "cutting-edge" reputation, as characterized by State Representative Kip Holden, the Labor-Neighbor Project and Louisiana Communities United would have to challenge more directly the injustices that Holden pointed out: poverty, pollution, and corporate welfare. Perhaps this is the progressive potential that Labor-Neighbor has yet to fulfill.

Recently union leaders from the PACE/United Steel Workers union local were in the process of rebuilding the Labor-Neighbor Project. They were hopeful that the coalition could continue its organizing after the expected hiring of a new organizing director who could bring back the skill and purpose lacking in recent years (Malek-Wiley, personal communication, September 23, 2004; King, interview, March 24, 2005).

LABOR-ENVIRONMENT POLITICS IN LOUISIANA: AN EXPLANATION

I now look at how crisis called forth a new politics for labor in Louisiana in ensuring its survival and building strength for the future. The ongoing success of labor-environmental politics in Louisiana is due to three important factors: the regional character of the petrochemical industry; the regional character of the state; and the class experience of labor and community. Future success must consider several additional factors: the dampening effect of local political culture; the complexities of moving from narrow to broader agendas; building coalition capacity; maximizing multiscale resources; and building multiclass, progressive coalitions.

The Regional Character of the Petrochemical Industry

The regional character of the petrochemical industry not only helped bring about a labor-community politics, it also provided an ongoing framework for labor-community campaigns. That the industry was relatively fixed in place, was largely governed by interests from outside the state which did not always lend themselves to straightforward representation by a monolithic trade association, and created a crisis of worker and environmental health, provided political opportunities for unions and community organizations. Petrochemical politics, and a loose neoliberal government regulation, contributed to an environmentally unsustainable, one-sided, resource extraction economy, with continuing extremely uneven economic development in industrial areas.

The Louisiana labor-environmental project was initiated in the 1980s as a response to a petrochemical corporation's politics employed to face the crisis of Fordism. The crisis of Fordism manifested itself in Louisiana, as it did nationally, as excessive rigidity of capital accumulation. It brought intense international competitive pressures on the petrochemical industry to rationalize production. At the same time, the Fordist crisis represented an environmental crisis for Louisiana after four decades of petrochemical and oil industry pollution. BASF and other companies responded to rigidities in Fordist production with strategies of flexibility, such as automation, operating at speed-up and overcapacity, and replacement of permanent workers with temporary contract labor as a way of increasing profits and reducing operating costs. In this climate of flexible response, BASF's lockout of OCAW members was a cost-cutting strategy designed to force wage and benefit concessions and to replace permanent union employees with nonunion permanent and contract workers.

But the industry faced a high level of contradictions in its own operations, namely, the extensive degradation of work and community environments, that is, the conditions of production and reproduction. Public perception also reflected the view that the industry was harming the environment and public health, which ultimately threatened the ability of Louisiana's business climate to attract new companies. The industry, therefore, had legitimacy and image problems. Declining environmental, health, and safety conditions, unfair treatment of workers, and the petrochemical industry's legitimacy problem helped to create opportunities for effective community and labor resistance. For OCAW International and other unions in the petrochemical industry, the industry's post-Fordist strategy of flexibility represented a critical moment, as they sought to stem the tide of union elimination in the industry. In this situation, OCAW International's intellectual leadership was crucial to its ability to deal with the crisis facing the local union in Geismar. Owing to the international union's extensive experience in fighting lockouts, building coalitions, and facing aggressive corporate practices with strategic campaigns, OCAW was acutely aware of the political-economic circumstances. Based on the union's awareness and experience it was able to devise strategies to build power and intervene in the state environmental regulatory process to challenge BASF. OCAW's leadership and its multi-scale resources played an important role in the union's ability to exploit the industry's contradictions, manifested in its legitimacy problem.

On the question of the petrochemical industry's politics of flexibility, the Louisiana case is hardly unique. What makes the case unusual, however, is the petrochemical industry's lack of ability to be geographically flexible. Production capital has often used geographical mobility, sometimes embodied in the practice of job blackmail, as leverage against workers and local governments. In addition to the crisis endemic to the petrochemical industry across the United States, Louisiana's petrochemical industry is particularly vulnerable to concerted labor-community resistance because it is relatively place-bound as a result of reliance on local water transportation and local sources of oil, gas, and mineral resources, such as salt brines, integral to the chemical-building process. Petrochemical facilities are part of elaborate, extensive, highly integrated, and highly capital-intensive production complexes. They are the epitome of immobility. Louisiana's petrochemical companies, thus, could hardly back up threats of capital and job flight with actual geographical mobility. Petrochemical industry politics, as such, were necessarily local. The industry had to face the labor and environmental crises that it helped create in a local setting. For the industry, the cost of degrading the conditions of work and environmental quality—that is, the cost of undermining the conditions of production, the second contradiction of capitalism (J. O'Connor, 1988)—was eventual resistance by labor, community, and environmentalism.

Apart from the material practices the petrochemical industry used to face the crisis, such as union busting and automation, the industry also used ideological practice. The Louisiana petrochemical industry sought to resolve the crisis of degraded production conditions in part by ideologically representing the environment and workers as properties of capital. In this way, industry sought to gloss over the class tensions—the class material relations—that generated the Fordist crisis in the first place. BASF's representation of OCAW as having no constitutional rights as labor, the Geismar area companies' subtle assumption that they had greater claim than the community on the local environment, and those companies' claim to the necessity of tax-exempt use of their industrial space, demonstrate the industry's symbolic incorporation of labor, environment, and local space into its private production sphere. Such ideological domination of nature by capital (M. O'Connor, 1993), was well-practiced by the petrochemical industry during the Fordist era, yet intensified with the industry's flexible response to the Fordist crisis. The petrochemical industry's claim to environment, labor, and space derives in part from Louisiana's long history of resource extraction and capital's privileged use of resources. The petrochemical and oil industries, headquartered largely outside of Louisiana, have long assumed that Louisiana was a resource colony, in part by acquiring the old sugar plantation property along the Mississippi, which gave it a perceived natural right over land and labor. The oil industry challenged Huey Long's excise tax assessment on oil exports by symbolically incorporating Louisiana's oil resources into its domain. The ten-year industrial property tax exemption continues to be a manifestation of industry's claim to industrial space and nature in Louisiana.

Given that most petrochemical corporations operating in the state gave primary allegiance to companies' ownership and financial bases of operations outside of Louisiana, they did not always work in unison, in step with their trade associations in the state. Rather, there was potential for division, if one company's practices were seen as harming the overall business climate in the state. In addition, there was a long-standing public perception that outside-based petrochemical and oil companies were not returning enough of their wealth to the general public welfare, a perception that Huey Long and progressive-era reformers addressed with the institution of an excise tax on oil. These factors meant that civil society organizations could challenge the industry on a local or statewide scale, over tax breaks and pollution issues. Indeed, the public perception of Louisiana's petrochemical industry as a largely "outside," if not foreign, economic force, allowed OCAW and the community to pressure BASF at numerous points at several scales in the early struggle against the company. During the lockout, the union applied sufficient pressure to other petrochemical companies to prompt them in turn to pressure BASF to lift the lockout. The union thus found and exploited weaknesses in the petrochemical community, which to a large degree stemmed from the foreign or outside status of most of the petrochemical companies. Not even a state-level trade association, the Louisiana Chemical Association, could prevent divisions from emerging.

The petrochemical industry's flexible response to the Fordist crisis helped heighten already uneven urban development in Louisiana, thereby fostering land-use conflict and the growth of grassroots environmentalism. Petrochemical-based agglomeration economies and urbanization, well-developed during the Fordist era, were intensified under the strategy of flexible accumulation in a process of accelerated uneven development (see Harvey, 1989; Lipietz, 1992; and Smith, 1990). Louisiana's primary industrial cities—New Orleans, Baton Rouge, and Lake Charles—had expanded since the 1970s, leading to urbanization of previously rural areas around periurban, primarily petrochemical, industrial facilities. This resulted in increasing conflict between residential and industrial land uses. Accelerated, uneven development placed cities in greater competition with one another for economic growth, forcing urban areas to find new ways of regulating crisis, demanding flexible strategies and new urban political alliances (Mayer, 1991). The demand for local innovation in crisis regulation has broadened the political space for labor and community organizations to influence local decision making. The evolution of labor-community collaboration in Louisiana must therefore be seen in the context of intensified uneven development.

The turn to flexible accumulation by the petrochemical industry—with its rationalization of production and contracting-out of permanent jobs, leading to escalating toxic hazards—posed a real threat to unions in the industry and neighboring communities. Post-Fordism presented a general crisis for labor in the petrochemical industry, as the restructuring process reduced union membership dramatically since the mid-1970s. The BASF lockout, taking place after a long series of union elimination efforts by the petrochemical industry, represented a critical moment for OCAW International to attempt to stem the tide of union-busting. Industrial restructuring forced all unions to finally confront their own rigidity, in particular their reliance on hierarchical business unionism to sustain union membership and political power. Post-Fordist restructuring prompted a growing realization on the part of unions that their dwindling political power could only be resuscitated through creative strategies such as those involving community and social movement allies.

The structure of post-Fordism itself facilitated the strategic alliance between labor and environment in Louisiana, in part by providing for a relatively smooth adoption of environmental consciousness by OCAW leaders and rank-and-file members. Post-Fordism represents a continuation of environmental crisis emerging in the Fordist period, but with a shift to widespread "environmental management" and "environmental consciousness" not present even during the late 1960s and early 1970s. Post-Fordist regulation is characterized by an ideological incorporation of nature by capital (M. O'Connor, 1993), involving broad public support for state and corporate command-and-control management of ecological resources and problems. For command-and-control management to succeed required legitimation of its ability to regulate environmental crises; this legitimation was evident in the creation of "environmental consciousness" within civil society. Such an environmental consciousness, generically created in popular consumer culture, did not involve any particular critique of capitalism as the source of environmental crisis; rather, it simply represented an awareness of pollution and the need for more aggressive regulation. This was the context for the emergence of an environmental consciousness among OCAW members during the BASF lockout. Given the post-Fordist greening of public opinion, already in progress by the early 1980s, the development of a new environmental awareness among OCAW members should be regarded as an important development, yet by no means a profound, radical redefinition of the union.

In labor-community campaigns after the BASF lockout, the Labor-Neighbor Project and allies exploited the regional character of the petrochemical industry— its relative space-boundedness, its tendency to export most of its enormous wealth, and its outsider status. Many of Labor-Neighbor's initiatives were environmental-justice campaigns that focused on the unequal distribution of environmental hazards and environmental benefits: the campaigns to stop the siting of a PVC production facility, make industry to pay for a municipal water system and air-monitoring network, stop a hazardous waste recycling facility, stop the siting of a regional airport, and make industry hire local workers. Some of the campaigns had an explicitly spatial strategy that capitalized on issues of uneven development and environmental harm, such as the lack of public works infrastructure, high levels of pollution, and the right to know about environmental harms through environmental monitoring. Campaigns targeting corporations for their current or future practices, seeking greater corporate accountability to the community, were often met by strong corporate opposition, particularly if the companies were already spatially fixed, with huge capital investments in their facilities. This was the case in Labor-Neighbor's "good neighbor" negotiations with chemical plant managers over corporate funding for a water/sewer system and air monitoring system in Geismar. These campaigns challenged corporations on several vulnerabilities: their place-boundedness and their public image as outside players that needed to return more to the community in exchange for exporting wealth. Corporate opposition was also fierce in the municipal incorporation campaign by Labor-Neighbor allies in Geismar in 1997.

In the early 1990s, the Louisiana Coalition for Tax Justice, Labor-Neighbor's sister organization, adroitly campaigned to overturn long-standing corporate subsidies that seriously impaired local and state-wide budgets. LCTJ played on the outside character of many of the corporations, characterizing them as robbing the state and the citizens of tremendous wealth that ought to go toward strengthening the social and fiscal health of communities. LCTJ depicted corporations as sucking resources out of the state while being heavily subsidized by Louisiana citizens. Corporations responded with strong lobbying, which overturned the environmental scorecard. Although LCTJ withered in the late 1990s, the issue of corporate welfare remained a huge debilitating factor in equitable economic development.

The environmental justice campaign to stop Shintech in 1997-1999, in which the Labor-Neighbor Project played an important organizing role, exploited the regional character of the petrochemical industry and the neo-liberal character of the state to halt the construction of Shintech's PVC production facility in a low-income community of color in Convent. Although Shintech's facility was not yet constructed, thus not yet fixed in place, the campaign played on Shintech's public image as another foreign corporation that was seeking to take Louisiana's wealth while returning very little to the common good. The campaign used environmental justice arguments of no further overburdening of a community already overburdened by polluting petrochemical facilities. At the same time, the campaign pressured a state environmental agency that was in disarray—due to the Department of Environmental Quality's poor leadership and lack of a protection mission—to refuse to issue an air permit to Shintech. The campaign exploited political opportunities to force the state to block industry in Convent. Shintech ultimately succeeded in constructing its PVC facility in Donaldsonville near Baton Rouge by avoiding a situation where opposition could be mustered.

In summation, the regional character of the petrochemical industry—as geographically inflexible, governed by outside interests, non-monolithic, and degrading working and living conditions—provided an ongoing framework for labor-community collective action. The petrochemical industry's politics of flexibility and ideological control derived from its ability to confront its local situation, which was crisis-laden. To the extent that the industry was geographically inflexible, it had to devise a politics which would hide that inflexibility. Broader uneven urban development, combined with the industry's decades-long environmental degradation and its rationalization of the production process, created ongoing conditions of crisis for the industry. While petrochemical capital is necessarily global, the unique constraints of geographic inflexibility in Louisiana are paramount in defining the industry's political strategies toward labor and community.

The petrochemical industry's regional character also highlights the capacity of labor-community collaboration to have an impact, however limited, on capitalist development. Under proper intellectual leadership and sustained by adequate skill and financial resources, labor-community projects can achieve remarkable successes, as demonstrated by the Labor-Neighbor Project's ability to understand acutely the strengths and vulnerabilities of the petrochemical industry and to mobilize people to challenge destructive industrial development and promote projects in the public interest. During the lockout and throughout the 1990s, Labor-Neighbor Project leaders and organizers were a model of informed and astute leadership that developed creative and fruitful strategies for building labor-community power and furthering corporate and governmental accountability.

The Regional Character of the State and Political Culture

Labor-community mobilization was also enabled by the regional character of the state, in particular, its relative openness. Louisiana's permeable neoliberal state is an ensemble of contested strategies (Jessop, 1990a), among them strategies for petrochemical development and environmental protection. As in other states, Louisiana state strategies generally favored capitalist development while allowing environmental and labor crises to persist, particularly during the Fordist period, the era of rapid petrochemical industrial development. State government is a complex set of struggles, framed by the relative power of industry, government players, unions, and civil society organizations (B. Miller, 1992). Government thus is constrained by the power of industrial capital, which, in Louisiana, most often privileged capitalist development strategies over strategies of environmental protection, worker protection, and equitable economic development. The state, as such, is strategically selective (Jessop, 1990a).

In Louisiana, the state was part of the crisis of Fordism. The alternating periods of reform and neopopulist (and corrupt) state administration since the Huey Long era (Maginnis, 1984) can be explained as state strategies that were open and contested, emerging from economic crisis and the balance of class and social forces. The tension between neopopulist and reformist state administrative ideologies provided political openings for community and working-class institutions to influence the development of state strategies. As the crisis of Fordism settled in nationally, antiunion forces in Louisiana finally succeeded in establishing a state open-shop (right-to-work) strategy in the early 1970s. As the gateway of corporate access to production conditions (J. O'Connor, 1988), the ensemble of state projects gave industry virtually unlimited freedom to pollute until the late 1970s. For lack of an effective indigenous environmental movement, state environmental regulatory projects lagged more than a decade behind national environmental protection efforts. Prompted by the sensational toxic asphyxiation of a truck driver at a toxic dump at Bayou Sorrel in 1978, the environmental crisis finally entered the broader public consciousness, creating for the state a legitimation crisis concerning environmental protection. State laxness in environmental protection provided an opening for then-diffuse grassroots environmentalism, which several years later forced the creation of new state projects in the form of the newly-created Department of Environmental Quality. The crisis of Fordism and its related environmental crisis created political opportunities for institutional experimentation in civil society, such as the growth of grassroots environmentalism. It was the shifting nature of state strategies—underscored by rhetorical administrative shifts from neopopulism to reform since the Long era—that provided frequent openings for the influence of alternative labor and community initiatives in confronting capitalist crises.

Political opportunities were facilitated sometimes by allies or supporters in state agencies and the legislature, sometimes by disarray within agencies, and by frequent lack of coordination between state projects, such as environmental protection and economic development. Allies within Louisiana's state apparatus, particularly within the Department of Environmental Quality and the Attorney General's office during a reform administration in the late 1980s and early 1990s, assisted labor-community campaigns against petrochemical companies. Union-community obstruction of industry operating permits, as well as alternative strategies such as the environmental scorecard—linking industry tax breaks to environmental performance—achieved gains during this period. Environmental justice campaigns, such as the campaign to stop Shintech, successfully blocked environmental permitting in part because of the strong legal challenges and disorganization within the Department of Environmental Quality. Political opportunities in Louisiana, as elsewhere, are highly unstable, shifting from one gubernatorial administration to the next. Indeed, state agency allies under the reform administration of Buddy Roemer (1987-91) were more abundant than under the business-as-usual Edwards (1991-1995) and Foster (1995-2003) administrations. As expected the Labor-Neighbor Project and its movement allies experienced less governmental responsiveness under Edwards and Foster, who were less keen about environmental protection.

Louisiana is characterized by corrupt, elite-driven, authoritarian tendencies, albeit with streaks of reform. Such a context makes it possible for the state to obstruct local and statewide labor-community initiatives. This was evident with the overturning of the environmental scorecard in 1992, as a more conventional, corrupt administration assumed power. It was also evident when, in 1998, the Republican governor, stung by the success of the grassroots campaign to stop Shintech, due in part to the legal assistance provided by the Tulane Environmental Law Clinic, pushed through a statewide policy curtailing the ability of the Tulane clinic to assist environmentally impacted communities in pursuing legal action against industrial polluters. Thus while the Labor-Neighbor Project and its allies took advantage of openings in the state process to conduct local and statewide initiatives, those openings sometimes closed, when corporations pushed hard enough on political elites to force changes in policy or laws, particularly when the governor ushered through a statewide policy change. The highly centralized

192 / LABOR-ENVIRONMENTAL COALITIONS

character of Louisiana government, then, meant that the governor could use a spatial strategy of his own, passing a statewide initiative, to undermine the local successes of the environmental movement and its allies.

In contrast to the avenues for labor-community collaboration provided by the state, the regional political culture has often had a dampening effect on movement mobilization. Louisiana maintains a persistent, elite, political culture, supported by a strong ideology that corruption and an overly centralized government should be tolerated in exchange for low taxes ("tooth-fairyism"), which militates against coordinated outrage (Maginnis, 1984). The state demonstrated a tendency to be very closely allied with corporations, to the point of ignoring the environmental health consequences of poorly regulated industrial development. Moreover, the state even sought to circumscribe the ability of civil society organizations to challenge petrochemical development, as was the case when the governor successfully changed state laws to limit the public outreach that university law clinics could offer to poor and middle-income communities, as a response to the Tulane Environmental Law Clinic's pivotal role in the successful campaign to stop Shintech from building a plastics production facility in the low-income community of Convent. The governor's ability to dictate state policy and laws in support of industry and against public interest organizations underscores the highly centralized structure of Louisiana government and the lack of an effective progressive front to challenge such autocratic decisions.

State intervention in crises actually favored workers and the public only after intense pressure on government or campaigns against corporations. Labor-community pressure prompted the governor to intervene in the BASF lockout after five years, helping to force an end to that conflict. Labor-community campaigning helped raise the issue of corporate welfare, prompting the governor to push through a policy linking industrial tax exemptions with good environmental performance, the environmental scorecard. Labor-community pressure on a disorganized Department of Environmental Quality forced the agency to refuse a critical environmental permit to Shintech, causing the company to abandon its plan to build a plastics facility in a low income community of color. Allies in government, particularly in the 1980s and early 1990s, and subsequent disorganization within some state agencies, provided opportunities for labor and community to pressure the state to institute pro-environmental and pro-community strategies.

Louisiana has a unique political culture, infused with colorful, corrupt public officials and a highly centralized, yet permeable state government. The permeable state is comprised of selective strategies that change with the balance of political parties and their ideologies (Jessop, 1990a). Louisiana's permeable, neoliberal state has generally provided opportunities for labor-community projects to influence public policy. On the other hand, the prevailing culture of tolerance for corruption, combined with the very powerful role the governor plays, makes it difficult for social movements to build up a progressive front against a powerful governor who is hostile to progressive alliances.

The Class Experience of Labor and Community

Labor-community coalitions come about and succeed because of class experience gained from confronting difficult working or living conditions. Unions very often build communities of solidarity when confronting an economic crisis (Calhoun, 1988; Cumbler, 1974; Fantasia, 1988). From a Gramscian perspective, collective class experience gained from confronting difficult material conditions, such as a strike or lockout or harsh living conditions, can provide working class organizations with the intellectual leadership necessary to build solidarity to deal with the economic crisis. Such class experience is vital to informing leaders which strategies they should use, such as building coalitions or a focus on environment or worker health. A union's class experience, in particular, is manifested in the breadth of its political agenda. Class experience can also engage bridge builders and call up resources. OCAW brought to the situation a class-experienced union with sufficient resources at the national and local levels. The prominent historical factor was the full engagement of OCAW's international union, which provided invaluable strategic class experience and resources. OCAW International's leadership on workplace health and safety and environment in trade unionism is rooted in the union's early experience in heavy, hazardous industry. OCAW built its experience in health, environment and coalition-building beginning with its struggles for better working conditions in mines and oil fields in the 1930s, continuing through its campaign to create OSHA in the 1960s, a strike against Shell in 1973, and a series of corporate antiunion offensives during the late 1970s and early 1980s. Faced with the BASF lockout, OCAW International strategists applied the union's progressive tradition—above all, its broad political agenda and an openness to experiment with new coalitions and strategies.

Apart from the international union's strategic experience, both the union local itself and the regional representative had survived corporate lockouts before. Indeed, the International's regional representative, Ernie Rousselle, brought invaluable experience in union militancy from a forty-four-month lockout at American Cyanamid in New Orleans in the 1970s, particularly the knowledge that community coalitions are necessary to sustain a union during a lockout. As an OCAW local union leader at American Cyanamid, Rousselle helped lead union efforts to gain solidarity from community institutions and local government officials. Local 4-620, for its part, had waged an eight-month strike against BASF in 1970 and had weathered a brief lockout by the company in 1980, neither of which could hardly prepare the local for a lengthy lockout. Union local leaders were quite savvy in developing a class behavior quickly among the membership during the early stages of the BASF lockout. Local 4-620 leaders and members learned quickly that BASF sought to divide the union and thus found ways to counteract the company's strategies. Out of the union members' lockout experience grew a culture of family solidarity, led mainly by the Women's

Support Group, which served as a vital connection to community institutions such as churches during the lockout.

OCAW International's class experience and coalition-building capacity set themselves apart from the general lack of militant unionism in Louisiana in the 1970s and 1980s. OCAW's capacity to forge an environmental-community coalition came largely from the progressive tradition of its International, not from a current militant union culture in Louisiana, which was not coherent enough to provide a militant tradition for OCAW Local 4-620. However, the influence of a long history of militant, inclusive unionism in New Orleans must be factored in, despite the fact that Louisiana was a right-to-work state where narrow business unionism had held sway in the labor community for decades. New Orleans' history of militant, inclusive trade unionism distinguished Louisiana from the rest of the right-to-work South, and helped shape OCAW's 44-month coalition building struggle against American Cyanamid in the 1970s. It also helped shape the labor and religious solidarity with OCAW that emerged from New Orleans during the BASF lockout. OCAW's strategy of coalition-building, or inclusiveness, stood in contrast to business unionist strategies of exclusion and single-minded focus on workplace economic issues, which were unable to challenge an aggressive post-Fordist industrial restructuring. Louisiana's historical confrontation between exclusive and inclusive unionism provides a context for the shift from the rigid, exclusive politics of dominant business unionism to OCAW's politics of inclusion.

In addition, class experience is shaped by communal bonds to place, in this case a shared space within an unevenly developed industrial corridor in the Louisiana river parishes, containing numerous pockets of poverty in close proximity to petrochemical facilities. The shared space of workers and community residents in the river parishes provided an important foundation for the emergence of the OCAW-community coalition during the BASF lockout. Many of the union members also lived in the parish, within a few miles of their work.

Community leaders in Louisiana brought an important class experience to their relationship with the union, although they were probably not more predisposed to political coalition with labor than their counterparts in other states. Civil rights organizations were no more collaborative with unions in Louisiana than elsewhere (Fairclough, 1995). There was, however, readiness on the part of some environmentalists and African-American community residents to work with a predominantly white union on environmental issues during the BASF lockout. That readiness must be attributed to both structure and agency; that is, to the severity of underdevelopment and the environmental crisis in the mid-1980s and to organic intellectual leadership, seasoned in social justice struggles, within the environmental and rural residential communities. Community leaders were deeply familiar with the region's uneven development and degraded environmental quality. Leaders from African-American and Acadian ethnic communities in the river parishes were conscious of the long history of exploitation of their communities by local elites. Some community leaders were experienced civil rights activists. Many worked at area industrial facilities and some were even trade unionists, and thus were familiar with the industrial workplace and conditions for workers. Several leaders, women and men, became early environment justice activists. Thus, the bridge to the initial coalition formation was a shared sense of place and understanding for the region and its problems, and the emergence of community bridge builders. Early community bridge builders from Geismar had a social justice background, familiarity with industrial workplaces, or a particularly clear understanding of the connection between production and consumption issues, between the industrial workplace and community issues. The civil rights and union experience of one particular early community leader in Geismar, Amos Favorite, was critical to building union-community ties. Later leaders, such as Rev. Welma Jackson of Ascension Parish and Pat Melançon of St. James Parish, leaders in Louisiana Communities United, understood the production-consumption connection and the political importance of a union-community political project.

One of the most significant bridge builders was a statewide grassroots environmental leader, William Fontenot, who did not come from or reside in the river parishes, but from years of work in building grassroots organizations around the state had developed class experience, a deep understanding of the production-consumption link. Fontenot helped forge OCAW's initial relationship to Ascension Parish community leaders during the lockout. He had long been adept in connecting with community leaders and industrial workers around the state over industrial pollution and hazardous waste site issues. During the lockout he helped the union formulate strategy to exploit the industry's image problem and other contradictions. He was a crucial intellectual leader whose understanding of Louisiana politics, industrial economy, and appropriate political strategy proved vital to the success of labor-community collaboration during and after the lockout. Fontenot continued to mentor the Labor-Neighbor Project throughout the 1990s. His extensive participation in the labor-community coalition process demonstrates the strength of multi-class alliances, which draw on the knowledge and experience of leaders of different class backgrounds. One might consider Fontenot as an archetype of intellectual leadership in building counterhegemonic projects.

OCAW's early partner in the Labor-Neighbor Project, the National Toxics Campaign, also provided significant class experience to the project's organizing. NTC, a national grassroots environmental network, brought skills of rigorous community organizing and nonprofit management to Labor-Neighbor, skills that benefitted the organization over the long run, even after the demise of NTC in 1993. The astute mentoring of seasoned organizing supervisor Stan Holt and the adept, tireless organizing of coordinator Dan Nicolai brought vital class experience to the project. The value of a national community organizing network to the project's vitality was no more in evidence than when Labor-Neighbor got into trouble in 2001. No level of local community resources and union resources could stabilize Labor-Neighbor after its organizing skills and networking, embodied in its organizing supervisor and coordinator, had left town. The class experience provided by a community organizing network was a critical component to the project's class capacity to mobilize.

It was not just the class experience of labor and community in Louisiana that allowed it to mobilize. Rather, it was as well due to sufficient structural opportunities, and the class capacity of the labor-community coalition to take advantage of those opportunities. One such opening was community residents' and union members' shared sense of place due to the relatively close proximity of their respective homes. Another opening was the perception that industry was largely foreign, a perspective based largely on the fact that most petrochemical and oil companies have out-of-state or foreign headquarters. Another structural opportunity was the frequent lack of organized resistance by state government and industry to labor-community initiatives, rendering industry and the state vulnerable to such initiatives. This was especially the case during the BASF lockout, but occurred again later, particularly during the campaign to stop Shintech. Finally, there are often open avenues through a permeable state government for labor-community to apply sufficient pressure on industry, such as in the case of environmental permitting, where labor-community pressure can hold up a company's environmental permits.

In a complex interaction of structure and agency, the class experience of labor-community exploited sufficient structural openings to conduct environmental and social justice campaigns. In each of OCAW's and Labor-Neighbor's political successes—breaking the lockout, winning a water system for Geismar, restricting hazardous waste truck traffic, stopping Shintech—the labor-community coalition skillfully used the shared sense of place, openings in local government, the outside character of petrochemical companies, and the lack of organized resistance to challenge the state and industry and win concessions.

OTHER SUCCESSFUL LABOR-COMMUNITY COALITIONS

To assess some of the important factors in shaping labor-community and labor-environmental coalitions I will attempt to draw some broad comparisons between the Louisiana coalition and other successful long-term alliances from recent years.

Jobs with Justice, founded in 1987, is a national network of activists and includes chapters in forty cities in twenty-nine states. Jobs with Justice builds community solidarity among labor, faith-based, community, and student organizations for a wide variety of union and worker struggles, including fights for job security and to protect workers' right to organize. Jobs with Justice applies an explicit class approach to workers' rights struggles, viewing them as part of a broader campaign for social and economic justice.

The Labor-Community Strategy Center in Los Angeles grew out of a United Auto Workers local's campaign to keep the Van Nuys, California, General Motors production facility open in 1987. Although the facility was ultimately closed, the labor-community alliance forged during the campaign was expanded to address a wide variety of environmental and economic justice issues, including air pollution and environmental justice in Los Angeles, true mass transit for working people, immigrant rights, as well as race, gender, and poverty. Today the Strategy Center regards itself as "think tank/act tank" and a national school for strategic organizing.

The Calumet Project in northwest Indiana, founded in 1984, is a labor-church-community coalition that grew out of a campaign to keep an aging steel plant open in Northwest Indiana. The project has since taken on a wide variety of environmental and worker issues in the Calumet region.

The Silicon Valley Toxics Coalition, founded in 1982 in San Jose, Calif., has from its inception been a bridge between health, environment, production, and social justice. SVTC has been a pioneer in integrating worker health and safety, environmental justice, and cleaner production organizing in the electronics industry. It forged international links on electronics production hazards and cleaner production strategies, such as extended producer responsibility.

The New Jersey Work Environment Council conducts campaigns on sustainable and safe jobs and the environment, and also provides technical assistance and training. Part of a national network of Coalitions for Occupational Safety and Health, it has a board comprised of leading grassroots environmental leaders, labor activists, and community activists.

The Citizens Environmental Council in New York State, founded in 1983, has grown into a statewide environmental coalition with more than 100 environmental, civic, and labor organizations, as well as 18,000 individual members. CEC's focus has been on pollution in the community and workplace. For many years, CEC put on an annual labor-environmental conference.

EMERGING COALITIONS ON PRECAUTION

Apart from the aforementioned longer-term labor-community coalitions, there are a number of alliances, from regional projects to national networks, organized around issues of precautionary action and prevention, that have emerged in the past few years. These include Clean Production Action, the Just Transition Alliance, the Blue-Green Working Group, the Alliance for a Healthy Tomorrow in Massachusetts, and the Apollo Alliance. All of them draw on network flows of strategies, ideas, and skills. Unions have played a variable role in each of these efforts.

Clean Production Action, for example, emerged in the late 1990s as a national network of activists promoting pollution prevention, cleaner production, and precautionary strategies. The network benefitted greatly from a link between experienced environmental organizers and cutting-edge policy strategists, many linked to universities. It provided a good framework for teaching activists the fundamentals of clean production. It had support and frequent participation from several union health and safety programs, including the Steelworkers, the United Auto Workers, and the Canadian Auto Workers.

The Just Transition Alliance formed in the late 1990s as an extension of OCAW/PACE's "jobs and environment" educational campaign and environmental justice networks' keen interest in the subject. It represents a melding of social unionism and environmental justice activism. It supports various campaigns oriented toward sustainable production, while drawing on leading policy on clean production.

The Blue-Green Working Group formed in 1996 at the prompting of the AFL-CIO under John Sweeney and several national environmental organizations. It became a frequent Beltway discussion group of twenty-forty national environmental and labor organizations, taking on issues of energy and climate change, toxics, and just transition. Blue-Green reached a temporary impasse in 2000 when the United MineWorkers and several building trades unions refused to support the Kyoto Protocol.

The Alliance for a Healthy Tomorrow is a coalition of environmental, public health, and labor organizations in Massachusetts founded in 2001 after three years of organizing and education on the precautionary principle. AHT's labor representation has been largely COSH and union health and safety activists. AHT consistently engaged the state AFL-CIO in dialogue about precaution strategies and ultimately won the state labor federation's support of several bills introduced to the state legislature, including a healthy cleaners bill and a bill calling for an "Act for a Healthy Massachusetts," which would set up a precautionary framework for substituting safer chemicals for ten toxic chemicals plaguing worker and public health. Winning the support of the building trades labor council was the critical hurdle in galvanizing union support for the Act for a Healthy Massachusetts. Critical in gaining state union leadership support was the organizing effort of COSH organizers, Clean Water Action organizers, and policy strategists from the University of Massachusetts Lowell, a hub of precautionary and occupational health policy and activism. The primary bridge builder from the state AFL-CIO had previously worked closely with Western MassCOSH on worker safety issues in western Massachusetts. In all its proposals, AHT has sought to include union and worker voices in considering the economic impact of precautionary actions on workers and communities.

The Bay Area Working Group is a coalition of environmental, consumer, public health, and labor activists that campaigned to help get the San Francisco Board of Supervisors to adopt the country's first city-wide environmental precautionary regulatory policy in June 2003, for the city and county of San Francisco (Rachel's Environment and Health News, 2003). Environmental and public health activists in and outside of San Francisco government, with help from precaution activists around the country, marshaled the campaign, gaining the support of the San Francisco Labor Council along the way. While this cannot be recognized as an overt labor-environmental coalition, the environmental and public health grassroots did build bridges on this issue with the labor council, which has supported environmental and peace initiatives in the past.

The Apollo Alliance is perhaps the most recent national labor-environmental effort, focusing on job creation and energy independence. Initiated by the Institute for America's Future and the Center on Wisconsin Strategy, the Apollo project proposes a government-led $300 billion ten-year plan, including government and industry investment in improved transportation technology and options: high efficiency factories buildings and infrastructure; expanded renewable energy development; smart urban growth; and preservation of regulatory protections (Apollo Alliance, 2004). Apollo has gained the support of numerous national unions, including the United Mine Workers, the Steelworkers, PACE, and several transport workers unions, including the International Association of Machinists and the Transportation Workers Union. It claims to have the support of environmental consumer advocacy organizations as well as socially responsible businesses. The Apollo project is driven in part to strengthen the Democratic Party, but also to develop a clear alternative to the antilabor and antienvironmental policies of the Bush administration.

Each of these projects is an effort to advance clean production in one form or another. Their success in bringing together labor and environment depends on developing a common agenda, and avoiding divisive issues. The Blue-Green Working Group faced setbacks while developing a common agenda on climate change, which presented an economic threat to several unions. Other projects have steered clear of such pitfalls by working on cleaner production issues that don't pose an immediate economic threat to workers. Labor involvement in precaution or clean-production campaigns revolves around the linking of worker and public health. Indeed, this recalls the early collaboration of worker and public health advocates during the Progressive Era. One can say that precaution campaigns, when conducted inclusively and carefully, bring back the original spirit of labor and occupational and public health collaboration, where health was the bridge.

SIMILARITIES BETWEEN COALITIONS

The previous labor-community and labor-environmental coalitions have demonstrated a number of similarities. First, they emerged where there was environmental or economic hardship, or both, and targeted failed regulation and lack of accountability. Government regulation failed to protect environmental health and economic livelihood. Corporations suffered from a general lack of accountability. Thus labor-community campaigns emerged to force corporate accountability and governmental responsibility, and thereby shape a new regulatory mode, more democratic and accountable to the public. Campaigns targeted corporate subsidies, corporate environmental and safety violations, and corrupt decision making.

Second, all labor-community projects are shaped by the collective experience of the coalition actors and by the degree of networking with outside organizations, which may support and inspire the coalition with successful models applied elsewhere. Projects learn from and adapt such concepts and strategies, from good neighbor agreements to clean production knowledge to precautionary strategies. Successful models, such as the Silicon Valley Toxics Coalition and the Los Angeles Labor-Community Strategy Center, maintain a consistent focus on governmental and corporate accountability. They also remain well networked, both nationally and internationally, to ensure the flow of ideas and strategies.

When compared to other successful models, the Labor-Neighbor Project demonstrates both strengths and weaknesses. First, the project succeeded when it committed itself to promoting government and corporate accountability. Campaigns with a focus on social justice—be it tax justice or environmental justice—drew a great degree of citizen energy and passion. The Labor-Neighbor Project, on the other hand, suffered when it did not make accountability and justice central to its campaigns. By not keeping its focus on corporate welfare and tax justice, the project lost an important framework for its organizing. Accountability and justice should be central elements of any campaign taking on government and corporations in an impoverished, environmentally burdened region. Successful urban, regional, and national labor-environmental coalitions all make governmental and corporate accountability the core focus of their organizing work.

Second, capacity building of staff and leaders is vital to the long-term success of a coalition. Labor-Neighbor succeeded when it educated and trained both its staff and leaders, both politically and in the details of sustaining a nonprofit labor-community organization. When the project did not adequately educate its union and community leaders about the importance of their coalition and how to best carry out its work, the organization suffered. Long-term coalitions such as Silicon Valley Toxics Coalition spend a good deal of effort on educating their leaders and staff about political issues and organizational dynamics.

Third, the Labor-Neighbor Project succeeded when it was well-linked with national and regional organizations and networks. Such links provided new and proven skills, ideas, and strategies for its staff and leaders. Labor-Neighbor's connection to the National Toxics Campaign in the early 1990s gave the project training and ongoing mentoring in community organizing for its staff, valuable understanding of strategies such as good-neighbor agreements, and professional support on environmental policy, such as pollution prevention and right-to-know. The NTC partnership brought the Labor-Neighbor coordinators into contact with successful organizing projects and activists from around the country. Moreover, the project's connection to OCAW International brought a greater understanding of health and safety concerns, as well as "jobs and the environment" thinking, including the concept of Just Transition, to the project's staff and leadership. It is not surprising that the project foundered when its links to national and regional organizing networks withered. Coalitions taking on campaigns of corporate and governmental accountability are greatly strengthened by a close relationship to organizing networks.

CHALLENGES FOR A NEW SPATIAL POLITICS OF LABOR-COMMUNITY

The future success of labor-community mobilization in Louisiana and elsewhere also needs to consider the following factors, which flow from the regional character of capital and government, and from the class experience of labor and community: the complexities of broadening agendas and building urgency; the dampening effect of local political culture; building coalition capacity; maximizing multiscale resources; and building multiclass, progressive coalitions.

Building Broader Common Agendas

The Labor-Neighbor Project moved from a narrow agenda to a broader one over time. Forging a broader agenda involved the danger of avoiding larger controversial issues, such as corporate welfare. A shift to mass-based (often church-based) organizing—with an emphasis on finding common issues, often noncontroversial—tends to avoid questions of class and distribution of wealth. These are the trade-offs of doing mass-based organizing versus issue-led, progressive coalition-building.

At any stage of development in a coalition, forging a common agenda is an open and contingent process. This process can involve sometimes tense interactions between union members and community leaders, but generally will lead to a greater awareness about the environment and community and labor solidarity. A common agenda is often broader than the separate interests brought to the coalition. In the course of solidarity building, the union expanded its agenda from a narrow focus on jobs and wages to include issues of environmental and community health, the use of contract labor and the resultant increase in workplace accidents, and corporate welfare. Moreover, in Louisiana a shared sense of place enabled union members and the community to develop overlapping, though different, interests and identities. The collaborative process brought out a range of community and worker concerns to be considered and prioritized.

Coalition politics—continuous creation of a broader common agenda—also involves the potential for a new spatial politics. It is distinct from the separate politics of labor and community. It is potentially more about production and reproduction and their intersection. This politics represents an opportunity for the community to address issues of production and working conditions, and an opportunity for labor to address issues of environmental protection and

202 / LABOR-ENVIRONMENTAL COALITIONS

community improvement. It represents an opportunity for worker and community concerns to be seen within a production-reproduction relationship. In the collaborative process, there is the potential for community residents to redefine "community" interests to include workers, the industrial workplace, and the production sphere. Industrial workplace hazards, workplace hiring, and company tax exemptions all become community issues as they had not been before. Labor has the potential to redefine itself to include community, workplace, and ambient environments. The issues of concern to the community—a municipal water system, local hiring, after-school recreation—all become issues of concern to labor activists. It draws on labor's knowledge about toxic production and its democratic process, and draws on community's broad base, leadership, and knowledge of community, to create a process-oriented, broader organizational agenda, rather than single-issue campaigns.

The Louisiana coalition experienced a shift in spatial strategies from the BASF lockout to the formation of the Labor-Neighbor Project. During the lockout, the union's larger spatial strategy was mirroring BASF's politics, which guided the union's spatial politics. It was much more spatially extensive, targeting companies, and shoring up environmental and community allies from around the state. The focus was not on building a substantial local base of community activists. After the lockout, there was a shift to spatially intensive politics, because the union's collaboration was place-specific, emerging most strongly out of the space of the union's workplaces and surrounding communities. The union's politics shifted naturally to encompass longer-term relationship building as both a means and an end; therefore, the focus on community organizing. The institutionalization of this spatially narrower coalition politics involved the conscious development of a democratic process within the project itself and within organizations that the project helped start. As the project progressed, it developed explicit spatial strategies to build power, such as strategies that guided the campaigns for a municipal water works, municipal incorporation, a twenty-four-hour air-monitoring network, and a parish ban on hazardous materials truck transport.

Labor-community's changing spatial strategies must ultimately face corporate and state politics, which tend to be reactive to the forces of civil society, often moving to a higher scale to obstruct labor-community. As the union expanded its political activities after the lockout, capital politics continued to be reactive, even matching the spatial scale of the union's initiatives. The environmental movement's success at getting a reform governor to institute a statewide policy of an environmental scorecard was ultimately challenged and overturned through industry pressure and a newly elected and corrupt governor. Corporate politics appeared to march in step with the intensity of labor-community politics. Although capital politics effectively slowed some of the political initiatives of the Labor-Neighbor Project, it was unable to halt or disrupt the process of labor-community collaboration. In general, state government, acting in coordination with capital, moved to a higher scale in order to obstruct. Such was the case with the governor attempting to undermine the Tulane Environmental Law Clinic, branding it as an "extremist" organization. While corporations and the state government have succeeded in hindering progressive politics, the process of labor-community collaboration continues. Job blackmail, racial and gender divisions, and class ideological differences at one time or another threatened to harm the creation and maintenance of the labor-community collaborative process, but the collaborative impetus was strong enough to overcome these obstacles.

Creating Urgency

In Louisiana as in numerous other instances, an economic crisis for labor is usually the trigger for labor-community collaboration. In an economic crisis, the group that is best-organized with the most available resources, and the most directly affected, which is most often labor, is the party that begins the search for allies (Moody, 1990). An economic crisis can create union militancy, which then turns to community bridge builders. The economic urgency of impending plant closings initiates the coalition-building process, such as in the case of the Labor-Community Strategy Center in Los Angeles and the Calumet Project in Indiana. In those cases and in the case of the OCAW-community coalition in Louisiana, labor brought the greatest urgency to building an alliance, although both community and labor bridge builders most likely sought to develop a connection with one another simultaneously.

Once the collaborative process starts, the coalition takes on a broader range of issues. A problem that coalitions face once they reach a certain maturity, however, is how to maintain a level of urgency in the coalition's organizing, or how to re-invigorate the organization with a sense of urgency when it reaches slow points in its mobilization efforts. The Louisiana Labor-Neighbor Project faced this question of instilling a sense of urgency in its organizing, particularly in recent years, when it underwent major staff and leadership changes. Creating a sense of urgency goes back to the question of the class capacity of the organization to avail itself of all the resources available to it. Intellectual leadership of labor, community, and movement organizations is vital in recognizing the political economic conditions creating crisis for labor or community organizations and in developing political strategies for confronting that crisis. That intellectual leadership flowed from the experience of OCAW, both locally and nationally, and key community leaders, who were well versed in struggle. The case of OCAW and the Labor-Neighbor Project is fundamentally about class leadership struggling over a material crisis. Labor's class leadership, in tandem with the astute class leadership of key community bridge builders, provided the sense of urgency to build labor-community collaboration. Class leadership was a central component in defining labor-community politics and shaping its agenda, and both labor and community leaders exhibited class leadership and experience in struggle by initiating the collaboration.

Building Coalition Capacity

Labor-community ultimately must build coalition capacity—including leadership skills and an understanding of nonprofit organization operational responsibilities—among its union and community leaders to thrive. Labor-community must ultimately find new urgent issues in order to capture the interests of union rank and file and community residents. Moreover, building coalition capacity requires long-term strategic planning and developing a long-term strategic relationship among the coalition partners. In the Labor-Neighbor Project, OCAW/ PACE's commitment to fund the project demonstrated its awareness of the political importance of an ongoing coalition. Yet, funding of a project by a coalition partner does not necessarily indicate that its leaders grasp the importance of commitment of energy and time to campaigns and building the coalition. To make a coalition work over the long run requires active capacity building, involving an ongoing discussion and continuous political education, particularly among the union rank and file and leadership, but also among community members and leaders. Capacity building to enhance the political education of coalition members and leaders also demands the right combination of resources and strategies, derived from multiple scales, from the local to the national.

Capacity building brings a coalition from a narrow to a broader agenda. During the BASF lockout, for instance, OCAW's intellectual leadership sought to enhance the class capacity of its membership to strengthen the union in its fight against the company. Union leadership and union international strategists helped members understand the class dimensions of the fight within the context of BASF's international politics. Union and community bridge builders helped bring about the involvement of community and environment in the union's politics. Capacity building by community and union bridge builders also brought the community to support the union, helping community leaders grasp the connection between industrial production and declining environmental health, between production and consumption. The contentious practice of solidarity building with a wary community, together with environmental awareness of union strategists, helped raise a new environmental consciousness among union members.

The Labor-Neighbor Project illustrates both the power of agency and the limits of agency. It demonstrates that it takes a high degree of organizing skill for such a coalition to work. Such skilled persons must be able to build coalition capacity in unions and the community. Building coalition capacity among the organizations' leaders and staff is essential to building a democratic organization, that in turn is strong enough to face stiff challenges such as personnel changes. Skilled organizers must also be able to recognize and exploit political opportunities to build the organization and advance a progressive agenda. Such opportunities would include persistent social problems such as poverty, pollution, underdeveloped public services, and lack of living wage jobs. Organizers would do well to take advantage of reformist tendencies in government and gain the trust and assistance of reformist government officials to advance progressive social campaigns.

At the same time, the project demonstrates the limits of agency, meaning the constraints on coalition organizers and leaders. Maintaining a high level of organizing and leadership skills is extremely difficult. Leaders need to be developed and organized by good organizers. Organizers require good mentoring. While national organizations and networks can more readily provide such resources, weathering staff changes can be extremely tenuous. Even with good organizers, building and maintaining capacity of leaders is difficult, given the differing ways that member organizations function and lend support to the coalition. Organizers face the constant threat of breakdowns in communication, as well as the constant need to inspire leaders to live up to their obligations as leaders and coalition partners. The decline of the Labor-Neighbor Project illustrates the importance of maintaining intellectual leadership and class capacity in organizations particularly when organizations are experiencing a change in leadership. The goal is to build new institutions with the capacity to survive staffing changes and other organizational challenges. This is a tall order and it raises the issue of the importance of building a progressive movement that can assist in sustaining class capacity of local projects. Gramsci's notion of intellectual leadership and class capacity takes on geographic meaning when we consider the difficulty in building durable coalition capacity. The experience of the Labor-Neighbor Project demonstrates that effective intellectual leadership and class capacity for building a counterhegemonic project must be multiscale. Responsibility for harnessing resources, developing strategy, and providing leadership rests with national organizations—labor, environmental, and other social movement—as well as local labor-community projects.

Maximizing Multiscale Resources

The history of the Labor-Neighbor Project demonstrates the importance of maintaining and effectively using multiscale resources. The labor-community project was from its inception a multiscale organizing project. During the BASF lockout, the community was just one tactic in the union's multiscale repertoire against the company. Yet, the union's local campaign was central because of the relative place-boundedness of BASF's politics in Louisiana. It was the union's community strategy that revealed and played up environmental violations among petrochemical and other industrial firms, thereby fostering pressure by other Louisiana industrial facilities on BASF to end the lockout. With the creation of the Labor-Neighbor Project after the lockout, the project's coordinators received organizer training from the project's national network. Thus, the project did not rely only on local resources, such as OCAW's financial commitment and leadership.

The project's overall decline since 2000 represented a decline in multiple-scale leadership. Its collaborative connections had become exclusionary. It remained too place-bound, too isolated from other communities and counterhegemonic projects. Its coordinator was isolated. Previously the project's link to OCAW International was a vital national connection that could potentially inform the project about changes in the national industrial economy. But OCAW's progressive brain trust, a national-scale resource, was out of the picture after 2000. Similarly, the outside mentoring for the project coordinator had been a vital resource. Once the supervisor left, there was no mentor or organizer training for the new coordinator. Having access to national intellectual and financial resources had been extremely important in developing effective strategies.

This highly ambitious coalition lacked a progressive network in the state to sustain it, provide it with organizers, mentor it. What was originally conceived and supported by national organizations (OCAW and NTC), in the end outlasted those organizations, but was left unsupported. Critical coalitions need national support from such networks, labor or otherwise. The lack of a progressive front in Louisiana was most palpable in the troubles faced by the Labor-Neighbor Project and the decline of the Louisiana Coalition for Tax Justice. When progressive projects falter, ideally there would be a network to step in to help out. In the case of the Labor-Neighbor Project, outside network assistance could play a role in ensuring that coalition capacity building could commence again, with the intent of investing the leaders and board members in the project again. Capacity building should ensure that leaders and board members will stay invested, and that labor and community representation on the board is broad and balanced.

Making Long-Term Progressive Strategy

The Labor-Neighbor Project, at its peak in the late 1990s, had done remarkable work at building an organizational base. What remained to be done was the next step: conducting broader campaigns against failed regulation, corporate welfare, and underdevelopment. Waging progressive campaigns is exceedingly difficult when one lacks the support of a network. Labor-Neighbor had the organizational skills to engage in statewide campaigns on progressive policy. It was much better at mass-based organizing than the Louisiana Coalition for Tax Justice. But at the time of its staff changes, Labor-Neighbor had not yet done the strategic capacity building to prepare for a larger campaign to take on corporations or the state. While the project did important mass-based organizing, the statewide progressive-- front organizing, such as LCTJ's campaign on corporate tax welfare, faltered. Labor-Neighbor had local agendas but no statewide campaigns. If Louisiana Communities United and Labor-Neighbor were the "cutting-edge" organizations that State Representative Kip Holden had claimed they were, they should have challenged more of the injustices that Rep. Holden had pointed out: poverty, corporate welfare, pollution. Labor-Neighbor's successes were at the local level.

Apart from the campaign against Shintech, its issues had become generally too nonconfrontational. Progressive campaigns have to work at multiple scales, and they must more often than not be confrontational. Challenges by corporations and state government at the state level slowed the work of the Labor-Neighbor Project and the environmental movement in Louisiana. But that just means that the effort by the labor-community initiatives must be more concerted and capacity building and multiscale resources better.

The Labor-Neighbor Project made superb inroads into leadership development and building a mass-based organization. Much remains to be done: rebuilding the mass base and consolidating a statewide effort to challenge corporations and the state on economic justice issues. No organization in Louisiana is currently doing this. To make this happen, the project would have to expand beyond being largely a working-class coalition, to include middle-class organizations as much as possible. Post-Hurricane Katrina labor-community mobilization in New Orleans shows signs of building such a progressive project.

Each of the coalitions described previously has doubtless dealt with the preceding factors: the regional character of capitalist politics; the regional character of the state and political culture; the class experience of labor and community; creating broader agendas; creating urgency; building coalition capacity; maximizing multiscale resources; and developing longer-term progressive strategy. Such coalitions have been successful because they have negotiated the previous factors to create broad-based organizations that draw effectively on class-based leadership and multiscale resources. Working-class-based coalitions have greater potential for success over time and greater potential to broaden their agendas. Middle-class environmental-labor coalitions have tended to be short-lived. But an increasing variety of labor-community coalitions is developing, taking on a broad range of economic issues, such as the preservation and creation of living-wage jobs. One thing is certain, longer-term labor-environmental coalitions must broaden the definition of environment to include economic and quality-of-life issues. At some point, they must challenge capital and the state over questions of taxation, pollution, jobs, health, and safety.

BUILDING SUCCESSFUL COALITIONS

What then does it take for labor-community and labor-environmental coalitions to thrive, to address crises for labor, community, and the environment? The answer is that they are able to do so by integrating issues of production and reproduction, and environmental and economic justice. This study has demonstrated that one such labor-community coalition, the Louisiana Labor-Neighbor Project, did so with important success. Its success, however, was historically specific and may not be easily replicable. Among other factors, a place-bounded petrochemical industry, an innovative, coalition-experienced International union, and a working-class, ethnic community with a leadership coming from churches and earlier civil rights struggles, helped to ensure the project's success. Moreover, the development of labor-community collaboration was greatly facilitated by the circumstances of uneven development in the river parishes' petrochemical corridor. A lack of equitable economic development, including jobs and public services, provided the basis for expanded collaboration after the lockout's end. Given this success, we should ask: Is the Louisiana case unique or is it replicable in other places? What does it take to win?

First of all, it takes a crisis to initiate coalition building. Often there are several crises at once, namely economic and environmental health. If an economic crisis—such as a threatened plant closing or labor-management standoff—is present, labor is likely to be the group first affected by the crisis and the first party to seek to collaborate. In Louisiana, however, labor and community bridge builders looked for each other at the same time, due in part to the presence of serious economic and environmental crises. For an environmental health crisis to initiate labor-community collaboration, more likely than not, labor's interest in collaboration will link worker health to the health of the community environment. As others have noted, worker-community health is a tried-and-true coalition issue (Levenstein and Wooding, 2000).

When the economic or environmental urgency has passed, does the impulse for mutual aid simply decline or stop? What is then the impetus for collaboration? Class identity of leaders and partner organizations is vital to developing long-term political education that can raise awareness and understanding about the political importance of labor-community coalitions. But once the initial economic or environmental urgency passes, the logic of mutual aid may subside, unless the coalition broadens its agenda to consider a wider range of economic and environmental issues. Such was the case with the Labor-Community Strategy Center in Los Angeles and the Calumet Project in northwest Indiana. Both projects expanded from a plant-closing crisis to take on questions of pollution and environmental justice, employment and job security, and poverty, while the Labor-Community Strategy Center became a preeminent voice for environmental and economic justice.

Second, it takes the expansion from a narrow agenda to a broader social justice agenda. Initially, a project begins with a modest agenda of keeping the plant open or retaining jobs. This then expands to include a broader range of issues, such as promoting economic development or environmental health protection. As a coalition broadens its agenda, it often expects an openness and flexibility of organizational form and strategy. It involves campaigns that seek to be broad and inclusive and which at a minimum build trust between labor and community leaders.

Third, a successful labor-community coalition needs effective mobilization of resources, or in other words, an effective deployment of class capacity. But it takes more than militancy. It also requires sufficient political opportunities in industry and government, which the coalition then takes advantage of. This also entails an effective use of political opportunities. Effective resource mobilization involves a continuous dialogue among parties, as well as ongoing capacity building, or political education. It means aspiring to a high level of skills, such as leadership or organizing.

Fourth, a successful, long-term, labor-community coalition must challenge a global capitalist agenda with its own broad-based grassroots agenda from below, as argued by Brecher and Costello (1996). Successful coalitions will work to link their broader grassroots agendas with other coalitions in the United States and internationally, providing international solidarity whenever possible. Such networking is vital to spreading successful progressive strategies to other coalitions, and "from the margins to the center of organizing" (Fine, 1998). It represents a return of social unionism.

Social unionism requires an ongoing commitment by unions and community leaders. That commitment is to build coalition capacity, by developing leaders, doing political education among the rank and file and core of leaders, developing and drawing from multiscale resources. It requires the capacity to develop a class identity, which defines the differences and common points held by coalition partners, while defining who the enemy is (Moody, 2001). Labor-community needs to define itself as a progressive organization, which seeks to build mainstream support, by recruiting mainstream institutions such as religious organizations and a broader array of unions.

Labor-community needs to live up to the potential of a new spatial politics, where production and reproduction issues are integrated, and organizing is conducted at multiple scales, while drawing on national resources and networks. We can learn from the experience of the Labor-Neighbor Project, which in 2002 stopped working toward this potential of a new spatial politics. Labor-community's new spatial politics is more about a process than about specific campaigns. It requires great skill to work; that is why it can easily fail.

CONCLUSION

How far can such a labor-community coalition realistically go in shaping policy and building political power for working people? What defines the Louisiana case is not so much its successes as its particular process of coalition building. The Louisiana Labor-Neighbor Project and coalitions like it are limited by their spatial politics in their capacity to shape policy and build power. Nonetheless, such projects are all about building democracy in local places and spaces. The Labor-Neighbor Project and coalitions like it are a response to crises of global capitalism, yet are at the same time constrained by such crises. Building local democracy is a vital part of intervening in crisis, ensuring that the institutions which regulate crisis in local spaces balance diverse interests with a common agenda, the essence of coalition building. Yet, building local democratic crisis-mediating institutions is strongly constrained by uneven development and a lack of national and international movement building. The next logical steps for local labor-community politics, then, are to build a network of projects, create national and international solidarity, and develop long-term strategies for lessening uneven capitalist development (Brecher and Costello, 1996; Lipietz 1992). Such a network could help prevent isolation of projects, particularly when the collaborative process breaks down. We are seeing such network building in the global justice movement and in campaigns for fair trade and a living-wage. We saw it in the global peace movement against the U.S. invasion of Iraq in 2003. We have seen the labor-community networking of local initiatives around chemical right-to-know during the 1980s. We are seeing a growing networking and solidarity around local and statewide environmental health campaigns on the Precautionary Principle. For some local labor-community projects, building such networks may seem a long way off, yet cumulative labor-community coalition work has made important progress.

While the Labor-Neighbor Project and other coalitions have influenced local policy and built local power, their impact on national politics is far less tangible. Policies that could broadly strengthen labor-community relationships, such as Just Transition and the Precautionary Principle, face overwhelming odds at the federal level in the current regulatory climate. Yet, such policies are being advanced in a growing number of local campaigns and hold promise for forging local labor-environmental collaboration. Successful local labor-community coalitions, particularly Jobs with Justice, have turned community coalition-building into routine practice and accepted strategy at the AFL-CIO and many labor councils around the country. Many national unions are redefining themselves as community institutions and broadening their constituencies to include natural allies in communities and social movements.

We should be encouraged by the wealth of local experiments in labor-community collaboration, which have drawn successfully from important resources in national networks, and have built an ever-growing repertoire of strategies and an experienced body of bridge builders. The past forty years, but in particular the time since the decline of labor-management accord in the early 1970s, have witnessed a growing need and role for labor-social movement alliances from the local to the international levels to challenge reckless corporations, compromised and unaccountable governments, and a wide range of social injustices. The continuing development of these alliances and of the networks that strengthen them and amplify their successes should be a priority in campaigns to strengthen civil society in the United States. The coalition-building process, involving labor, community, and social movements, is an essential part of broadening progressive political practice and strengthening democracy in this country and elsewhere.

References

Aglietta, M. (1979). *A Theory of capitalist regulation*. London: New Left Books.

Angel, D. (2000). Environmental innovation and regulation, in G. Clark, M. Feldman, & M. Gertler (Eds.), *The Oxford handbook of economic geography* (pp. 607-624). New York: Oxford University Press.

Apollo Alliance. (2004). *New energy for America: The Apollo Jobs Report*. The Institute for America's Future and the Center on Wisconsin Strategy. www.apolloalliance.org

Bacharach, S., Bamberger, P., & Sonnenstuhl, W. (2001). *Mutual aid and union renewal: Cycles of logics of action*. Ithaca, NY: ILR Press.

Baton Rouge Advocate. June 23, July 2, July 27, August 16, 1993; April 9, 2002.

Baudrillard, J. (1981.) *For a critique of the political economy of the sign*. St. Louis: Telos Press.

Baudrillard, J. (1975). *The mirror of production*. St. Louis: Telos Press.

Becnel, T. (1980). *Labor, church, and the sugar establishment*. Baton Rouge: Louisiana State University Press.

Berman, D. (1979). *Death on the job: Occupational health and safety struggles in the United States*. New York: Monthly Review.

Boggs, C. (1976) *Gramsci's Marxism*. London: Pluto Press.

Bourgeois, R. (1997). Oil, Chemical and Atomic Workers Local 4-620, Baton Rouge, LA. Address at Louisiana Communities United annual convention, Gonzales, LA, November 15, 1997.

Boyte, H. (1980.) *The backyard revolution: Understanding the new citizen movement*. Philadelphia: Temple University Press.

Braverman, H. (1974). *Labor and monopoly capital: The degradation of work in the twentieth century*. New York: Monthly Review Press.

Brecher, J., & Costello, T. (1996). *Global village or global pillage*. Boston: South End Press.

Brecher, J., & Costello, T. (1990). Labor-community coalitions and the restructuring of power, in J. Brecher & T. Costello (Eds.), *Building bridges: The emerging grassroots coalition of labor and community* (pp. 325-345). New York: Monthly Review.

Brenner, R., & Glick, M. (1991). The regulation approach: theory and history, *New Left Review, 188*: 45-120.

Bronfenbrenner, K. (2001). Changing to organize: Unions know what has to be done. Now they have to do it. *The Nation, Sept. 3/10*: 16-20.

Bullard, R. (Ed.). (1993). *Confronting environmental racism: Voices from the grassroots*. Boston: South End Press.

Bullard, R. (1990). *Dumping in Dixie*. Boulder, CO: Westview.

Burawoy, M. (1985.) *The politics of production: Factory regimes under capitalism and socialism*. London: Verso.

Burke, W. (1993). Breakup of the National Toxics Campaign, *In These Times*, May 3-17.

Burke, W. (1992). Poisoning the National Toxics Campaign, *In These Times*, October 28.

Calhoun, C. (1988). The radicalism of tradition and the question of class struggle, in M. Taylor (Ed.), *Rationality and revolution* (pp. 129-175). Cambridge: Cambridge University Press.

Carleton, M., Howard, P., & Parker, J. (Eds.). (1988). *Readings in Louisiana politics*. Baton Rouge: Claitor's Publishing Division.

Carroll, W. (1989). Restructuring capital, reorganizing consent: Gramsci, political economy, and Canada, *Canadian Review of Sociology and Anthropology, 27*(3), 390-416.

Castells, M. (1983). *City and the grassroots: A cross-cultural theory of urban social movements*. Berkeley: University of California Press.

Chapman, K. (1992). *The international petrochemical industry: Evolution and Location*. Cambridge, MA: Blackwell.

Chary, L. K. (1997). Pollution prevention and income protection: Fighting with empty hands—A challenge to Labor, in C. Levenstein and J. Wooding (Eds.), *Work, health, and environment: Old problems, new solutions* (pp. 446-457). New York: Guilford.

Clark, G. (1981). The employment relation and the spatial division of labor. *Annals of the Association of American Geographers, 71*, 412-424.

Clark, G., Gertler, M., & Whiteman, J. (1986). *Regional dynamics: Studies in adjustment theory*. Boston and London: Allen and Unwin.

Cobb, J. (1982). *The selling of the south: The southern crusade for industrial development, 1936-1980*. Baton Rouge: Louisiana State University Press.

Cobble, D. S. (1993). *Women and unions: Forging a partnership*. Ithaca, NY: ILR Press.

Cockburn, C. (1984). *Brothers: Male dominance and technological change*. London: Pluto.

Commission for Racial Justice, United Church of Christ. (1987). *Toxic wastes and race in the United States*. New York: United Church of Christ.

Commoner, B. (1990). *Making peace with the planet*. New York: Pantheon Books.

Cook, B., & Watson, J. (1984). *Louisiana labor: From slavery to right-to-work*. Lanham, MD: University Press of America.

Cumbler, J. (1979). *Working-class community in industrial America: Work, leisure, and struggle in two industrial cities, 1880-1930*. Westport, CT: Greenwood.

Cumbler, J. (1974). Labor, capital, and community: The struggle for power. *Labor History, 15*, 395-415.

Davis, M. (1986). *Prisoners of the American dream*. London: Verso.

Debray, R. (1973). Time and Politics, in R. Debray, *Prison writings* (pp. 87-160). London: Allen Lane.

Dickerson, J. (1991). Gulf Coast Tenants Organization, Baton Rouge. Interview, November 20, 1991.

Donnelly, P. G. (1982). The origins of the occupational safety and health act of 1970. *Social Problems, 30*(1), 14.

Dowie, M. (1995). *Losing ground: American environmentalism at the close of the twentieth century*. Cambridge, MA: MIT Press.

Early, S. (1998). Membership-based organizing, in G. Mantsios (Ed.), *A new labor movement for the new century* (pp. 82-103). New York: Monthly Review.

Epstein, B. (1990). Rethinking social movement theory. *Socialist Review, 90*(1), 35-65.

Escobar, A. (1995). From organism to cyborg: Elements for a postructural political economy of ecology. Amherst, MA: Amherst College, unpublished manuscript.

Evans, A. (1994). Community Outreach Organizer, Tulane Environmental Law Clinic, New Orleans, LA. Interviews: March 7, 1991; December 1, 1993; October 28, 1994.

Faber, D. (Ed.). (1998). *The struggle for ecological democracy: Environmental justice movements in the United States*. New York: Guilford.

Faber, D., & O'Connor, J. (1993). Capitalism and the crisis of environmentalism, in R. Hofrichter (Ed.), *Toxic struggles: The theory and practice of environmental justice* (pp. 12-24). Philadelphia: New Society Publishers.

Fainstein, N., & Fainstein, S. (1985). Economic restructuring and the rise of urban social movements, *Urban Affairs Quarterly, 21*(2).

Fairclough, A. (1995.) *Race and democracy: The civil rights struggle in Louisiana, 1915-1972*. Athens: University of Georgia Press.

Fantasia, R. (1988). *Cultures of solidarity: Consciousness, action, and contemporary American workers*. Berkeley and LA: University of California Press.

Faue, E. (1991). Paths of unionization: Community, bureaucracy, and gender in the Minneapolis labor movement of the 1930s, in A. Baron (Ed.), *Work engendered* (pp. 296-319). Ithaca, NY: Cornell University Press.

Favorite, A. (1992). Environmental activist, Geismar, LA. Interview, January 14, 1992.

Femia, J. (1981). *Gramsci's political thought*. Oxford: Clarendon Press.

Ferguson, T., & Rogers, J. (1986). *Right turn: The decline of the democrats and the future of American Politics*. New York: Hill and Wang.

Ferris, D., & Hahn-Baker, D. (1995). Environmentalists and environmental justice policy, in B. Bryant (Ed.), *Environmental justice: Issues, policies, and solutions* (p. 67). Washington, DC: Island Press.

Fine, J. (1998). Moving innovation from the margins to the center, in G. Mantsios (Ed.), *A new labor movement for the new century* (pp. 119-146). New York: Monthly Review.

FitzSimmons, M., Glaser, J., Mor, R. M., Pincetl, S., & Rajan, C. (1991). Environmentalism and the American liberal state. *Capitalism Nature Socialism, 2*(1), 1-16.

Fletcher, B. (2005). Debate over the future of the AFL-CIO: More heat than light. Common Dreams News Center, June 4, www.commondreams.org

Foley, B. (1992). Class, *Rethinking Marxism, 5*(2), 117-128.

Foner, P. (1974). *Organized labor and the Black worker: 1619-1973*. New York: Praeger.

Fontenot, W. (2002). Environmental Affairs Representative, Louisiana Office of the Attorney General, Baton Rouge. Interviews: March 13, 1991; November 17, 1997; March 3, November 18, 1998; October 12, 2002.

Foster, J. B. (1993). The limits of environmentalism without class: lessons from the ancient forest struggle in the Pacific Northwest. *Capitalism, Nature, Socialism, 4*(1), 11-41.

Foucault, M. (1980). *Power/knowledge*. Brighton: Harvester.

Frank, D. (1995). A small circle of friends, Review of Sklar, Kathryn, Florence Kelley and the Nation's Work, *The Nation, 260*(22), 797-800.

Frank, D. (1991). Gender, consumer organizing, and the Seattle labor movement, 1919-1929, in A. Baron (Ed.), *Work engendered* (pp. 273-295). Ithaca, NY: Cornell University Press.

Gaudet, C., & Gaudet, K. (1991). Environmental Activists, St. Gabriel, Louisiana. Interview, October 2, 1991.

Geiser, K. (1977). *Reform school reform: The nature of change in a social policy biography*. Unpublished Ph.D. Dissertation, Massachusetts Institute of Technology.

Gersuny, C. (1981). *Work hazards and industrial conflict*. Hanover, MA: University Press of New England.

Gibbs, D., & M. Healey, M. (1997). Industrial geography and the environment. *Applied Geography, 17,* 193-201.

Gordon, D. (1977). Class struggle and the stages of American urban development, in D. Perry & A. Watkins (Eds.), *The rise of the sunbelt cities* (pp. 55-82). Beverly Hills: Sage.

Gottlieb, R. (2001). *Environmentalism unbound: Exploring new pathways for change*. Cambridge, MA: MIT Press.

Gottlieb, R. (1993). *Forcing the spring: The transformation of the American Environmental Movement*. Covelo, CA: Island Press.

Gramsci, A. (1971). *Selections from the prison notebooks*. London: Lawrence and Wishart.

Grantham, D. (1983). *Southern progressivism: The reconciliation of progress and tradition*. Knoxville: University of Tennessee Press.

Green, G. (1986). Labor in the western oil industry. *Journal of the West, 25*(2), 14-19.

Gremillion, E. (1991). Oil, Chemical and Atomic Workers Local 4-620, Baton Rouge, LA. Interview, August 5, 1991.

Grossman, R. (1985). Environmentalists and the labor movement. *Socialist Review, 15*(4-5), 63-88.

Gutman, H. (1963). The worker's search for power: labor in the Guilded Age, in H. W. Morgan (Ed.), *The guilded age* (pp. 38-68). Syracuse: Syracuse University Press.

Habermas, J. (1991). A reply, in A. Honneth & H. Joas (Eds.), *Communicative action* (pp. 214-264). Cambridge, MA: MIT Press.

Habermas, J. (1984). *The theory of communicative Action*. Boston: Beacon Press.

Hair, W. (1988). Rob them! You bet!, in M. Carleton, P. Howard, & J. Parker (Eds.), *Readings in Louisiana politics* (pp. 316-340). Baton Rouge: Claitor's Publishing Division.

Hair, W. (1969). *Bourbonism and agrarian protest: Louisiana politics, 1877-1900*. Baton Rouge: Louisiana State University Press.

Hamilton, C. (1993). Environmental consequences of urban growth and blight, in R. Hofrichter (Ed.), *Toxic struggles: The theory and practice of environmental justice* (pp. 67-75). Philadelphia: New Society.

Harvey, D. (2003). *The new imperialism*. Oxford: Oxford University Press.

Harvey, D. (1996). *Justice, nature, and the geography of difference*. Malden, MA: Blackwell.

Harvey, D. (1993). Class relations, social justice and the politics of difference, in M. Keith & S. Pile (Eds.), *Place and the politics of identity* (pp. 41-66). London: Routledge.

Harvey, D. (1991). Flexibility: Threat or opportunity? *Socialist Review, 21*(1), 65-78.

Harvey, D. (1989). *The condition of postmodernity*. Oxford: Blackwell.

Harvey, D. (1982). *The limits to capital*. Oxford: Blackwell.

Hasten, A. (2002). Louisiana Communities United leader, White Castle, LA. Interviews: November 16, 1997; October 21, 2002.

Hays, S. (1959). *Conservation and the gospel of efficiency: The progressive conservation movement, 1890-1920*. Cambridge: Harvard University Press.

Heiman, M. (1996). Race, waste, and class: New perspectives on environmental justice. *Antipode, 28*(2), 111-121.

Heiman, M. (1990). The local defense of residence: a progressive challenge to the liberal environmental agenda, Carlisle, PA: Department of Environmental Studies, Dickinson College, unpublished paper.

Heiman, M. (1989). Production confronts consumption: Landscape and social conflict in the Hudson Valley. *Environment and Planning D: Society and Space, 7,* 165-178.

Herod, A. (1991). The production of scale in United States labour relations. *Area, 23*(1), 82-88.

Hirsch, J. (1983). Fordist security state and new social movements. *Kapitalistate, 10/11,* 75-88.

Hofrichter, R. (Ed.). (1993). *Toxic struggles: The theory and practice of environmental justice.* Philadelphia: New Society.

Hofstadter, R., & Wallace, M. (1971). *American violence: A documentary history.* New York: Vintage Books.

Holden, M. "Kip." (1998). State Representative, Baton Rouge, LA. Keynote address, Louisiana Communities United annual convention, Gonzales, LA, November 21, 1998.

Holt, S. (1998). Consultant, Louisiana Labor-Neighbor Project. Personal communication, November 21, 1998.

Horwitt, S. (1992). *Let them call me rebel: Saul Alinsky, his life and legacy.* New York: Vintage.

Houck, O. (1986). This side of heresy: Conditioning Louisiana's ten-year industrial tax exemption upon compliance with environmental laws. *Tulane Law Review, 61*(2), 289-377.

Industrial Areas Foundation. (1978). *History and principles.* New York: Industrial Areas Foundation.

Jackson, Rev. W. (1997). Louisiana Communities United leader, Gonzales, LA. Interview, November 17, 1997.

Jameson, F. (1984). Postmodernism, or the cultural logic of late capitalism. *New Left Review, 146,* 53-92.

Jeansomme, G. (1990). Huey P. Long: A political contradiction. *Louisiana History, 31*(4): 373-385.

Jenkins, J., & Perrow, C. (1977). Insurgency of the powerless: Farm worker movements (1946-1972). *American Sociological Review, 42,* 249-268.

Jenson, J. (1989). "Different" but not "exceptional": Canada's permeable fordism. *Canadian Review of Sociology and Anthropology, 26*(1), 69-94.

Jessop, B. (1990a). *State theory: Putting capitalist states in their place.* University Park, PA: Pennsylvania State University Press.

Jessop, B. (1990b). Regulation theories in retrospect and prospect. *Economy and Society, 19*(2): 153-216.

Jonas, A. (1998). Investigating the local-global paradox: corporate strategy, union local autonomy, and community action in Chicago, in A. Herod (Ed.), *Organizing the landscape: Geographical perspectives on labor unionism* (pp. 325-350). Minneapolis: University of Minnesota Press.

Judkins, B. (1986). *We offer ourselves as evidence: Toward workers' control of occupational health.* New York: Greenwood.

Kallick, D. (1993). What it means to fail. *Social Policy, 24,* 2-5.

Katznelson, I. (1981). *City trenches: Urban politics and the patterning of class in the United States.* Chicago: University of Chicago Press.

Kazis, R., & Grossman, R. (1982). *Fear at work: Job blackmail, labor and the environment.* New York: The Pilgrim Press.

Keil, R. (1995). The Green Work Alliance. *Capitalism Nature Socialism, 6*(3), 63-76.

King, N. "Duke." (2002). Oil, Chemical and Atomic Workers Local 4-620, Baton Rouge, LA. Interviews: November 20, 1991; December 19, 1995; November 17, 1997; October 15, 2002.

Kirkland, L. A. (1991). Environmental activist, Plaquemine, LA. Interview, October 24, 1991.

Laclau, E. (1977). Fascism and ideology, in E. Laclau (Ed.), *Politics and ideology in Marxist theory.* London: New Left Books.

Laclau, E., & Mouffe, C. (1985). *Hegemony and Socialist Strategy.* London: Verso.

Lake, R. (1996). Volunteers, NIMBYs, and environmental justice: Dilemmas of democratic practice. *Antipode, 28,* 160-174.

Lappé, F. M. (2005). Time for progressives to grow up: Beyond Lakoff's strict father versus nurturant parent, a strong community manifesto. Common Dreams News Center, www.commondreams.org.

Latour, E. (1985). *The creation of the Louisiana Department of Environmental Quality: Administrative reorganization and public policymaking.* Unpublished MA Thesis, Louisiana State University.

Lee, C. (1990). The integrity of justice: The evidence of environmental racism. *Sojourners, 19*(2), 22.

Lerner, S. (2005). *The struggle for environmental justice in Louisiana's chemical corridor.* Cambridge, MA: MIT Press.

Leonard, R., & Nauth, Z. (1990). Beating BASF: OCAW busts union-busters. *Labor Research Review, 9*(2), 34-49.

Levenstein, C., & Wooding, J. (2000). *The point of production.* Amityville, NY: Baywood.

Lipietz, A. (1992). A regulationist approach to the future of urban ecology. *Capitalism Nature Socialism, 3*(3), 101-110.

Lipietz, A. (1988). New tendencies in the international division of labor: Regimes of accumulation and modes of regulation, in A. Scott & M. Storper (Eds.), *Production, work, and territory* (pp. 16-40). London: Unwin Hyman.

Lipietz, A. (1987). *Mirages and miracles.* London: Verso.

Louisiana Coalition for Tax Justice. (1992). *The Great Louisiana Tax Giveaway: A study of Louisiana's "10-year" industrial property tax exemption.* Baton Rouge, LA: Louisiana Coalition for Tax Justice.

Louisiana Environmental Action Network. (2002). www.leanweb.org

Maginnis, J. (1992). *Cross to bear.* Baton Rouge: Darkhorse Press.

Maginnis, J. (1984). *The last hayride.* Baton Rouge: Gris Gris.

Malek-Wiley, D. (2004). Delta Chapter, Sierra Club, New Orleans. Interview, April 3, 1991; personal communication, Sept. 23, 2004.

Mann, E. (1993). Labor's environmental agenda in the new corporate climate, in R. Hofrichter (Ed.), *Toxic struggles: The theory and practice of environmental justice* (pp. 179-185). Philadelphia: New Society Publishers.

Mantsios, G. (Ed.). (1998). *A new labor movement for the new century.* New York: Monthly Review.

Marable, M. (1983). *How capitalism underdeveloped Black America.* Boston: South End Press.

Mattera, P. (1992). *World class business: A guide to the 100 most powerful corporations.* New York: Henry Holt.

Mayer, J. (1994). Organizer, Pacific Institute for Community Organizations. Interview, October 15, 1994.

Mayer, M. (1991). Politics in the post-Fordist city. *Socialist Review, 21*(1), 105-124.

McAdam, D. (1982). *Political process and the development of Black insurgency 1930-1970.* Chicago: The University of Chicago Press.

McCarthy, J., & Zald, M. (1977). Resource mobilization and social movements: A partial theory. *American Journal of Sociology, 82,* 1212-1241.

McWhinney, G. (1988). Louisiana Socialists in the early twentieth century, in M. Carleton, P. Howard, & J. Parker (Eds.), *Readings in Louisiana politics* (2nd ed., pp. 341-358). Baton Rouge: Claitor's Publishing Division.

Meier, A., & Rudwick, E. (1979). *Black Detroit and the rise of the UAW.* New York.

Melucci, A. (1985). The symbolic challenge of contemporary movements. *Social Research, 52*(4), 789-816.

Melucci, A. (1980). The new social movements: A theoretical approach. *Social Science Information, 19*(2), 199-226.

Merkel, M. (1983). *The Labor Union Handbook.* New York: Beaufort.

Merrill, M. (1997). Accepting a challenge: A response to Lin Kaatz Chary, in C. Levenstein & J. Wooding (Eds.), *Work, health, and environment: Old problems, new solutions* (pp. 458-460). New York: Guilford.

Miller, B. (2000). Geography and social movements: Comparing Antinuclear Activism in the Boston Area. Minneapolis: University of Minnesota Press.

Miller, B. (1992). Local-central state relations and geographically shifting political opportunity structures: The Cambridge, Massachusetts anti-nuclear weapons movement during the most recent cycle of protest. Paper presented at *Conference on Empowering Political and Economic Transformations*, Boulder, Colorado.

Miller, B. (1990). *Space, time, and new social movements: The socio-spatial dynamics of the Boston area peace movement.* Minneapolis: Department of Geography, University of Minnesota. unpublished paper.

Miller, M. (1980). Labor on the move: The future, in M. Miller (Ed.), *Working lives: The southern exposure history of labor in the south* (pp. 352-369). New York: Pantheon.

Miller, R. (1991-92). Policy Analyst, Oil, Chemical and Atomic Workers. Baton Rouge, Louisiana. Personal communications, (1991-92).

Minchin, T. (2003). *Forging a common bond: Labor and environmental activism during the BASF lockout.* Gainesville: University of Florida Press.

Moberg, D. (1990). Putting out the fire with gasoline in the petrochemical industry. *In These Times, 15*(5), 12-13, 22.

Moody, K. (2001). Reply to Kate Bronfenbrenner. *The Nation*, Sept. 2/10.

Moody, K. (1997). *Workers in lean world: Unions in the international economy.* London: Verso.

Moody, K. (1990). Building a labor movement for the 1990s: cooperation and concessions or confrontation and coalition, in J. Brecher & T. Costello (Eds.), *Building bridges: The emerging grassroots coalition of labor and community* (pp. 216-228). New York: Monthly Review.

Moody, K. (1988). *An injury to all: The Decline of American Unionism.* New York: Verso.

Morris, I. (1992). Environmental activist, Geismar, Louisiana. Interview, March 13, 1992.

Nast, H. (1994). Review of Michael Keith and Steve Pile (Eds.), 1993. *Place and the Politics of Identity*, New York: Routledge, in *Annals of the Association of American Geographers, 84*(4): 767-769.

Navarro, V. (1991). The limitation of legitimation and fordism and the possibility for socialist reform. *Rethinking Marxism, 4*(2), 27-60.

Navarro, V. (1983). Work, ideology and science: The case of medicine, in V. Navarro & D. Berman (Eds.), *Health and work under capitalism: An international perspective* (pp. 11-38). Amityville, NY: Baywood.

New Orleans Times—Picayune. (1991) February 20.

Nicolai, D. (2002). Coordinator, Louisiana Labor/Neighbor Project, Baton Rouge, LA. Interviews: May 10, November 30, December 12, 1993; January 28, October 26, November 20, 1994; January 26, July 28, November 30, 1995; October 28, 2002.

Noble, C. (1993). Work: The most dangerous environment, in R. Hofrichter (Ed.), *Toxic struggles: The theory and practice of environmental justice* (pp. 171-178). Philadelphia: New Society Publishers.

Noble, C. (1990). OSHA at 20: Regulatory strategy and institutional structure in the work environment. *New Solutions, 1*(1), 30-42.

Noble, C. (1986). *Liberalism at work: The rise and fall of OSHA*. Philadelphia: Temple University Press.

Obach, B. (2001). *Labor and environment: A study of social movement alliance formation.* Cambridge, MA: MIT Press.

Oberschall, A. (1973). *Social conflict and social movements*. New York: Prentice Hall.

O'Connor, J. (1994). Is sustainable capitalism possible?, in J. O'Connor (Ed.), *Is Capitalism Sustainable?* (pp. 152-175). New York: Guilford Press.

O'Connor, J. (1988). Capitalism, nature, socialism: A theoretical introduction. *Capitalism, Nature, Socialism, 1*, 11-38.

O'Connor, M. (1993). On the misadventures of capitalist nature. *Capitalism Nature Socialism, 4*(3), 7-40.

Offe, C. (1985). New social movements: Challenging the boundaries of institutional politics. *Social Research, 52*(4), 817-868.

Oil, Chemical and Atomic Workers. (1988) *Locked out*. Video. Washington, DC: Organizing Media Project.

Orr, M. (1995). Executive Director, Louisiana Environmental Action Network, Baton Rouge, LA. Interview, December 20, 1995.

Page, J., & O'Brien, M.-W. (1972). *Bitter wages: Ralph Nader's study group report on disease and injury on the job*. New York: Grossman.

Peck, J. (1996). *Work place: The social regulation of labor markets*. New York: Guilford.

Peet, R., & Watts, M. (1996). Liberation ecology, in R. Peet & M. Watts (Eds.), *Liberation ecologies: Environment, development, social movements* (pp. 1-45). London: Routledge.

Peet, R. (1984). Class struggle, the relocation of employment, and economic crisis. *Science and Society, 48*(1), 38-51.

Piven F., & Cloward, R. (1977). *Poor people's movements*. New York: Vintage Books.

Plotke, D. (1990). What's so new about new social movements. *Socialist Review, 20*(1), 81-102.

Plotkin, S. (1984). Property, policy, and politics: Towards a theory of urban land-use conflict. *International Journal of Urban and Regional Research, 11*, 382-403.

Poulantzas, N. (1978). *State, power, socialism*. London: Verso.
Preteceille, E., & Terrail, J. (1985). *Capitalism, consumption, and needs*. Oxford: Basil Blackwell.
Prothro, J. (1988). The early period in constitutional developments in the office of governor, in Louisiana, in M. T. Carleton, P. H. Howard, & J. B. Parker (Eds.), *Readings in Louisiana politics*. Baton Rouge, LA: Claitor.
Pulido, L. (1996). A critical review of the methodology of environmental racism research. *Antipode, 28*, 142-159.
Pulido, L. (1995). "People of color," identity politics, and the environmental justice movement." Pasadena, CA: University of Southern California, Department of Geography, unpublished manuscript.
Rachel's Environment and Health News. (2003). San Francisco adopts the Precautionary Principle. #765, March 20. www.rachel.org
Rixner, I. (1997). Community activist, Gonzales, Louisiana, Interview, November 17, 1997.
Robert, T. (1991). Environmental activist, Burnside, Louisiana. Interview, April 4, 1991.
Robinson, W. (1998). Oil, Chemical and Atomic Workers Local 4-620, Baton Rouge, LA. Interview, March 4, 1998.
Rose, F. (2000). *Coalitions across the class divide*. Ithaca, NY: Cornell University Press.
Rosner, D., & Markowitz, G. (1991). *Deadly dust: Silicosis and the politics of occupational disease in twentieth century America*. Princeton, NJ: Princeton University Press.
Rosner, D., & Markowitz, G. (1989). Safety and health as a class issue: The Workers' Health Bureau of America during the 1920s, in D. Rosner & G. Markowitz (Eds.), *Dying for work: Workers' safety and health in twentieth-century America* (pp. 53-64). Bloomington, IN: Indiana University Press.
Rousselle, E. (1991). OCAW International Representative, Baton Rouge, Louisiana. Interview, August 2, 1991.
Roy, A. (2004). *Public power in the age of empire*. Open Media Pamphlet Series. New York: Seven Stories Press.
Saunders, P. (1981). *Social theory and the urban question*. New York: Holmes and Meier.
Sayer, A., & Walker, R. (1992). *The new social economy: Reworking the division of labor*. Cambridge, MA: Blackwell.
Schafer, K. (1993). *What works: Local solutions to toxic pollution*. Washington, DC: The Environmental Exchange.
Schneider, B. (1998). Oil, Chemical and Atomic Workers Local 4-620, Baton Rouge, LA. Interview, March 3, 1998.
Siegmann, H. (1985). *The conflicts between labor and environmentalism in the Federal Republic of Germany and the United States*. New York: St. Martin's.
Slatin, C. (1999). *Training for action: The political economy of the Superfund worker training program*. Lowell, MA: University of Massachusetts Lowell. Unpublished Doctoral Dissertation.
Smith, N. (1990). *Uneven development* (2nd ed.). Oxford: Blackwell.
Storper, M., & Walker, R. (1989). *The capitalist imperative: Territory, technology, and industrial growth*. New York: Basil Blackwell.
Summers, J. (1991). OCAW president, Vista Chemicals, Lake Charles, LA. Interview, April 25, 1991.

Szasz, A. (1991). In praise of policy Luddism: Strategic lessons from the hazardous waste wars. *Capitalism Nature Socialism, 2*(1), 17-43.

Tarrow, S. (1983). *Struggling to reform: Social movements and policy change during cycles of protest.* Ithaca: Cornell University Press.

Templet, P. (1992). Former Secretary of Louisiana Department of Environmental Quality, Baton Rouge, LA. Lecture at LSU Law School, February 24, 1992.

Tilly, C. (1978). *From mobilization to revolution.* Reading, MA: Addison-Wesley.

Touraine, A. (1985). An introduction to the study of social movements. *Social Research, 52*(4), 749-788.

Vann, L. (1991). Oil, Chemical and Atomic Workers Local 4-620, Baton Rouge, LA. Interview, November 21, 1991.

Walker, R. (1981). A theory of suburbanization: Capitalism and the construction of urban space in the United States, in M. Dear & A. Scott (Eds.), *Urbanization and urban planning in capitalist society* (pp. 383-429). New York: Methuen.

Williams, R. (1977). *Marxism and literature.* Oxford: Oxford University Press.

Wills, J. (1998). Space, place, and tradition in working class organization, in A. Herod (Ed.), *Organizing the landscape: Geographical perspectives on labor unionism* (pp. 129-158). Minneapolis: University of Minnesota Press.

Women's Support Group. (1991). Oil, Chemical, and Atomic Workers. Interview, August 4, 1991.

Wooding, J. (1989). *Dire states: Workplace health and safety regulation in the Reagan/ Thatcher era.* Unpublished Ph.D. Dissertation, Brandeis University.

Wooding, J. (1990). Dire states: Health and safety in the Reagan-Thatcher era, *New Solutions, 1*(2), 42-53.

Yates, M. (2001). The "new" economy and the labor movement. *Monthly Review, 52*(11), www.monthlyreview.org

Young, I. M. (1990). The ideal of community and the politics of difference, in L. Nicholson (Ed.), *Feminism/postmodernism* (pp. 300-323). New York: Routledge.

Young, R. (1986). Industrial location and regional change: The United States and New York state. *Regional Studies, 20*(4), 341-369.

Index

For Product Safety Concerns and Information please contact our EU
representative GPSR@taylorandfrancis.com
Taylor & Francis Verlag GmbH, Kaufingerstraße 24, 80331 München, Germany

www.ingramcontent.com/pod-product-compliance
Ingram Content Group UK Ltd.
Pitfield, Milton Keynes, MK11 3LW, UK
UKHW052030210425
457613UK00032BA/477